THE BRIDGE
THAT SAVED
A NATION

THE BRIDGE THAT SAVED A NATION

BERGEN COUNTY, NEW BRIDGE AND THE HACKENSACK VALLEY

To my good friend Manfred

KEVIN W. WRIGHT
WITH DEBORAH POWELL

AMERICA
THROUGH TIME®
ADDING COLOR TO AMERICAN HISTORY

For Kevin, I know we will meet again some sunny day.

America Through Time is an imprint of Fonthill Media LLC
www.through-time.com
office@through-time.com

Published by Arcadia Publishing by arrangement with Fonthill Media LLC
For all general information, please contact Arcadia Publishing:
Telephone: 843-853-2070
Fax: 843-853-0044
E-mail: sales@arcadiapublishing.com
For customer service and orders:
Toll-Free 1-888-313-2665

www.arcadiapublishing.com

First published 2019

ISBN 978-1-63499-165-0

Typeset in 10pt on 13pt Sabon
Printed and bound in England

Preface

This place.

This place has fascinated us since 1981 when we first set foot here at the state historic site, the Zabriskie-Steuben House. We lived at the eighteenth-century, Jersey-Dutch sandstone mansion along the tidal Hackensack River for sixteen and a half years. My husband, author and historian Kevin W. Wright, tells the compelling, multi-layered New Jersey history beginning with the geography of the Hackensack valley, followed by the Original Peoples, Jersey-Dutch settlers, the American Revolutionary War at this crossroads, Major-General Baron von Steuben's role, and the post-Revolutionary War. He relates the efforts to save the house and site as residents of Bergen County awakened to the landscape around them changing from farmland to residential and industrial development in the early 1900s. He researched the Bergen County Historical Society's fabulous artifact collections that the Society began acquiring in 1902 and now displays at the museum site. I included a selection of photographs from and of the collections. Kevin often told our history through writing and speaking at lectures and tours. He spoke to thousands and people began connecting to this place. My husband of forty years was writing this book when he died in October 2016. I picked it up when I could and started to stitch it together, adding some segues and fleshing out a couple of parts but the book is his writing. I included a chapter, "An Incomplete Record: Free Africans, Enslavement, and Indentured Servants," that Kevin wrote in 1996, updated in 2007, that he did not get to add to the book. I created three maps and selected seventy-seven images to include and wrote captions for each. In some ways, this book raises more "heat than light" to quote him. I look forward to working on uncovering some of the mysteries in the future. Kevin had three books published on New Jersey history but he persevered to write this book in 2016.

Kate Reilly was invaluable for her perceptive feedback, editing, and punctuation. I thank Jim Smith for editing suggestions and support. Kevin was in awe of Jim's enthusiasm for New Jersey history and interpretive initiatives. Many thanks for help with the book: Todd Braisted (Kevin references his research), Christine George,

Cindy Piano, Patricia Daurizio, Carol Restivo, John and Linda Heffernan, Linda Masullo, Jim Bellis, Rosemary Jerkovich, Lucille Bertram, Teaneck Public Library, and the many stalwart friends who have supported us through the years. All royalties from the sales of this book benefit the Bergen County Historical Society.

Contents

Introduction:
Historic Gateway

New Bridge nestles at the geographic and cultural heart of Bergen County, New Jersey, where the stream-laced boundaries of River Edge, Hackensack, New Milford, and Teaneck intersect, 7 miles west of the George Washington Bridge, and a quarter of a mile north of Route 4. With minor modern adjustments, these civic boundaries perpetuate the bounds of seventeenth-century Indian deeds and a demarcation between two distinct indigenous communities: the Hackensacks and Tappans.

Standing 15 miles inland at the narrows of the Hackensack River, New Bridge memorializes a wooden drawbridge, first built in 1744, which, as the nearest river crossing to Newark Bay for half a century, funneled overland traffic between Manhattan, its agricultural outskirts, and the vast interior of North America. At this strategic node, the narrow Hackensack escapes its hilly confines to join the sea. In 1882, W. Woodford Clayton described the "dwindled stream" north of New Bridge as "only a tributary of the ocean-fed Hackensack." Below New Bridge, the stream broadens at places to 500 feet.

It is nothing short of a miracle that we may presently sit and converse upon the remarkable survival of this storied place where history was made, it being so precariously planted in the core of one of America's premier suburban counties. Such amazing occurrences rarely (if ever) happen by pure circumstance, so a great deal of stubborn commitment was and is involved in its preservation. Yet credit where credit is due: its perpetuation is largely attributable to the purposefulness and perseverance of our oldest county cultural institution, the Bergen County Historical Society, founded in 1902. The Society is joined in this endeavor by partners; the Department of Environmental Protection/the State of New Jersey, the Blauvelt Demarest Foundation, and the County of Bergen, River Edge, Teaneck and New Milford, working through the Historic New Bridge Landing Park Commission.

Steady pulses of their interest and advocacy have shown people are willing to support a historic site in New Jersey. Every now and again, a dose of serendipity helps the cause, but the outcome is truly worth it. Today, Historic New Bridge Landing

Park remarkably preserves a scenic fragment of the Jersey Dutch countryside, strategically situated at the narrows of the Hackensack River and famed for its compelling role in the American Revolution—indeed, we may confidently suggest this hallowed spot survived more of the American Revolution than any other place in America. Its distinctive antique dwellings, artifact collections, and leafy backwater landscapes are uniquely reminiscent of a vanished folk culture, dependent upon the tidal river as a commercial artery and as a self-renewing source of nourishment and industrial power.

1

Groundwork

Cloistered by the Hudson Palisades, whose summits give grand spectacle to Manhattan's skyline, Bergen County occupies the northeast corner of New Jersey, one of America's most attractive, if misunderstood, states. From the beginnings of pioneer agriculture through the sprawl of a commuter age, this suburban plain has progressed from highly cultivated to most populous.

While it may never be settled, I favor the hypothesis that Bergen is named for the great natural wonder of the Hudson Palisades; "Bergen" is ancient terminology for "an elevated border of a river" or "certain rocks elevated perpendicularly above the water."[1] A Dutch village atop Jersey City Heights, laid out in 1658, was named Bergen for its hilltop vantage, lending its name to the surrounding county in 1683. Up until 1840, when Hudson County separated, this was old Bergen. From the neighborhood of the original village, the Palisades climb steadily in height, impinging upon the waterfront at Weehawken, and stacking an imposing barrier reminiscent of a walled cloister—hence the lingering Dutch name of *Klooster*, or Closter, mountain to the north.[2]

Peeling back the sediments of long ages in search of the groundwork for this story, we glimpse how landforms shape our culture and destiny. Bergen County occupies a gently fluted plain, nearly 20 miles wide, which declines southeast from Bald Mountain in Mahwah—the highest elevation in Bergen County at 1,164 feet above sea level—until it finally unrolls beneath the reedy tides. Some 25 million years in the making and another 180 million years in the baking, the pebbly, reddish brownstone of this remnant continental rift basin was quarried and stacked to make Bergen County's distinctive Dutch cottages and churches as well as the fashionable brownstones of Hoboken and New York City.

This shale-and-sandstone valley, technically the Newark Basin, extends along the Delaware River from Trenton north to Holland, New Jersey, and continues along the southeast margins of the Highlands to Suffern, New York. It is a tilted and eroded swath of Late Triassic lowland, whose sedimentary foundation incorporates pebbles, mud, and sand, carried by mountain streams that slowly filled a deep rift valley, perhaps 10 to 50 miles wide, during the breakup of the supercontinent of Pangæa. This rock wedge has an estimated thickness of 20,300 feet along the border with the Highlands but thins eastward until it finally disappears entirely under the Hudson River. Cretaceous sedimentary rocks of the inner coastal plain overlap its southeastern boundary, which runs from Trenton to near the outlet of Lawrence Brook, below New Brunswick, and northeast to the Arthur Kill, 3 miles northeast of Woodbridge.[3]

Conglomerate is found where Mesozoic streams abandoned their heaviest burden of pebbles and gravel along the base of the Highlands, notably between Lebanon and Pottersville, New Jersey. Sand and mud rode the onrushing waters farther and evidence of ripple marks, mud cracks, raindrop impressions, and reptilian tracks indicate deposition in and about lakes.[4] Varying conditions over time nuanced the composition of the bedrock. From the Palisades southwest into Hunterdon County, the sandstone is "compact, hard, and well-adapted for building," but between the South Branch of the Raritan and the Delaware River, it has a more shaly character that "taken from whatever depth, readily disintegrates into loam more fertile than that formed from the harder stone."[5] Along these lines, geology and geography shape culture.

As the supercontinent ruptured over the span of 2 million years, lava flared through fissures. It first erupted in long, deep lakes, forming the pillow lavas found in Paterson's Upper New Street Quarry. The upturned and exposed edges of three extrusive lava flows form the semicircular trap ridges called the First, Second, and Third Watchung Mountains. In contrast, the coarse-grained diabase of the Hudson Palisades indicates a molten sheet or sill of magma that intruded flat beds of sedimentary rock at depth, cooling slowly. It was subsequently upturned and exposed at the surface, presenting a steep escarpment for 30 miles along the western shore of the Hudson River from New York Bay northward to Haverstraw, New York, where it finally bends inland on a hooked course to the Highlands.[6]

As North America separated from northwest Africa along the heated rift giving birth to the Atlantic Ocean, the crust thinned, fractured, and pulled apart, allowing massive blocks of terrain to slide down along faults. Thus, the Ramapo Mountains rose as adjacent sedimentary beds of the Newark Basin slipped down along the Ramapo Fault. The edge of the buried sill of the Palisades was raised from the depths. Rocks of volcanic origin, being harder and more resistant to erosion, prominently endure as trap ridges or hills, but anyone crossing the grain of the intervening lowland rides a roller-coaster, up and down a mild succession of narrow sandstone ridges. One such ridge lies between Harrington Park and Ridgefield Park, declining southward in height from about 60 to 40 feet. Another, primarily of sandstone, extends south from Emerson into Maywood, dividing the Hackensack and Saddle Rivers. This ridge rises again in the Fairmount section of Hackensack as Red Hill and continues south into Rutherford. Historian Frances A. Westervelt summarized this topography and its consequences to a honking migration of automotive commuters in 1923:

> Roads running east and west cross the ridges and depressions, whereas those up
> and down the valley follow the valleys or ridges. The ridges gradually become lower

Photograph of Frances A. Westervelt, president of BCHS, 1914–1915. (*Bergen County Historical Society Collections*)

towards the southwest and the valleys widen out into flats, coalescing about the southwestern end of the ridges, which gradually disappear. At the south junction of the west and middle branches of the Saddle River, near the New York line, is the south end of a ridge. Tea Neck, near Hackensack, and the ridge at Arlington, disappearing at East Newark, are other examples.[7]

So the major streams flow south, the rails and roads tracing their valley slopes.

Up until 1931, when State Route 4 connected Paterson to the George Washington Bridge, most roads running east and west were generally aimed at choke points in the intervening streams, where natural circumstances favored a ford, mill dam, or landing—in other words, those locations most advantageous for the first bridges. But if an unwitting wayfarer chose to continue east, climbing the western slope of the Palisades, the path inevitably culminated at the precipice of the Palisades with its dreamy vision of Manhattan, beckoning tantalizingly below, so near but so unreachable by wheel or hoof.

The actual escarpment of the Palisades soars 530 feet above the Hudson River at its highest point in New Jersey. Its crest declines uniformly to the south

The Palisades and Hudson River, Barber & Howe, *Historical Collections of the State of New Jersey* (Newark N. J., Benjamin Olds for Justus H. Bradley, 1844).

from 547 feet near Closter to 440 feet above Huyler's Landing, to 263 feet at Guttenberg, to 183 feet at Weehawken, to about 40 feet at Bayonne, touching sea level at Bergen Point on the north side of the Kill van Kull, opposite Staten Island.[8] Above Weehawken, opportunities for passing between summit and shore were rare and precarious, being little more than foot trails snaking down offsets or cloves in the perpendicular cliff-face. Landings under the cliff were located at Bulls Ferry (Guttenberg and North Bergen), Moore's or Burdette's (Edgewater), the Lower Closter or Huyler's (Alpine), Closter (Alpine), and Sneden's (Palisades, New York). Better options, however, lay south and so the earliest roads connecting Manhattan to its trans-Hudson hinterland—indeed, by the nexus to the interior of the continent—branched from the Hudson River landings at Paulus Hook (Jersey City), Hoebuck (Hoboken), and Weehawk (Weehawken) onto what is now Tonnelle Avenue through Hudson County, squeezing between the Hackensack Meadowlands and the rocky crest of the Palisades.

All might have been worse (that is to say, so very much more uneven) if not for glacial lobes repeatedly lumbering into our latitude over the past several million years, only to shrink away in balmier interludes. The most recent resurgence, beginning about 75,000 years ago, eventually inundated one-third of North America, lowering sea level by nearly 400 feet. Pressing its most southerly advance through the Hackensack valley, it climaxed approximately 21,750 years ago. About 16,000 years ago, the icy mantle began to waste away, haltingly conceding on average about 60 to 100 feet yearly in its retreat. It abandoned a stony cushion of boulders, gravel, sand, and clay, not only as ground till, but piled in various landforms, filling voids and smoothing rough edges.

An outwash plain of water-sorted sand and gravel fills the Saddle River Valley, extending south from Saddle River through Paramus and westward to Hohokus Brook. A sandy plain, cut by Pascack Creek and Musquapsink Brook, extends eastward to Rivervale and southward to Emerson. Another covers Fair Lawn, and some of the most pronounced kames in the state of New Jersey frame a pitted flat, about two square miles in extent, adjacent to Franklin Lake.

Whaleback ridges of fine glacial sediments, called drumlins, define the rolling topography of the northern Hackensack valley. Usually a quarter to half a mile in length, but seldom rising more than 30 to 50 feet in height, they swarm in parallel belts, creating a fluted terrain with small lakes and swamps occupying the troughs. Summit Avenue rides the crest of a drumlin that extends from the bend in Kinderkamack Road at the intersection of New Milford Avenue in Oradell, running south to Continental Avenue below Roosevelt School in River Edge. Fifth Avenue in River Edge marks the axis of another, extending from just north of Continental Avenue south to St. Peter the Apostle Church. Cherry Hill in River Edge is another notable example—Bogert Road rides its crest. Another lies east of Forest Avenue between Soldier Hill Road and Ridgewood Avenue on the boundary between Paramus and Oradell. Just north of this, the Hackensack Golf Club occupies yet another drumlin, which extends north nearly to Ackerman Avenue in Emerson. Spring Valley Avenue rides the crest of another between Oradell Avenue and Soldier Hill Road. Yet another forms the spine of Berdan Heights in Fair Lawn between Fair Lawn Avenue and Berdan Avenue.

Summer's gleam sent meltwater cascading down crevasses in the ice, piling boulders, cobbles and gravel in subglacial streambeds called eskers. These rocky ridges, some standing 25 feet high, snake across valley bottoms and along hill slopes. In 1892, glaciologist Rollin Salisbury noted the rarity of eskers, not only in New Jersey, but in most glaciated regions, adding, "Nowhere do they find better development than in the vicinity of Ramsey in Bergen County."

Yet there are deeper concerns. A well drilled in the rear of the new Consolidated Market Company at 153 Main Street, Hackensack, in July 1909, bored through 212 feet of solid clay without reaching bedrock. Similar borings confirm a void in the sandstone and shale bedrock, infilled with silt, clay, sand, gravel, and cobbles, that plumbs depths approaching 265 feet in places. Indeed, if these glacial sediments were removed, the Hackensack valley would cradle a deep rock bay, extending north to Old Hook Road and continuing northeast nearly to the state line.[9] Thus the Hackensack Meadowlands owe their origin to being a catch basin for sediment-rich meltwaters impounded between the receding ice front and a morainal ridge to the south.

In its earliest incarnation, proglacial Lake Bayonne formed behind a morainal dam about 30 feet high, extending across the Arthur Kill between Staten Island and New Jersey. When this huge glacial embankment eroded, the lake dropped to the level of a diabase sill situated about five miles north, creating a new spillway for proglacial Lake Hackensack. Deltas of sand and gravel in Oradell, Westwood, and Englewood mark the mouth of feeder streams. Proglacial Lake Paramus formed when glacial deposits dammed the Passaic Valley between Clifton and Rutherford, just north of Route 3, impounding meltwaters in the Saddle River Valley. This reservoir drained through Musquapsink Brook, below Westwood, when that outlet was freed of ice. Ice also dammed the headwaters of Goffle Brook, temporarily creating Proglacial Lake Hohokus. Meltwaters were similarly impounded in the Pond Brook Valley at Franklin Lakes until released through the deglaciated Ramapo and Pond Brook Valleys in Oakland.

The suspension of fine clays released from the waning ice turned meltwaters a milky white. Summer layers of sand and silt accumulated on the lake bed, capped by winter veneers of fine clay. Counting these seasonal varves in the clay pits of Little Ferry brickyards indicated this cold-water reservoir existed for at least 2,550 years before the ice sheet withdrew north of Haverstraw, New York.[10] From colonial times onward into the first third of the twentieth century, this body of Late Pleistocene, red-burning clay proved reliable for brick manufacture and consequently was mined and fired at ten major brickyards. Workable clay beds along the Hackensack River vary in depth, from 20 feet at Hackensack to 98 feet at Little Ferry.

By 17,500 years ago, the glacier receded far enough north to allow proglacial Lake Hackensack to drain northeast through Sparkill Gap into the Hudson River, thereby exposing the former lakebed clays, south of Moonachie, to erosion. The Passaic and Saddle Rivers temporarily flowed eastward from Garfield, forming a delta fan at Hackensack, and drained through the north-flowing Hackensack River. Yet relieved of an immense burden of ice, the land slowly rose about 3.5 feet per mile northward of a hinge pinned at the terminal moraine at Perth Amboy, gradually restoring the valley's southward slant. Due to isostatic rebound, the Passaic, Saddle and Hackensack Rivers assumed their southerly flow about 6,500 years ago, forming new terraces, such as those along the Teaneck bank of the river south of New Bridge.

Sea level rose as waning ice sheets fed the oceans, reaching 43 feet below its present level 6,000 years ago and 33 feet below its present level by 5,000 years ago. The rate of rise markedly slowed 4,000 years ago, so that sea level stood 16 feet below its present level 3,000 years ago and 9 feet below present level 2,000 years ago. Atlantic white cedar invaded the Hackensack estuary during a warm spell called the Medieval Climatic Optimum, lasting from 950 to 1150 CE, when sea level likely reached its present stand. Thus, the Hackensack River became a tidal race, reaching inland from the head of Newark Bay to Van Buskirk Island (New Milford Avenue, Oradell). Yet the onset of cooling at the start of the Little Ice Age caused sea level either to stabilize or intermittently decrease over the next seven centuries. Since the close of the Little Ice Age—often dated to around 1850—sea level in New York Harbor has risen 15 inches.

The Hackensack River originates as a collection of insignificant brooks rising on South Mountain, below West Haverstraw, New York. Damming its headwaters formed Lake Lucille in 1928. Descending 34 miles south to its outlet in Newark Bay, the stream collects several tributaries as it courses along the western talus of the trap rock Palisades. The east and west branches unite in Lake DeForest, a reservoir created in 1966. Nauraushan Brook enters Lake Tappan, north of Convent Road in Rockland County. From its perch 150 feet above and half a mile back from the Hudson River, Rockland Lake also contributes. Continuing southward, Pascack Brook is its principal freshwater tributary in Bergen County. From 45 feet in elevation at the New York state line, the river drops to tide level at New Milford Avenue in Oradell, where a bench mark formerly recorded an elevation near the train station at 16.8 feet.[11] Before extensive modern alteration, salt meadows and white-cedar bottoms covered 19,850 square miles of estuary, spreading 4 miles wide and nearly 10 miles long; more recently, its drained marshes piled with garbage were renamed the Hackensack Meadowlands.

Since 1951, travelers in great number have sped across the miry barrier of the Hackensack Meadowlands on the New Jersey Turnpike—this roadway accommodated 232 million vehicles in 2015. We forget how, unbridgeable and nearly impassable in former times, this vast wetland impeded transit. However, that did not stop some from trying. To facilitate the export of copper ore from his North Arlington mine to the Bristol copper and brass works, Colonel John Schuyler invested £3,000 of his own money to build a 3-mile causeway of cedar logs running from the ferry steps on the Passaic River through cedar swamp, over the meadows and marshes of New Barbadoes Neck, to a ferry landing on the west bank of the Hackensack River. As work neared completion in 1772, the legislature authorized a lottery to raise £1,000 to cover the log causeway with gravel to prevent its destruction by fire. Despite its combustibility, this corduroy road obviated the tedium of a 15-mile detour around the marsh and therefore attracted "the Inhabitants of the Northern Parts of Sussex, Morris and Essex, in passing to and from New-York, by Paulus-Hook."[12] Scows served as ferries.

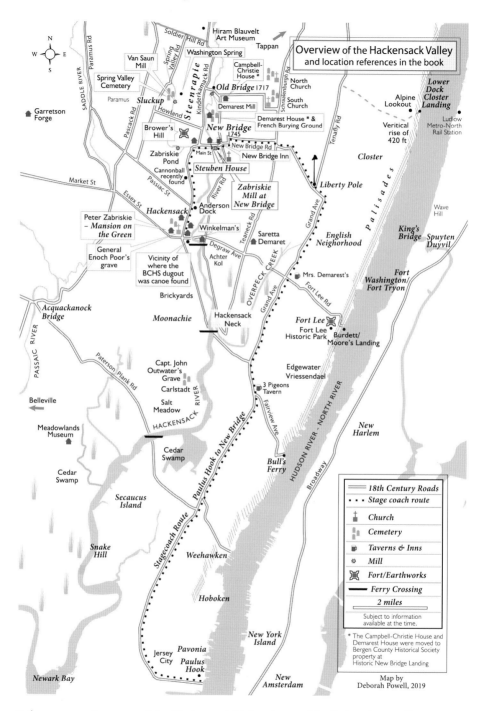

Reference overview map of the Hackensack Valley. (*created by Deborah Powell*)

Old Fort Lee road is the earliest described pathway circumventing the northern fringe of salt meadows flanking the Hackensack River and Overpeck Creek. Captain David De Vries walked this way "to Ackingh-sack" in August 1642, hiking from his plantation at Vriessendæl (Edgewater) "to see how far the colony of Heer Vander Horst had advanced." Though no longer continuous in name or route, being superseded by arteries feeding the George Washington Bridge, its former track may be traced today: It originated at a landing on the Hudson River in Edgewater, rising as River Road through a fault or offset in the Palisades to become Main Street in Fort Lee; it continues west as Fort Lee Road in Leonia, and, resuming west of Overpeck County Park, becomes Fort Lee Road and East Fort Lee Road in Bogota. West Fort Lee Road brings it to a bend in the Hackensack River and the Court Street Bridge. Crossing the river, Court Street intersects Main Street in Hackensack, a corner lot significant as the site of the Bergen County Courthouse.

Main Street in Hackensack is another ancient trail, branching westward as Passaic Street to Paramus Road, or crossing the Saddle River on Red Mill Road. This was once the principal road into the backcountry, leading around the Wagaraw bend in the Passaic River to Totowa. Thence it passed the Highlands along the route approximately now taken by State Route 23 from Pequannock to Port Jervis, New York.[13] A major branch crossed the Finger Lakes region to Lake Ontario at Oswego, New York.

Main Street, Hackensack, also continues north, to join Kinderkamack path. The earliest spelling (1686) is Kindokameck, an approximation of the Algonquian word Wenhakamike or Linhakamike, meaning "upland" or "top of the hill." The Jersey Dutch corrupted it to Kinderkamack and the road does indeed climb to the top of the hill in northern Oradell and Emerson before joining Old Hook Road.

Returning to the old Fort Lee road, we find it intersected two north–south arteries. A seventeenth-century deed refers to a Teaneck Path, now Teaneck Road, which joined the Tappan Path (1696) on the present route of Washington Avenue in Bergenfield and Schraalenburgh Road to the north. To the west, the old Fort Lee road intersects River Road in Bogota, which traces the east bank of the river north through Teaneck and New Milford to the Oradell Flats. Its antiquity and popularity is attested because it was widened from two to four rods in 1718. According to a road survey, dated November 23, 1717, it began on the Hackensack River at a place known as Winkelman (Winckleman), a neighborhood surrounding the intersection of River Road and West Fort Lee Road in Bogota.

Winkelman was Captain De Vries' destination in 1642. Why? Because Meyndert Meyndersen van Keren, Baron Nederhorst, had received a patroonal grant of land in the Hackensack valley the previous year. That winter, Nederhorst's agent Johannes Winkelman arrived upon Staten Island with farmers and livestock to establish "another colony behind the *Col*." (Bogota, NJ). Winkelman placed his outpost "nearest the Indians in order to trade with them easily," choosing a location along the Hackensack River in present-day Bogota. Here dugout canoes at the western terminus of the old Fort Lee trail ferried traders and travelers across the river on their trek between backcountry and Manhattan.[14] In May 1642, Winkelman supervised construction of a *bouwhuys*, 43 feet wide by 90 feet long, so close to the native village of Achinkeshacky that the colonists' cattle, wandering in the woods without a herdsman, "frequently came into the corn of the Indians which was unfenced on all sides, committing great damage there;" provoking "complaints" and "revenge on the cattle without sparing even the horses, which were valuable in this country."[15]

Cornelis Jansen Coelen (Cool) was engaged to operate the farm, but it did not last long. Routinely plied with alcohol and cheated, the neighboring native villagers fiercely attacked Winkelman's trading post on the night of September 27, 1643.[16] Five soldiers, five boys, and a servant defended the wooden structure with its thatched roof until attackers set it ablaze; its defenders narrowly escaping in a canoe, carrying only their firearms. On November 3, 1643, Sergeant Pieter Cock and Roeloff Jansen testified the following, after the Achter Col colony had been burnt:

> It was impossible to go there by land or by water to examine the place and its condition, because of the great number of savages, who burn and slay whatever they can lay hold of in the woods, on the Kil or elsewhere.[17]

An expedition was eventually mounted to retrieve "some iron work and ordnance" the attackers had sunk in the Hackensack River.

So we find the native village of Achinkeshacky seated at a crossroads in Bogota and likely near a canoe ferry over the Hackensack River, opposite what became and remains the county seat. Native villages were conveniently situated:

> Near the water sides, at fishing places, where they plant some vegetables; but they leave those places every year on the approach of winter, and retire to their strong places, or into the thick woods, where they are protected from the winds, and where fuel is plenty, and where there is game and venison.[18]

I suspect Achinkeshacky, or Ackingsack, soon corrupted to Hackensack, may be an approximation of *Achsinnigeu hacki*, meaning stony ground.

Counterbalancing the insurmountable Palisades to the east and an impassable swamp to the south and west, a tidal artery tapping the heart of a rich agricultural country was an economic asset of incalculable value, especially for moving bulk freight in an age of execrable mud lanes and stony, rutted roads. The Hackensack River has a mean tidal range of about 4.4 feet with spring tides averaging 5.3 feet and neap tides averaging 3.4 feet. A natural conveyor belt, the tide flows about 20 mph. Shallow-draft vessels of 40-ton burden could navigate 20 miles inland between March and December. With the tide, farmers and merchants sailed the fruits of their labor to city market and brought back whatever goods they might afford for their subsistence or adornment.[19] The tide also powered several gristmills.

A relatively self-contained geologic and cultural basin shaped the economy and folk culture of its inhabitants. The Jersey Dutch tilled and harvested advantageously proximate to the booming port of New York City, straddling piers of world trade on the Hudson River, where farmer and cosmopolitan commingled. They were proverbially noted for their bent for navigation, industriousness, thrift, and creature

The halberd was in the
dugout canoe when it
was found. The halberd
was not donated to the
Bergen County Historical
Society. (*Photo in Bergen
County Historical Society
Collections*)

A 15-foot white oak dugout canoe found in 1868 during an excavation for a cellar where Col. Garret C. Ackerman was constructing a house, now the location of the County Administration Building in Hackensack. (*Artifact in the Bergen County Historical Society Collections, photo by Deborah Powell.*)

comforts. Though chatting an archaic dialect, they imbibed the latest controversies, fashions and gossip of the Old World. Yet for the most part they seemed to keep their own company, maintaining a conservative rurality in webs of close kinship, proving ever capable of being both big-hearted and small-minded.

2

Indigenous Peoples

European adventurers who first penetrated the tidal bays, ascended the great rivers, and explored the Great Lakes and beyond did not intrude upon any peaceable kingdom. There was much bad blood in the northeastern woodlands—ancient feuds, unending wars of vendetta, and wars of extermination. Arrayed in opposing leagues, Iroquoian nations resided from the head of tide on the Hudson River, to the shores of the Great Lakes, and south along the Susquehanna River to Chesapeake Bay. Their numbers reflected the successful development of a small-kernel corn that produced "more and better flour in proportion," but that began to ripen about the middle of August.[1] This short-season variety suited the northern winter and fed growing populations, gathered in fortified hilltop towns, residing in bark-sheathed, bent-frame lodges, capable of storing hundreds of bushels of corn. Though constantly battling one another for dominance or survival, several of these Iroquoian chiefdoms positioned themselves to intercept and control the new Transatlantic trade in firearms for beaver skins.

Policy favors money, and peltries came from inland tribes of Susquehannocks, Senecas, Mohawks, Adirondacks, and Hurons.[2] In 1635, Father Jean de Brebeuf reported, "twelve other nations, all settled and numerous," besides the Hurons, spoke Iroquoian languages.[3] These included the Seneca, the Onondagas or "mountain people," the Ohioans, the Oneidas, the Maquaas, or Mohawks, and the Susquehannocks, also known as Minquas.[4] Some were better positioned than others to monopolize the most important trading outposts of Dutch, English, Swedish, or French merchants, but it often took wars of terror to compel submission from the original native coastal residents.

For reasons in the interest of all parties concerned, it became important to control and police the Hudson River corridor, lifeline of the exchange of beaver skins for weapons. For competitive advantage over rivals in adjacent New France and New England, Dutch traders at Fort Orange (Albany, New York) chose to favor and arm the Mohawks as the centerpiece of their diplomatic and commercial strategy.

The traders began to furnish firearms.[5] On February 22, 1643, a Mohican war party of eighty or ninety warriors, all armed with muskets, descended from Fort Orange to levy a contribution upon the Wickquasgeck and Tappan, and other adjacent villages. In the dead of night, they fell upon the native communities, forcing hundreds to flee through deep snow to seek protection on settlers' farms at Vriessendæl (Edgewater) and around Manhattan. The refugee column included "those of Hackingsack" and even many Esopus Indians from what is now Kingston, New York. Those at Vriessendæl continued after dawn to the Oysterbank at Pavonia (Jersey City). Most camped on the west edge of Jan-the-Laugher's Point at the mouth of Mill Creek, while others crossed to Curler's Hook on the East River. Yet instead of refuge, they found mayhem.

In the small hours of February 26, 1643, Director-General Wilhelm Kieft sent soldiers to murder or capture the unarmed and unsuspecting asylum seekers in their makeshift camps on Manhattan and Pavonia. At Jan-the-Laugher's Point in Jersey City, Kieft's goons massacred about eighty Indians, young and old alike, some in their sleep, most by slashing, and some by burning. Toddlers were tossed into the frigid waters of the Hudson River. Enraged survivors burnt four outlying Dutch plantations, killing ten colonists. The house of Johannes Winkelman at Achter Col (Bogota, New Jersey) was not spared.

Under the watchful eye of Mohawk enforcers, Oratamin (Oratam), Sachem at Achinkeshacky, agreed to a truce on April 22, 1643, acting also on behalf of native communities at Croton-on-Hudson, Ossining, Tappan, and on Long Island. Other river tribes soon followed suit. But the impetuous and stingy Dutch governor skimped on the customary compensation to injured parties, thereby goading the aggrieved to settle accounts by vendetta. Disruption of the beaver trade was threatened when, some 50 miles up the river from Manhattan, Wappingers began seizing Dutch boats in August 1643, killing crewmen and seizing cargoes.[6] With international backing on both sides, a battle for the Hudson was beginning.

Alarmed, New Amsterdam's newly elected advisory council of eight men decided to hire 150 English settlers on western Long Island under command of Captain John Underhill to augment the fort garrison, burgher guard, and armed citizenry organized into militia companies. However, Director-General Kieft's poor judgment left outlying farmsteads exposed, it simply being ineffective to garrison each one. Under pretense of trading pelts, nine Tappans slew several soldiers at Jacob Stoffelsen's farmhouse at Ahasimus (Jersey City) on October 1, 1644, then burned four farms at Pavonia (Jersey City). In response, New Amsterdam's small army took the offensive, raiding and destroying Indian villages near Greenwich (Connecticut), Tarrytown, Massapequa, and on Staten Island. Native casualties are unverifiably estimated at 750. The Mohawk ambassador Sisiadego brokered another peace treaty on August 30, 1645, with Oratamy (Oratam), chief of Achkinkeshacky (Hackensack); Pennekeck, chief at Achter Col (Newark Bay); Sesekemu, chief at Rechgawawanck, (Rockville Center, Long Island); Willem, chief at Tappan; and Pacham, chief of the Tankitekes, who were also empowered to speak for neighboring tribes.[7]

Mohawk and Seneca warriors destroyed a Huron town of about 2,000 inhabitants in July 1648. Eight months later, an army of 1,000 warriors inflicted

Image of a warrior from what is now Edgewater, NJ, selected from a larger drawing. (*David P. deVries, Korte Historiael, ende Journaels Aenteyckeninge, Hoorn: Symon Cornelisz Brekegeest, 1655*)

Large 1921 bronze bust of Oratam by John Ettl of Leonia. Oratam died in 1666. No known image was created of him during his lifetime. (*Artifact in the Bergen County Historical Society Collections, photo by Deborah Powell*)

another devastating blow, dispersing the Hurons to distant places. After half a century of warfare, the Mohawks next forced the Mohicans, their neighbors and rivals at Fort Orange, into tributary status in 1629. At this juncture, Reverend Johannes Megapolensis described the Mohawks as "the principal nation of all the savages and Indians hereabouts ¼ who have laid all the other Indians near us under contribution."[8]

When Fort Orange was built near the head of the tides and navigation on the Hudson River, the Mohawks inhabited the west bank, while the Mohicans resided on the east bank along Sturgeon's Hook and Fisher's Hook. Patroon Kiliaen van Rensselaer once described the Mohicans as a free and rich nation, over 1,600 strong, who had their own distinct Algonquian dialect. Their territory spread over 34,000 acres of mountain, valley, marsh and forest, rich in game, fish, and fowl, and included about 2,400 acres of cleared riparian land, standing normally three to five feet above the water, but annually enriched by the overflow of spring freshets. Defeated in 1629, they sold their lands to Kiliaen van Rensselaer in 1630–31.

Writing in 1628, when a fort of good quarry stone was being raised, the Reverend Jonas Michaelius noted, "The business of furs is dull on account of the new war of the (Mohawks) against the Mohicans at the upper end of this river. There have occurred cruel murders on both sides. The Mohicans have fled and their lands are unoccupied and are very fertile and pleasant."

Manatthans occupied the east side of New York Bay. After the sale of their home island 1626, the original inhabitants of Manhattan took up residence across the river on Bergen Neck.

Speaking a distinct dialect, the Sanhicans occupied the rich crescent of tidal lowlands fronting Raritan Bay, Staten Island, and Newark Bay as far north as the head of tides on the Hackensack and Passaic Rivers. Their territory was shaped like an arrowhead, its broad base formed by the wetlands bordering Newark and Raritan Bays and its point at the head of tides on the Delaware River at Trenton.[9]

The Susquehannocks were bound to Mohawk hegemony on the Hudson, which allying with or subjugating the various river tribes. As these tribes raised corn and pumpkins, often in great quantities, and produced other commodities for trade, they did not participate significantly in the beaver trade. The Susquehannocks (or Minquas, as the Dutch called them) seized control of trade routes via the Schuylkill and Minquas Kill, leading from the great forest to Dutch and Swedish trading posts on Delaware Bay and River. Yet the beaver trade on the Delaware River suffered for want of trade goods, with neither the Dutch or Swedes steadily providing their small outposts with cargoes. In July 1650, the Susquehannocks were evenly divided in their opinions: one half favoring the Swedes, who readily supplied their faction with muskets, powder, and lead; and others who favored the Dutch and sought armaments from their South River factor.

Sesekemu, chief of Rechgawawanck (Rockville Center, Long Island), Willem of Tappan and Oratamin (Oratam) and Pennekeck, chiefs at Achter Col, appeared at Fort Amsterdam on July 19, 1649, stating the Susquehannocks had asked them to live in friendship with Dutch, which they were willing to do. Throwing down beaver pelts with each promise made, Pennekeck thought it possible to live in peace, "forgetting on either side, what was past." Director-General Peter Stuyvesant expressed thanks for their offers of neighborly friendship and gave a small present worth about twenty guilders "to the common savages and some tobacco and a gun to the chief Oratamin, and so the savages departed well pleased."

Encouragement was given to establishing agricultural outposts on the mainland, opposite Manhattan. The directors of the Dutch West Indies Company granted Cornelis van Werckhoven a colony "beginning at Tappan, near the Colony of van Nederhorst and stretching northward through the Highlands" on November 7, 1651. Van Werckhoven instead chose to establish his colony on Long Island. Several land patents were issued in 1654 to prospective settlers for lands at Communipaw, Pavonia, and on the Kil van Kol. This population would not only provide the reinforcement the Dutch needed for their colonial population against their Indian neighbors, but also against the encroachment of New Englanders.

The Peach War

Nineteenth-century historical writers thought events took a sudden turn for the worse on September 15, 1655, because Hendrick van Dyck, who lived on the west side of Broadway, near the present site of Trinity Church, callously killed "one of the squaws for taking some peaches or other fruits from his garden." Contemporary accounts, however, only mention that Van Dyck was impaled with an arrow in his side while standing beside his garden gate at about 9 p.m. that evening.

The earliest reference to the Peach War is found, not in contemporary accounts, but in Washington Irving's fictional account of New Netherland, entitled *A History of New-York from the Beginning of the World to the End of the Dutch Dynasty*, by *Diedrich Knickerbocker*, first published in 1809. John Romeyn Brodhead tried to explain the name of the "Peach War" in his *History of the State of New York, First Period 1609–1664*, published in 1853:

> Ten years had passed away since Kieft's treaty at Fort Amsterdam, during which interval the relations between the Dutch and savages had generally been friendly. A new provocation now roused the red man to vengeance.
>
> Van Dyck, the superseded schout-fiscal, having killed a squaw whom he had detected in stealing some peaches from his garden, her tribe burned to avenge her death. The neighboring savages shared in the sentiment; and aware of the absence of the Dutch forces, they resolved to attack their defenseless settlements. A party of Mahicans, Pachamis, Esopus Indians, Hackinsacks, and Tappans, with some others from Stamford and Onkeway, supposed to number nineteen hundred, of whom five to eighteen hundred were armed, suddenly appeared before New Amsterdam in sixty-four canoes.[10]

During the hostilities, a farmhouse in Hoboken was set ablaze and then the whole of Pavonia, where everything was burned and every settler killed, except one. The 800 Indians who encamped at the tip of Manhattan now joined the others. Over the next three days, settlements upon Long Island were razed and Staten Island was cleared of people and houses.

By the time the fury subsided, fifty colonists were killed; another 100, mostly women and children, were captured; twenty-eight bouweries and plantations, together with 12,000–15,000 schepels of grain, were burned; and 500–600 cattle were either killed or taken. Councilor La Montagne stated the natives "of *Ahasimus (Harsimus Cove, Jersey City), Hackinkeshacky (Hackensack), Tappan* and others" participated in "this engagement and did the most damage to our people and committed the fearful cruelty of murdering seven men and women, whom they killed in cold blood." Hostages were taken and attempts for their return was negotiated.

The Ugly Mood Never Faded

In July 1663, when Oratam, sachem of Hackensack, was asked by the Dutch to sell Old Hackensack Neck, he answered, "that most of the young men of the tribe are out hunting, so that he has not been able to speak with them, but he has talked with the old warriors, who say, that they would not like to sell, preferring to keep a portion of it to plant, for they dare not go further inland for fear of being robbed by their enemies."[11, 12]

There is good documentary evidence to show that the Hackensacks were also closely related to the natives of Long Island and had their winter hunt there. As affirmed by De Rasieres in 1628, the "neighborhood of the Sancicans" was disturbed by "a state of constant enmity" with the Manhattans and related tribes, so much so that paths leading from Raritan Bay to the Trenton Falls were "but little used."[13] Between 1628 and 1634, the Sanhicans were driven away from the west shore of Raritan Bay by a band, known as the *Roaton* or *Raritanghe*, who had been expelled from the east bank of the Bronx River above Manhattan "by the Wappenos," and consequently fled across Staten Island and fought their way into the lower Raritan Valley. A treaty of peace was concluded between the Dutch and the Raritans in 1634, after which the Dutch "continued to trade with them by sending a sloop there every spring ¼"

3

Settlement of the Hackensack Valley

The East Bank: New Hackensack

To hopefully make it somewhat easier to navigate this tale, I have chosen to artificially separate the stories of the earliest settlements on the east and west banks of the Hackensack River at New Bridge, prior to the construction of the first bridge across the river narrows in 1744. So let us begin on the east side of the stream in the neighborhood where Teaneck and New Milford presently meet.

Confusingly for those who identify "Hackensack" with the city of that name on the west bank of the Hackensack River, the actual Indian village of Hackinkesacky, or Ahakinsack, was situated near the intersection of River Road and West Fort Lee Road in Bogota, where Johannes Winckleman, manager of the Achter Col colony, built a heavily framed and thatched roofed *bouwhuys* for a trading post in the spring of 1642. Consequently, Hackensack Township covered the ground between the Hackensack and Hudson Rivers between 1693 and 1871, when what remained of it was divided into Ridgefield, Englewood, and Palisades townships. The village of Hackensack on the west bank in what was New Barbadoes Township only officially became known as the city of Hackensack in 1921.

Having a maximum width of about 1 mile, Hackensack Neck was the name given to the peninsula between the Hackensack River and its major tributary, Overpeck Creek. Journeying seven miles from its most remote sources, the Overpeck enters the main stream at Ridgefield Park, opposite Little Ferry. An alluvial fan of marshes once sheltered small freshwater tributaries entering the creek from encompassing uplands. The Brack Meadows, which formerly extended north along the Overpeck to Fycke Lane in Teaneck and to Sheffield Avenue in the Nordhoff section of Leonia, were seasonally mown in former times for valuable crops of salt hay. In 1876, one historical commentator noted, "The valley of the Overpeck is tide meadow, every inch of which is cut for farming purposes." The favorable combination of well-drained upland and salt meadow led the same observer to praise these "well cultivated and productive lands." Early spellings include Awapough, Awapuck, or Aquapeake Creek, which seem to be approximations of either the Algonquian word "*wipochk*," referring to "a bushy place," or *wequa-peek* (in some dialects, *ukque-paug*), referring to "the head of the bay." It may also possibly be equivalent to the Massachusetts áupauk (Eliot), meaning "flooded or overflowed land" and referring to meadows that border a creek. The Overpeck has also been called the English Creek in reference to the English Neighborhood, later Englewood.

Hackensack Neck rises near the junction of the Hackensack River and Overpeck Creek, reaching 158 feet above sea level just north of Fort Lee Road in Bogota. It achieves a height of 173 feet in Teaneck near the intersection of Barr Avenue and Carrol Place, but subsides again to the north along New Bridge Road. French Creek (French Vale) rises from Fountain Spring and skirts the northern slope of Teaneck ridge before joining the Hackensack River at New Bridge. The French Creek, originally styled Hesawakey Brook, formed the southern boundary of the Demarest Patent. The Demarest deed of Indian purchase in 1677 required the concurrence of twenty-seven Tappan Indians, suggesting that a comparatively large number of Indian families cultivated this friable expanse of river plain. A cove still partly evident in Brett Park, and referred to as the "Old River" in some early deeds, is an

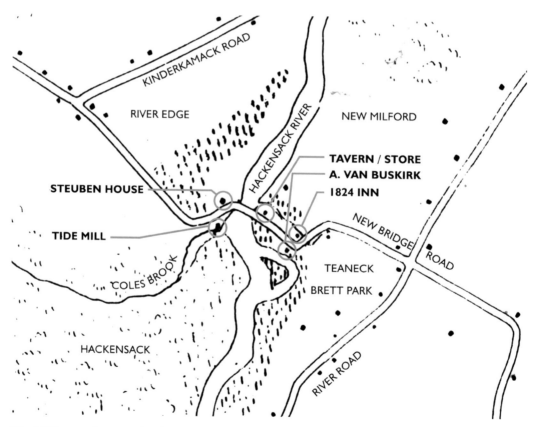

The 1839 coastal survey showing New Bridge, information text added by Deborah Powell.

"elbow" or abandoned meander of the stream. The 1839 Coastal Survey shows an island within this cove that apparently was once attached to the west bank. Erosion cut off this meander and the island has either vanished or been attached to the east bank (perhaps by human intervention).

The upland spine, lying east of the Hackensack River and where the back slope of the Palisades descends into the sandstone valley, was formerly known Schraalenburgh, a name that survives only on the road riding the crest of this ridge to the north. Schraalenburgh describes a "scrawny or narrow ridge." This is most evident where Schraalenburgh Road passes Haworth and the declivities on either side of the narrow ridge are immediately evident. Westward, sand dunes and deltas, left over from the shores of a proglacial meltwater lake, embank the east side of the river, continuing south of Old New Bridge Road. New Milford occupies the river plain, which the Tappan Indians once cultivated. River Road, running along the east side of the river from the Winkelman section of Bogota north to the Oradell Flats, superimposes a prehistoric footpath. When the road was widened in 1717, John Demarest also marked out a four-rod road leading westward to the Hackensack River at New Bridge, leading perhaps to a landing, a canoe ferry or ford. The "Road of New Hackensack that leads from the bridge east" was again surveyed in April 1745 across Peter Demarest's lands to the first bend in French Creek and then across Lawrence van Buskirk's upland (as near the brook as possible) before re-crossing the stream onto Peter Demarest's land again, and continuing east to Washington Avenue/Teaneck Road. This was the original route of New Bridge Road. It was re-aligned again in 1767 on the line dividing the farms of Peter Demarest, deceased, and Lawrence P. Van Buskirk, deceased. The east abutment of the original bridge, erected in 1744–45, stood about where the modern highway bridge crosses the Hackensack River into River Edge today. It wasn't until August 1753 that Peter Demarest, Jr., asked the highway surveyors to lay out a two-rod road "from Peter Demaris [*sic*.] to New Bridge so called, now that the said bridge being removed, we lay the way out from said road with a southerly course to a post, being four-panel fence from the dock, easterly from said dock, thence from said line westerly four rods wide." This is approximately the present route of Old New Bridge Road on the boundary between New Milford and Teaneck.

Tantaqua was listed as a native owner of lands surrounding the tidal estuary of the Hackensack River, from Newark Bay northward to New Bridge, in July 1668, February 1672, January 1676, September 1677, and November 1686. He was listed as a Sackamaker (chief) of the Hackensacks in April 1678. After selling the northern part of Teaneck (then known as New Hackensack) in 1677, he and his kinfolk moved westward across the Hackensack River. His last known residence was on the ground where the Steuben House now stands, which was called Tantaquas Plain in the 1680s. Cole's Brook, which enters the Hackensack River immediately south of the Steuben House, was originally called Tantaquas Creek.

According to a journal that he kept of his travels through the Middle Atlantic colonies in 1679–80, Jasper Danckærts, a Labadist missionary, met an old Hackensack sachem named Tantaqua at Danckærts' lodging in Manhattan. He described him as "a man about eighty years of age, whom our people called Jasper, who lived at Ahakinsack (Hackensack) or at Ackinon" (Acquackanonck). He was the brother of a sakemaker (chief) and was accompanied by a young man identified as a sakemaker's son. Danckærts' landlords related:

> When they lived on Long Island, it was once a very dear time; no provisions could be obtained, and they suffered great want, so that they were reduced to the last extremity; that God the Lord then raised up this Indian, who went out fishing daily in order to bring fish to them every day when he caught a good mess, which he always did.[1]

Possessing a "great affection for him," they gave him the name Jasper and considered him their "*nitap*, that is, my great friend." Reportedly, "he sometimes got drunk." In the Sanhican Lenape dialect, "*tinteywe*" means fire.[2]

In October 1679, Tantaqua explained to Jasper Danckærts a seemingly godless act of creation, taking a piece of charcoal from the fire and drawing upon the floor:

> He first drew a circle, a little oval, to which he made four paws or feet, a head and a tail. "This," said he, "is a tortoise, lying in the water around it," and he moved his hand round the figure, continuing, "This was or is all water, and so at first was the world or the earth, when the tortoise gradually raised its round back up high, and the water ran off of it, and thus the earth became dry." He then took a little straw and placed it on end in the middle of the figure, and proceeded, "The earth was now dry, and there grew a tree in the middle of the earth, and the root of this tree sent forth a sprout beside it and there grew upon it a man, who was the first male. This man was then alone, and would have remained alone; but the tree bent over until its top touched the earth, and there shot therein another root, from which came forth another sprout, and there grew upon it the woman, and from these two are all men produced. [3]

The southern tribes of Lenape told the same creation myth seventy years later, as recorded in July and August 1750 by Peter Kalm:

> A large turtle floated on the water. Around it gathered more and more slime and other material that fastened itself to it, so that it finally became all America. The first savage was sent down from heaven, and rested on the turtle. When he encountered a log he kicked it, and behold, people were formed from it. In every city (of the Red Men) there is ordinarily one family, which takes the name of 'Turtle.'[4]

An old Indian said that when God had created the world and its people, he took a stick, cast it on the ground, and spoke unto man, saying, 'Here thou shalt have an

Tantaqua's mark on a deed from January 6, 1676, for the sale of New Hackensack, extending from Old Hackensack north to French Creek at New Bridge, "adjoining to the Great Indian Field–called the Indian Castle" to Laurence Andriessen (Van Boskerk) & Company.

animal which will be of great service to thee, and which will follow thee wherever thou goest,' and in that moment the stick turned into a dog.[5]

On June 24, 1669, Governor Carteret confirmed a grant of 2,260 acres, lying between the Hackensack River and Overpeck Creek, to Sarah Kiersted, who had received it as a gift from the Hackensack sachem Oratam. On January 6, 1676, Tantaqua joined six other Hackensack sachems, namely, Cusquehem, Nechtamcepepeaw, Wansoughham, Kanagions, Anesachore, and Poughquickquarae, in the sale of New Hackensack, extending from the bounds of Old Hackensack northward to "a small kill or Vale (French Creek) adjoining to the Great Indian Field—called the Indian Castle" to Laurence Andriessen (Van Buskirk) & Company. In present terms, this tract extends from about the boundary between Bogota and Teaneck northward to French Creek on the present boundary between Teaneck and New Milford boundary. "The Great Indian Field—called the Indian Castle," located on the south side of the French Creek at New Bridge, refers to the high ground, above the river, including Roemer Woods and upper Brett Park. This is a rare reference to a palisaded Lenape fortification, or "castle" in New Jersey. In 1644, "three castles" at Wickquaesgeck, probably near Stamford, Connecticut, were "constructed of plank five inches thick, nine feet high, and braced around with balk full of port-holes."[6]

On April 10, 1682, Laurence Andriessen (Van Buskirk) of Minacques received a patent for 1,076 acres at "Hackensack," which lay north of the Kiersted Patent in Teaneck. According to the original survey, the bounds of this "tract of land upon the Hackensack River containing 1,076 acres" began:

With a stake planted by a small creek (French Creek) that parts David de Marais land from this—from thence running as the brook runs forty chains to a black oak

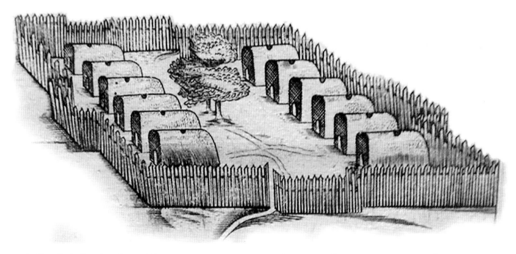

Palisaded Castle above Tappan, *A New Mapp of East and West New Jarsey being an Exact Survey Taken by Mr. John Worlidge*, 1698. (*Special Collections and University Archives, Rutgers University.*)

tree marked on four sides by a spring (near Spring Avenue in Bergenfield)—running thence East Northerly (actually southeast) 98 chains upon the edge of a great swamp to a white wood tree marked on four sides —thence running west 136 chains to the Hackensack River—and thence running North Northeast as the river runs 78 chains to the stake where it first began, Bounded on the Northeast part by John Demarest and part by a small creek (French Creek at the southern boundary of New Milford), southeast by a great swamp and the West Branch of Overpeck Creek (which flows southward from the Knickerbocker Country Club in Bergenfield through Mackay Park in Englewood), Southwest by a highway (most likely Fort Lee Road), and Northwest by the Hackensack River—allowance for barren land and highways is to remain for 900 acres English measure.

On December 31, 1695, East Jersey proprietor Robert Vanquillin, of Woodbridge, issued a quit claim to Thomas Lawrence (Van Buskirk), Derick Epkee (Banta) of New Hackensack, and to their partners for a certain lot lying between Old Hackensack and the lands of John Demarest (along the French Creek at New Bridge) and extending from the Overpeck Creek to the Hackensack River. This partnership was referred to as the Dutch Company.

The will of Laurence Andrise (Van Buskirk) was drawn on August 29, 1679 and proven on March 19, 1693. It names the children of his wife Jannetie Jans by her first husband, Christian Barents. They and their descendants owned property in the vicinity of New Bridge.

The Wood Church or Boskirk

On August 8, 1716, Laurence Van Boskerk (Van Buskirk) of Hackensack deeded a parcel of land in Teaneck in consideration of love and good will towards the Lutheran Church. This small tract was described as being "on Hackinsack Creek or River Joining a small River that Runs between the lands of Nicholas Lassure (Lozier), shoemaker, and the said parcel of Land." The deed survey began on the King's Road ten feet from the "small Run or Creek" and ran all along the small run of water "always Ten Foot from it to the mouth of the said River" to the "Great Hackensack Creek or River" and thence along the Hackensack River northerly 223 feet, from thence easterly to the King's Road on such a course that "the South Breadth from King's Road may fully be 163 Feet, the Beginning of this Breadth to be made on the Hackingsack River between Nicholas Lassure (Lozier), and the said Parcel of Land, only keeping Ten Foot distance from it as aforesaid." The grant of land was made on the condition that the Protestant Lutheran Congregation should build "a House for Divine Worship for the use of the Protestant Lutheran Congregation in and about Hackinsack" within the term of four years. The Reverend Justus Falkner, son of a Lutheran minister in Saxony, is credited with being the first pastor to several Lutheran congregations in New Jersey, each numbering about 100 communicants.[7]

Ordained by Swedish ministers, he arrived in New York on November 25, 1703. As late as February 27, 1704, Lutheran services were conducted in the barn of Cornelius Van Boskerk. A small wooden church was built sometime soon thereafter.

It is uncertain exactly when the small church was built, but the United Lutheran Congregation of New York and Hackensack sent out a blank call for a minister to the Holy Trinity Lutheran Church in London, promising the new pastor to pay for the expense of his journey, a salary of £60, a free residence, wood and light, and additional payments, ranging from several to as much as twenty shillings each, for funeral sermons, graveside prayers, for officiating at marriages outside and marriages at the house, for publishing marriage notices, and performing christenings. He was to spend summers in New York and winters in Hackensack.[8]

After making several visits, the Reverend Henry Melchior Muhlenberg recommended Reverend William A. Graaf to minister to the Lutheran congregations at Hackensack and Ramapo. He took charge in May 1760, making his home at Ramapo and traveling to the Hackensack congregation on alternate Sundays. In 1759, a lottery was held to raise money "for repairing of the Lutheran Church, in Hackensack." The winning tickets were drawn on December 11, 1759 at Shooter's Island, about two miles from Elizabethtown Point. The lottery managers were Lawrence Van Buskirk, Jacob Titsort, Johannes Demarest, Captain Jacobus Van Buskirk, Lawrence Van Horn, and John Vanorden. Reverend Graaf departed for Zion Church in New Germantown, Hunterdon County, in 1775. According to Reverend David Demarest, citing Muhlenberg's diary, "the first American-educated Lutheran minister in this country came from the Hackensack congregation."[9]

This was the twenty-two-year-old son of Captain Jacob Van Buskirk. On October 31, 1776, the records of St. Matthew's Church indicate that conditions at the country church in Hackensack Township were so deplorable, it was deemed necessary to transfer the church register to the New York church. In 1917, several antiquarians were removing dirt from atop a stone burial vault, when they unearthed a stone, broken and used for a capping stone, with twenty-eight letters about two inches high, woven into monograms similar in style to those on the eastern wall of the church on the Green. This stone, with another (that is upside down and may contain letters also) were no doubt in the church walls, representing "the founders of the church."[10]

A visitor to the site of the Lutheran Church at New Bridge in 1890 reported:

I visited the locality of the old Hackensack Lutheran Church. The site is on the east side of the river, about a quarter of a mile from the place called New Bridge. The point is a sandy steep shore between the water and the highway, scarcely seventy feet and at least twenty-five feet above the river. Formerly the plot was evidently wider than it is now, but it is clear that at least one-quarter of the churchyard has been washed away by reason of the caving in of the shore. Only four gravestones still remain and all bear the name Van Boskerk.

The church stood broadside along the road and had a pointed roof. It is probable that in the attempt to straighten the road some of the original space was lost. Now the place is overgrown with small trees, brush and ferns and it appears to have met with some consideration, though no fence protects it.

I met a very old man who said that he had always lived near New Bridge and could well remember the church before it was burned down. He had always thrown stones at it at bats. The structure was still in pretty fair condition; the roof leaked only here and there and the pulpit was good enough to preach in. When preaching had been done there he did not remember. One day as he was working in the corn field he saw smoke ascending and soon the interior was burned out. A spark from a brush fire in the neighborhood had set it afire.

"That took place, so they say, in 1812, for I was a boy and am now eighty-nine. Well do I remember Dr. Shaffer of New York in the summer of 1821 preached in the church-yard; he stood upon the ruins of the old church and tried to awaken a new interest in the old congregation, but he did not succeed. 'With the exception of this old man and a woman equally as old I found nobody that could give me any information.'"[11]

While little is now known of the Lutheran church at New Bridge, even less is known about a Lutheran parsonage (or perhaps only a parsonage lot) associated with it. On April 15, 1828, Peter Van Buskirk, John J. Van Buskirk and his wife, Catherine, and John J. Van Buskirk and his wife, Myselake of Hackensack Township deeded 2 acres, formerly belonging to the Lutheran Congregation and since descended by law to the parties of the first part, to Charles Cluss of Hackensack Township for $150. This lot was bounded north by a small brook, formerly and commonly called by the name of French Brook, east by lands of Charles Cluss, south by lands of Mabie, and west by the public road (that is to say, River Road) leading from Old Bridge to Winkelman's (in Bogota). This indicates the Lutheran parsonage (or parsonage lot) stood northeast of the intersection of New Bridge and River Roads in what is now known as the Roemer Tract in northern most Teaneck.

Peter Lawrence (Van Boskerk) acquired title to 356 acres of land on the east side of the river at New Bridge in 1697, which was bordered south by 240 acres acquired by his brother Lawrence (Van Boskerk). The Lutheran church deed of 1704 mentions the King's Road, later known as the road leading from Old Bridge to Old Hackensack and presently as River Road.

A quit-claim or release from East Jersey proprietor James Bollen to the heirs of John and David Demarest, Sr., dated September 15, 1720, refers to "Peter Demarest's land beginning on the mouth of a run or brook (that is to say, the outlet of French Creek into the Hackensack River at New Bridge) which divides the land of Pieter Van Boskerck & Pieter Demarest opposite the house of Johannis Ackerman." This proves Peter Van Boskerk owned the land straddling the present boundary of New Milford and Teaneck along Old New Bridge Road, lying south of the outlet of French Creek, in 1720. The "house of Johannis Ackerman" stood on the opposite side of the Hackensack River near the present intersection of Elizabeth Court and Main Street in River Edge.

Though unremembered today, Cornelius Wynkoop was perhaps the first merchant to settle in the neighborhood that later became known as New Bridge. A son of Benjamin Wynkoop and Femmetje Van der Heul, Cornelius was baptized in the Dutch Reformed Church in New York City on December 1, 1699. He married Elisabeth van der Spiegel at the Dutch Reformed Church at New York City on May 9, 1724.[12] They had four children. Cornelius and Elisabeth Wynkoop moved to New Hackensack between 1730 and 1736, most likely leasing land from Pieter Van Buskirk. The survey of an adjacent riverside tract, sold by Lawrence Van

Buskerk on April 24, 1736 to John Anderson, crossed "the Top of Mr. Wynkoep, his bolten (flour bolting) house." We know from newspaper advertisements that he lived at New Bridge in November 1745, where he operated a bakery, opposite to John Zabriskie's Mills. He occupied "a good Dwelling House Forty Feet front and Forty-two Feet long; a Bolting-House, a Bake-House, a Baker's Oven, and a Kitchen, and a Wharf for Vessels to load and unload at."[13] Two years later, on April 4, 1747, *The New York Gazette Revived in the Weekly Post Boy* advertised:

> A Very convenient House, for a Store-keeper and Bolter, of 40 Feet in Breadth and 42 in Length, four Rooms on a Floor, a very good dry Cellar and Cellar-Kitchen, a Bolting-House and Bolts, a Bake-House, Smoke House, Stable, Garden, and about 5 Acres of Land thereunto belonging, situate on Hackinsack River in the County of Bergen and Province of New-Jersey, navigable for Vessels of about fifty Tons; there is a very good Wharf at the Door for Vessels to load and unload.[14]

The last will and testament of Peter Boskerk, drawn on January 20, 1736, and proven September 8, 1738, provides an inventory of his lands, including those at what became New Bridge. He bequeathed his real and personal estate to his wife, Tryntje, during her lifetime but provided for the division of his property among his children after her decease. Regarding a tract of 600 acres at New Hackensack (Teaneck), then occupied by his sons Lawrence and Johannes: Lawrence was to receive the northeastern half (300 acres) bounded north by Peter Demarest, southeast by Teaneck Path (Teaneck Road) and partly by "land sold by me to my son Johannes," southwest by land of Jacob Van Boskerk, and northwest by the road (either the predecessor of New Bridge Road or River Road). His son Johannes received the southeastern part (300 acres) of the tract, bounded southwest by Benjamin Van Boskerk, northwest by the Teaneck Path, northeast by David Demarest, and southeast by Overpeck Creek. His son, Andries, received the 60 acres of upland and salt meadow, together with the mills, situated on the Kill Van Kull, whereon Peter Boskerk resided. His son Jacobus, born in 1705 at Constable's Hook, received the remainder of his homestead plantation in Bergen County. By codicil to his will, dated September 8, 1738, he left his sons, Andries and Jacobus, "an equal share of my brew kettle."

Peter Boskerk named four sons and four daughters in his will: Lawrence, Johannis (Hans), Willempty, Jannety, Andries (Andrew), Jacobus, Rachel, and Antje. His sons divided his lands according to his wishes—the division being made by deeds dated August 12 and 24, 1738, recorded November 9, 1764.

Lawrence Pieterse Van Buskirk inherited his father's portion of the New Hackensack Patent on the east side of the river at New Bridge in 1738. Construction of the New Bridge in 1744–45 clearly encouraged settlement and commercial development in this neighborhood. While the deed record is incomplete, county records covering the maintenance of the bridge refer to Lawrence Van Buskirk's ownership of these lands. For example, in 1765, the Freeholders ordered:

> That Lawrence Van Buskirk, Esq., and John Zabriskie do take the chains that are now on the New Bridge & dispose of them to the best advantage for the benefit of

the county and ordered that they shall buy good Pitched Ropes & fix upon the Draw Bridge & have said Bridge put in good repair.

Again in 1768, the Freeholders ordered, "that the Bridge commonly called the New Bridge between Lawrence Van Buskirk's, Esq. and John Zabriskie shall be repaired."

Lawrence Van Buskirk's real estate was divided among his heirs in 1767. Again, the records are incomplete, but we know that Lawrence Pieterse Van Buskirk had at least four children: Jacobus, Abraham, Andrew, and Elizabeth (wife of Isaac Vroom, Vroomen, or Roome). Three sons—Jacobus Van Buskirk, Abraham Van Buskirk, and Andrew Van Buskirk—were to play important roles at New Bridge in the years leading up to the American Revolution.

The Great Awakening fractured Jersey Dutch society into competing conservative (*Conferentie*) and liberal (*Coetus*) factions, often dividing families. Conservatives wanted their ministers trained in Holland and conducting services in Dutch. Espousing the value of the conversion experience and religious "enthusiasm," the liberals were eager to Americanize their church and to appeal to a younger generation. This split widened during the American Revolution, taking on an often-violent political dimension. The success of the Whig rebellion and the attainment of American independence drove away many loyalists or diminished (at least briefly) their social standing.

David Des Demarest

David Des Marest led a restless life. As a Protestant born at Beauchamp, in Picardy, he was forced to flee his homeland and join a French colony at Middleburg on the island of Walcheren, Zeeland. There, on July 24, 1643, he married Marie Sohier, daughter of Francois Sohier, a Walloon refugee from Nieppe.[15] Their eldest son, Jean, was born in April 1645. By 1651, they removed to Mannheim, on the Rhine, settling under the protection of Charles Lewis, elector of the Lower Palatinate, where they helped organize a French church.[16] Two sons were born during their stay at Mannheim, namely David in 1652 and Samuel in 1656.

With their place of refuge threatened with invasion by the Catholic Duke of Lorraine, David Demarest returned with other Huguenots to Holland. On April 16, 1663, the family boarded the *Bonte Koe* for transport to New Netherland, paying 175.10 florins as passage and board for husband, wife "& 4 Children of 18, 11, 6 and 1 years."[17] They first settled upon Staten Island, where they joined with other Huguenots in organizing a French congregation. In 1665, the Demarests took up lands at New Harlem. On May 1, 1670, David Des Marest was listed as owner of a house and farm lots totaling 16 acres of land. His son Jean married Jacomina, the daughter of Simon De Ruine, a Walloon from Landrecy in Hainault, in 1668. On March 3, 1671, Jean received his patent for a lot 26 yards wide, and 160 rods long, encompassing 13 acres. He also purchased a house lot and farm from Johannes La Montagne, with the crop sown thereon.[18]

In August 1673, David Demarest, Sr., was appointed *schepen*. David Demarest, Jr., purchased a vacant lot of the late Lubbert Gerritsen at an estate sale in July 1674.

The Demarests and their Huguenot neighbors organized a French congregation at New Harlem and engaged a preacher in 1674. Consequently, Governor Francis Lovelace, ordained that "the French of the Town of New Harlem should be free as to contributing to the Dutch *Voorleser*" and David Demarest ceased making "Free-will Contributions for the support and salary of the Voorleser of this Town ..." according to an agreement entered into on October 23, 1670 (though not signed by any Demarest).[19]

On October 3, 1676, Hendrick Jansen Vander Vin, Parish Voorleser or clerk at New Harlem, complained that his house was unfit for occupancy. Accordingly, it was ordered that the schoolhouse be adapted for his dwelling with the installation of a bedroom (*bedstede*), chimney and mantle, together with repairs to the doors and windows. It was further determined "to repair the old house the following spring." David Demarest, Senior, was assigned to work in "the loft," to put a lock on the door and to glaze the windows. David Demarest, Jr., however, refused to contribute towards the repairs and was ordered to pay twelve guilders to the Deacons and for court charges.

By this time, the Demarests were intent upon establishing a French colony upon the Hackensack River, to be settled by thirty or forty families, transported from Europe. David Demarest, Sr., and his son, David, sold their property at New Harlem to Paulus Richard, a New York merchant, on March 12 and April 12, 1677, respectively. David Demarest, Sr., reserved the use and occupancy of his house at New Harlem until May 1, 1677, on which date he planned to take his family, and Jacques Le Roe, to the site of their proposed colony.[20] On April 14, David Demarest appeared before the Mayor's Court, stating his intention to depart the town, but agreeing grudgingly to pay his arrears for the maintenance of Voorleser Vander Vin. To the magistrates, he remarked, "You people are my enemies, and seek but to drive me into costs."[21] On April 23, 1677, David Demarest, Jr., paid up his arrears. His father settled his accounts three days later.

On June 8, 1677, the Demarests completed their purchase of lands in the Hackensack valley from the Tappan Indians. Daniel Du Voor, Jean Durie, and Nicholas De Vaux soon joined David. On October 7, 1678, the seven adult members of the Demarest family, together with Jacques La Rou, united by certificate with the Bergen Reformed Church.[22]

In the gathering warmth of a May dawn in 1677, a small flotilla navigated a thick mist upon the waters of the Hackensack River. An incoming tide crept imperceptibly through reedy marshes and gloomy cedar swamps, urging the boats upstream. David Demarest, Sr., his sons and their families, joined by Jacques Larue, had packed their arks with the necessities of a new life on the frontier: several head of cattle, seed grain and agricultural utensils, hewn timbers to frame houses, meager household furnishings, and provisions for man and beast. The Demarests left no journal, and we are left to surmise the details of their voyage.

Daylight disclosed high ground to east and west, but this land had already been ceded to others; these Huguenot pioneers would have to travel inland for a dozen miles to stake their claim. Having passed the village of Bergen upon the heights, the river bent westward around the conical masses of Snake Hill and Little Snake Hill. A marsh creek set apart these trap rock sentinels from Panepack Neck and the island of Sikakes guarded by dark stands of white cedar.[23, 24] Perhaps they saw a faint curl of chimney smoke rising from a small stone house on the sandstone upland to the west, the lone residence for many miles.[25] Several wooded swells of ground, called Moenachia, Chestnut Island, and Peach Island, seemed to float amidst the Wolf Swamp and cedar bottoms, interlaced by marsh creeks.[26] Hereabout, the voyagers may have tried their hand at catching large snapping turtles in the tidal meadows. Shortly after passing a marsh-fringed eminence where the waters of Awapough joined the mainstream, a few charred timbers marked the former site of the ill-fated *Colonie van der Heer Neder Horst*.[27, 28] About 500 or 600 paces beyond, a few tumbling bark huts in an abandoned clearing, strategically situated upon a steep bluff on the east side of the stream, were all that remained of the Indian plantation of Achkinkes Hacky.[29] In 1643, the Hackensacks had been "full a thousand strong," but their numbers had declined precipitously. Upon selling the lower half of the peninsula in 1664, the dwindled population established their new *Uteneyik* (villages) farther north, near the headwaters of the West Branch of the Overpeck.[30] Pulled northward by the tide, the Huguenot colonist passed Warepeake, with its stately forest of sycamores, rapidly greening with the lengthening days.[31]

Rounding a large bend in the river the Red Hills and sandy bluffs converged at a place called Aschatking, narrowing the river's passage.[32, 33] The wooden palisades of an Indian fort stood atop a hill overlooking the Gessawakin, a small run of water that issued from an inland spring and curled westward to the Hackensack, marking the northernmost boundary of the Hackensacks.[34] Lands upon the east bank of the river known as New Hackensack, extending from Achkinkes Hacky north to the Indian fort, had been recently conveyed by the Hackensack sachems to Laurence Andriessen Van Buskirk and the Dutch Company.

Native fishermen were out in force with their seines, attempting to catch shad, striped bass, herring, yellow perch, eels, and sturgeon. Finally, the water-borne French colonists arrived at the head of the river plain and disembarked.

The Demarest assembled the precut framing timbers for a house, measuring about twenty-feet square, which they had carried with them from New Harlem.[35] The first house in which David Des Marest resided was located "on the East side of the Hackensack and doubtless very near to his mills at the Old Bridge," probably on the south side of River Edge Avenue in New Milford, just east of the present bridge.[36]

When Surveyor-General Robert Vauquellen surveyed 16 acres on the west side of the river for David Demarest, Sr., by warrant dated July 30, 1681, the property was bounded east by "the mill and mill-dam and the river." This was the first grant of land made to a European settler within the bounds of River Edge. David Demarest, Sr., immediately settled upon this land west of the Hackensack River and erected a gristmill, which stood on the river's edge, east of the intersection of Grove and Park Avenues. His wife Marie Sohier, and Jean's wife, Jacomyntie Dreuyn, both died before 1682, when they disappear from the records.

On March 23, 1683, the Governor's Council received a petition from David Demarest desiring "to have all the Timber in that Indian purchase for the supply of his saw Mill although the land not patented to him and his Sons." The Council agreed to issue patents for the lands duly surveyed to the Demarests but could not see any reason "to grant liberty to Cut the timber from the land he takes not up until further matters appears than what is yet manifested." On May 29, 1684, David and Samuel Demarest again petitioned the Council "setting forth that they have an Indian Deed of gift for a Tract of Land on Hackingsacke River containing 300 Acres or there about—Desire lib'ty that they have a Conveyance thereof—" to which the Council agreed upon the stipulation that a formal survey be made and quit-rents established.[37]

On October 15, 1684, the Governor and Proprietors of East Jersey purchased:

> A tract of land lying and being upon Hackinsack River, bounded on the south and east by Hackensack River and Korands land, a little below a great rock lying in the river, running from the said river northwest unto a place called Kaharos, from thence running along Peskeckie Creek northeasterly unto Metchipakos Creek, so running along the said Creek southeasterly unto Hackensack River, and so along the said river unto Korands land.[38]

The native owners were listed as Memmess (Memsha), a Tappan sachem, Seythepoey, Korand (Coovange), Mettachmahon, Rawtom, Jan Claes, Mendenmass (Mendewmass), Mettetoch, Hepenemaw, Marenaw (Mareque), and Hayamakeno (Hayankeno).[39] The buyers had to deliver ten waistcoats, eight kettles, six blankets, two stroudwaters, six guns, two pistols, five shirts, five pairs of stockings, ten quarts of gunpowder, sixty bars of lead, ten hatchets, ten hoes, sixty knives, an anker of rum, fifteen fathoms of white wampum, and four harpoons to the native owners and sellers of the land within one year. The deed was signed October 8, 1685, before Samuel Edsall, William Lawrence, Albert Saborasky (Zabriskie), Lawrance Andress (Van Buskirk), Kobus (the Indian who marked the trees), and Samuel Demarest.

On November 27, 1684, a Tappan elder named Korough (a sachem who resided within the precincts of present-day River Edge, and whose named is variously represented as Coovang, Corange, or Kovand) appeared before the Council to complain against David Demarest.[40]

After hearing both sides, the Council reprimanded the Demarests and ordered that they provide security for their good behavior in the future. Samuel Edsall and William Lawrence were appointed commissioners to investigate the disputed property and report back to the Council with their recommendations.

On January 5, 1686, East Jersey Proprietor and Governor, Gawen Lawrie received a patent for three parcels of land on the west bank of the Hackensack River: one of 1,520 acres lying north of David Demarest and bounded north and west by unsurveyed lands; another tract of 643 acres lying bounded south by John Demarest, north by David Demarest and west by unsurveyed land; and a third of 261 acres bounded north by David Demarest, south by Albert Zabriskie and west by unsurveyed lands.[41]

The West Bank

The valley still whispers old names, though some are entirely faded from maps and memory, such as Aschatking, Steenrapie and Kinderkamack, which hint at its original occupants. Aschatking is likely a corruption of *tachtschaunge,* or *woaktschachne,* describing the narrows of the river, where it flows out from the confining hills that shadow its headwaters. The farming neighborhood lying along the road leading from Old Bridge to New Bridge was curiously called Steenrapie, later corrupted into Stony Arabia. *Steen* is the Dutch word for "stone," which prompts some to mistakenly believe—as with the *kinder* in Kinderkamack—that these toponyms are of Dutch origin. Most likely, Steenrapie, which describes the hilltop neighborhood in northern River Edge, is an approximation of the Algonquian word, *Lenacki,* meaning "high ground, upland." The countryside atop the hill, extending from northern River Edge into Emerson, was anciently known as *Kinderkamack.* In its original form, *Kendocamack,* this place name is a Jersey Dutch approximation of *Wendokamike,* meaning "upland."

The Hackensack River lazily courses its valley, which is "marked by low ridges or swells of sandstone or shale which rise 100 to 200 feet above the general level of the broad depression in which they stand."[42] To the west, drumlin hills form the watershed between tributaries of the Hackensack and Saddle Rivers. Achieving a height of 497 feet, Chestnut Ridge in Montvale forms the head of this upland spine whose southward extension is crested by Farview Avenue through Paramus. Just south of Musquapsink Creek, Kinderkamack Ridge stands 170 feet above tidewater in Oradell. Momentarily breached by Cole's Brook near New Bridge, the ground rises again in the Fairmount section of Hackensack, passing southward through Hasbrouck Heights and Woodridge, before reaching the Passaic River. Along Route 17 South, the sandstone face of the ridge forms a steep embankment behind the Hackensack Meadowlands.

Overlooking the surrounding lowlands to the east, south and west, Cherry Hill in River Edge rises 113 feet above sea level. Beyond the shallow swale where Van Saun Park is now found, yet another ridge rises. In the eighteenth century, this was "the hill commonly called the Cacel Rugh at the road (now Howland Avenue) which leads from the New Bridge to Sluckup." *Kachgel Ruygte* derives from the Dutch words, *Kachgel,* meaning "stove", and *ruygte,* meaning a "thicket, bramble-bushes or shavings of wood", and translates as "Stove-Kindling." Several living springs feed brooks that descend the narrow vale between these ridges, concentrating in Van Saun mill pond before contributing their commingled waters to Cole's Brook and the Hackensack River.

Cherry Hill was first called Brower's Hill, after a family of that surname who lived along Main Street in River Edge at the foot of the slope. Following the brook that winds down the hill back to its several springs, the curious traveler would arrive at *Sluckup.* Sluckup has resisted interpretation—it was even humorously suggested in 1876 that the place earned its name when a cow "slucked up" a farmer's linen coat from a fence.[43] The Bantas, one of the earliest families to farm this valley of springs, came from Friesland on the North Sea, where they spoke a language that is Scandinavian in origin, more closely resembling Old English than Dutch. Old Norse had a word, *slakki* ("slack" in English), to describe a small valley or boggy hollow. In 1832, the old name was almost literally translated into the more euphonic Spring Valley. A wolf-pit reportedly was located east of Spring Valley Road, near the confluence of the upper branches of the Mill Brook, and within the present confines of Van Saun Park.

Van Saun and Herring Brooks feed Cole's Brook. A sandy loam predominates in this small vale, before changing to clay near the Hackensack River. Cole's Brook sneaks between Cherry Hill and Fairmount, blending into the Hackensack River just south of the historic Steuben House at New Bridge Landing. Its outlet served as a tidal reservoir to operate a gristmill between 1710 and 1852. David Ackerman's will, composed on October 2, 1710, described the alluvial flats on the west bank of the river as "Tantewagh's Plain." This is a corrupted form of the name of Tantaqua, a Hackensack sachem. Cole's Brook was styled Tantaqua's Creek in 1682. Hereabout, clay flats and cattail marshes, only 5 feet above sea level, are inundated by full-moon and spring tides. The Hackensacks cultivated the fertile river plain in this location. Another river plain, which the neighboring Tappans cultivated, was located north of New Bridge in the central and southern portion of the present-day Borough of New Milford.

The southeasterly view from New Bridge Landing, to where the Shops at Riverside now stand north of Route 4, encompasses a scenic bend in the river known as Rond (Round) Hook. It seems the Hackensack River once pursued a more sinuous passage through the narrows at New Bridge but, by a constant process of erosion and deposition, it has gradually straightened its ways, leaving behind mud islands and sloughs on either bank as the only evidence of its previous wanderings.

On the west bank of the Hackensack River at New Bridge, the history of land ownership begins with a Swedish immigrant named Cornelius Matthyszen Van Stockholm. Like the Van Buskirks who settled the opposite side of the river, he was Lutheran. Cornelis Matthyszen, from Stockholm, first appears in the records on February 26, 1661, when he married Barentje Dirks, a young woman from Meppel, at the Dutch Reformed Church in New Amsterdam.[44] The *Doop-Boeck* of the Dutch Reformed Church in New York records the baptisms of several children born to the couple, namely, Matthys Cornelisze, on January 18, 1665; Hendrick Cornelisze, on December 5, 1669; Catharina Cornelisze, on February 19, 1676; and "tweeling," or twins Sara and Rachel, on December 23, 1681. While the mother of the first three children is identified as Barentje, or Beertje, Dircx (Dirks), the mother of the twins was named Marritie Dircx, presumably the same woman (or a second marriage to a sister?).

Cornelis Matthyszen is listed among the earliest settlers of New Harlem, New York. In the spring of 1666, town records noted he had finished clearing the Church Lot. He is further mentioned as the first tenant of a farm set aside for the town's poor. Matthyszen was appointed an overseer on June 12, 1666, an office apparently similar to a justice of the peace. When his lease of the church land expired in 1667, he removed to Hellgate, where he resided for about ten years, after which he removed to the Hackensack valley. Interestingly, the first listing of thirty-two New Harlem heads of households, compiled in 1661, indicates their national stock: 34.37 percent French, 21.87 percent Hollanders, 12.5 percent Walloon, 12.5 percent Danes; 9.37 percent Swedes, and 9.37 percent German.[45] Like Cornelis Matthyszen, many of these New Harlem farmers would become prominent in the pioneer settlement of Bergen County.

Three months after the birth of their twin daughters in December 1681—the last of their children whose baptisms are recorded in New York—Cornelis and Beertje

Matthyszen moved across the Hudson River into New Jersey. On March 31, 1682, Matthyszen purchased 420 acres along Hackensack River and Tantaqua's Creek (Cole's Brook) from the East Jersey Proprietors. His son Matthys Cornelisze from New Harlem, then living at Hackensack, married Tryntje Hendricks of Bergen at Bergen Church on November 13, 1692. As indicated in the marriage records, he and his father resided on their riverfront tract at New Bridge. On October 29, 1695, Matheus Corneliuson (Matthys Cornelisze), son of Cornelius Matheus, of Hackensack River, sold the 420 acres to David Ackerman, of the same place. The property was then bounded north by lands of Albert Sobrisco (Zabriskie) and southeast by lands of Captain John Berry. Mathew Cornelisse (Matthys Cornelisze) was a Bergen County yeoman who resided at or near New Bridge on 125 acres when he died in 1748. Merchant Cornelius Wynkoop, of Hackensack, who lived across the river in what is now Brett Park, was named his executor. The inventory of his estate also mentions a bond from Jan Zabriskie.

David Ackerman hailed from the town of Berlicum in North Brabant, located in the Meierij region near the city of Hertogenbosch. The last will and testament of David Ackerman, of Hackensack, was composed on October 2, 1710 and probated on June 4, 1724.[46] He mentions his wife Hillegond, and their children, David, Johannes, and Mary. The inventory of his real estate included land on the west side of the road to Kindakemeck, as far as the Falls over Acquacenas (Acquackanonk, or Saddle River) Valley; a gristmill and land on the east side of the Kinderkamack road in what is now River Edge; and land in Tantewagh's Plains; grist and sawmills; and a house in New York City. He bequeathed hereditary right to his New York house lot to his daughter. His sons received his gristmills, sawmills, and other lands.

Johannes Ackerman, born in New York, married Jannetje Lozier, born in Hackensack, at the Hackensack Reformed Church on June 6, 1713. At the time of his marriage, Johannes Ackerman apparently erected a dwelling on the Steenrapie (Kinderkamack) Road, most probably near what is now the intersection of Main Street and Elizabeth Court in River Edge, and thereafter built a tidal gristmill where Cole's Brook debouches into the Hackensack River. This mill got its power from a man-made pond: the high tide was trapped in the mouth of Cole's Brook by a dam with a special gate that lay flat on the creek bed to admit the incoming tide and was raised by a pole to trap an artificial reservoir of water in the mill pond formed by the outlet of Cole's Brook. When the point of ebb tide was reached, the mill pond was slowly released through the mill's waterwheel to grind grain into flour or meal. On March 29, 1714, John Demarest bequeathed his son Peter "all that farm, situated on the east side of Hackensack River, opposite the House & Farm of David Ackerman, deceased."[47]

The tidal gristmill at New Bridge was of vital interest to farmers who wished to sell their grain at the best possible price; Grinding kernels into flour or animal feed tripled the value of the grain. A pair or run of heavy millstones did the work of grinding. The bottom or nether stone was fixed in the floor of the mill while the top or runner stone turned above it. The grain trickled from a large wooden holder or hopper through an eye or hole in the center of the runner stone. The spinning upper stone threw the kernels outward between the two rough stone faces, reducing

Half a millstone from Zabriskie's Mill at New Bridge. (*Photo by Deborah Powell*)

them to a fine meal. The flour dropped off the edges of the stones and was trapped in a circular wooden tub or husk surrounding the millstones. It fell down a wooden chute into a barrel or bag. A waterwheel turned the heavy millstone through a simple system of wooden axles and gears.

The last will and testament of Johannis Ackerman, of Hackinsack, was composed on April 23, 1738 and probated August 19, 1745. His widow and executrix Jannetie was to have use of his personal and real estate during her widowhood, but he ordered a division of his estate among sons David, Niclas, Gilyn, and Abraham after Jannetie's decease or remarriage.

New Bridge

While pioneer settlement of the central Hackensack valley began in the last quarter of the seventeenth century, a bridge was first built at the upper ford or crossing near Demarest's Mill in 1724, connecting River Edge and New Milford on what is now River Edge Avenue. Spanning the narrows of the Hackensack River at New Bridge was first proposed in 1743. On October 28, 1743, it was noted:

Painting of Grietje (Peggy) Ackerman Westervelt (b. 1756 in Paramus). Painting is *c.* 1810. Donated to BCHS by the David Ackerman Descendants.

Mr. (David) Demarest (of Bergen) and Mr. (Leonard) Gibbon (of Salem) brought up from the House of Assembly (to the Governor's Council), a Bill entitled an Act to empower the Inhabitants of the County of Bergen to erect and build a Draw or Swinging Bridge over Hackinsack River, for the Concurrence of this House (i.e. Council).

The Council approved on November 3, 1743.[48] As the Hackensack estuary was occupied by salt meadows, which were 4 miles wide and 10 miles long, covering 19,846 acres, the broad, marshy channel presented an impediment to spanning the river below its narrows at New Bridge. Thus, after its erection in 1744, New Bridge formed an indispensable link on the overland journey from Manhattan to Albany and the Great Lakes.

Construction of the New Bridge at the narrows of the Hackensack River in 1744 necessitated the survey of roads leading to the bridge from east and west. At Nicholas Ackerman's request, on March 9, 1744, surveyors of the highways laid out a road on land of widow of Johannis Ackerman:

Beginning at the Road of Stien Rabi [that is to say, Steenrapie Road, now Kinderkamack Road) and on the said land along the house of the deceased (Johannis Ackerman) as the Road goes to the Mills of the deceased, about an East course and thence North along Creek about 10 yards where the bridge is to be built, which Road we lay out 4 Rodd wide.[49]

Orders for repairs to the New Bridge, listed in the records of the Board of Chosen Freeholders, suggest a sliding drawbridge with a section of the deck being pulled

The 1836 colored pencil drawing of Old Bridge by John K. Demarest looking west. This is the only known image of a draw bridge over the Hackensack River. (*Artifact in the Bergen County Historical Society Collections, photo by Deborah Powell*)

horizontally on runners by a tackle and ropes. The work was completed by autumn as *The New York Weekly Post Boy* of November 11, 1745, carried Cornelius Wynkoop's advertisement of a storehouse, dwelling, commercial bakery, and wharf for sale "near the Bridge that crosses that River, and opposite to John Zabriskie's Mills."[50]

Jan and Annetje Zabriskie

As with any good mystery, the scant facts of the case yield more heat than light. Upon his own testimony, the marriage registry at Bergen listed Albert Zabriskie's birthplace as "Engh^estburgh." Yet no such place is known to researchers, some favoring Engelsberg in Austrian Silesia and others Angerburg or Insterburg in East Prussia.[51] The surname, however, possibly derives from Zborowiska or Zabrze, a Silesian town on the west bank of the Prosna River. Since Albert Zabriskie was Lutheran, his family may have been displaced by religious wars that swept central Europe. From his age at the time of his death, we calculate that he was born about the year 1638.

The curious name of the man with obscure origins appeared upon the passenger list of the *D'Vos* (The Fox), which arrived in New Amsterdam on August 31, 1662, where is recorded "Albert Saboriski, from Prussia."[52] Twenty-four years old when he disembarked (seemingly alone) in New Netherland, he is lost to history for a dozen years thereafter. He surfaces again from obscurity in 1675, when Albert

Zaborowsky was reported trading with the Tappans, notably Mamshier, their sachem, and Metetoch and Chechepowas, whereby these headmen became indebted to him.[53] At thirty-eight years of age, he married Machtelt Van der Linden, a maiden but sixteen years old, on December 17, 1676.[54] On October 11, 1680, the clerk of the Bergen Dutch Reformed Church noted that Machtelt, wife of Albert Sabarosky, had returned to the Lutheran faith which she had formerly forsaken.

On July 15, 1679, Albert Saboroscoe (Zabriskie) acted as interpreter with the native owners in the purchase of Aschacking, a tract of land at the head of New Barbadoes Neck, "near Warepeeck and a run of water commonly called Tantaquaes Creeke," that extended northwest "unto Sadle river." [55, 56, 57] He attempted to purchase land in this neighborhood and on April 12, 1682, was issued a survey for 380 acres lying upon the Hackingsack River. He got a patent for 444 acres along the Hackensack River and Tantaque Creek (Cole's Brook) on March 25, 1683, but when surveys were finally drawn, only 224 acres of this amount could be found unclaimed.[58] Albert *Saberasky* (Zabriskie) witnessed the purchase of land in the northern Hackensack valley and along Peskeckie Creek, conveyed by Tappan *sackemacker* Memsha, Mettatoch, and Seytheypoey to the East Jersey Proprietors on October 16, 1684.[59, 60]

Back on January 6, 1676, Laurence Andriessen (Van Buskirk) & Company had purchased "a tract of land called by the name of New Hackensack, bounded on Olde Hackensack and from thence running to a small kill or vale (later known as French Creek) adjoining to the Great Indian fielde called the Indian Castle to the northward" from the Hackensack sachem Tantaque.[61] It was subdivided into strips of land extending between the Hackensack River and the west branch of Overpeck Creek. On March 25, 1685, the East Jersey Proprietors conveyed 183 acres "upon the New Plantations upon the Hackensack River called by the name of New Hackinsacke" to Albert Sabboresco (Zabriskie) of Bergen, planter.[62] This tract was bounded southeast by the west branch of Overpeck Creek (now called Teaneck Creek) and northwest by the Hackensack River. Here he made his home. A year or so later, Albert Saberiscoe (Zabriskie) (with the Indian alias "Totlock") witnessed the sale by several Hackensack and Tappan sachems of a parcel of land "adjoining unto Captane Sandford's bounds, upwards pasaick River five rods beyond a run of water called by the Indians Warepeake, but the right name of the said run is Rerakanes & by the English named Sadle River," made November 29, 1686. [63, 64]

On January 5, 1686, Governor Gawen Lawrie (on behalf of Peter Sonmans) received a patent for three parcels of land on the west bank of the Hackensack River in what is now Oradell and River Edge: one tract of 1,520 acres; another of 643 acres; and a third of 261 acres.[65] On September 1, 1686, the East Jersey Proprietors conveyed two adjacent tracts of land to Albert Saberiscoe (Zabriskie): the first was described as 330 acres "called Coovange the Indian's land," extending between the Hackensack and Saddle Rivers, bounded north by land of Daniel River (the boundary line running along what is now Adams Avenue in River Edge) and south by his own land; the second tract of 250 acres also extended from the Hackensack River to the Saddle River, and was bounded south by land of Peter Sonmans and north by his own land. The deed survey for the southern tract began at two marked red oaks and a walnut tree, standing "by the path" (now Kinderkamack Road) at

People often ask us why we use the turtle for a logo. The turtle was designed for the Bergen County Historical Society by wildlife artist Charles Livingston Bull in 1928. The turtle ties into the creation story Tantaqua told. (*History of Oradell by Hiram B. D. Blauvelt, 1944*)

Bergen County, Where America Begins

the point where Kinderkamack Road and Jackson Avenue presently intersect. From here, the property extended southwest along the river and then about three miles northwest to the Saddle River. Today, Manning Avenue in River Edge runs along the southwest limit of this tract. On September 4, 1686, Albert Saberiscoe of Bergen deeded 450 acres, comprising the eastern side of these lands, to Richard Pope of Hackinsack. The portion conveyed extended from the Hackensack River west to Winocksack (Sprout) Brook, bounded north by land of Daniel River and south by lands also purchased by Richard Pope. On October 29, 1695, Albert Sobrisco of Hackinsack sold 224 acres on the west side of the Hackensack River to Jacob Vansan of New York.[66] The survey for this tract began at the north corner of the tract of land that David Ackerman purchased from Matheus Corneliuson fronting the Hackensack River and extended 2.25 miles northwest to a branch of the Saddle River (now called Sprout Brook), being bounded north by land patented to Gawen Lawrie in right of Peter Sonmans and south by land of David Ackerman.[67] The Council of the East Jersey Proprietors, meeting on November 11, 1695, agreed to the petition of Albert Zobrisco (Zabriskie) to grant a patent to Jacob Jansen for 229 acres sold him and for a warrant to lay out 200 acres wanting of his former patent upon the Saddle River. Jacob Vansan of New York City, boatman, received his deed for the same on November 29, 1695. This tract (now in River Edge) extended from Howland Avenue south to Reservoir Avenue; to the west, the original boundary line runs along the south side of Lexington Drive.

On June 1, 1702, Orachanap (*alias* Metachenak), Coovang and Nomerascon, Tappan Indians, conveyed a tract of 1,200 acres on the southeast side of Saddle River, called Weerommensa, to Albert Zaborowsky. This tract began on the northeast bounds of Claess Jansson Romyn's land (now Mill Road) and ran beyond his line to a great rock, from thence it ran in a straight line "up to a certain small run (Musquapsink Brook), which is Easterly just below a certain old Indian field or plantation, known by the name of *Weromensa*" (located in vicinity of intersection of Wierimus Road and Woodcliff Avenue) to a marked pear tree, from thence in a straight line (along present route of East Allendale Avenue and Woodcliff Lake Road) to certain wild cherry trees or a white oak, marked on three sides, from thence to the Saddle River and down the River to the beginning point, supposedly encompassing 1,200 acres.[68, 69] On March 29, 1708, Albert Zaborowsky of Hackingsack, yeoman, conveyed "the full, true and equal half" of this tract to Thomas Van Buskerk.

As interpreter, Albert Zabriskie negotiated a sale of land on the Passaic River by the native owners to George Ryerson of Pechqueneck, Francis Ryerson of New York City and Jurya Westervelt of Hackensack, by deed dated September 16, 1709. He died September 1, 1711, aged about 73 years, and was buried at Ackinsack, being survived by his wife and five sons: Jacob A., John A., Joost A., Christian A., and Henry. He left no will and his lands were apparently divided among his children the following summer. On June 11, 1712, Jacob Zabriskie of New Barbadoes, yeoman, sold the farm or plantation within New Hackensack, occupied by Albert Zabriskie during his lifetime, to John Zaborowsky (Zabriskie) for £300.[70] This tract began northwest on the Hackensack River and extended southeast to the Overpeck Creek, being bounded southwest by the line of Peter Vanderlinda and northeast by land of Eptkey Banta.

Jan Zabriskie was born at Hackensack about 1682. He first married Elizabeth Claes Romeyn on September 20, 1706. She died in 1712; he then married Margaretta Johns Durie. He produced four children by his first wife and another nine children by his second wife, namely Albert, Matilda, Nicholas, Christina, Elizabeth, John (Jan), Jacob, Elizabeth, Peter, Joost, Rachel, Cornelius, and Christian. Albert Zabriskie's farm of 183 acres at New Hackinsacke passed subsequently to Jan's son, Joost, in 1766.[71]

Jan Zabriskie was born in Hackensack in January 1716. He married Annaetjen Akkerman, born 1720, at the Hackensack Church on June 5, 1739. She was a daughter of Egbert Ackerman and Elizabeth Bryant. Twins named Jan and Elizabeth were born to the couple and baptized on September 3, 1741. Although no deed of the sale has survived, newspaper advertisements allow us to determine that Jan and Annetje (nee Ackerman) Zabriskie purchased the Johannes Ackerman farm in or about September 1745, shortly after construction of the first draw-bridge at the narrows of the Hackensack River.

In 1752, Jan Zabriskie built the oldest part of the Steuben House. Archeological explorations, paint and mortar analysis and careful detective work, conclusively demonstrate that the oldest part of the Zabriskie-Steuben House at New Bridge was a stone saltbox, 45-foot front and 35 feet, 10 inches deep, with front rooms flanking a center hall and three narrow rooms at the back of the house, comprising a kitchen, a milk room, and a root cellar, under a shed extension of the gable roof. The room on the north side of the hall was used as a parlor, while the large room on the south side of the hall was the Dwelling Room, where the family ate, worked and slept around the largest fireplace in the house. A winding, boxed or enclosed staircase led from the back of the hall into the garret. This upper story was located

Zabriskie-Kipp Homestead, the largest Bergen-Dutch sandstone dwelling built as a single unit. Erected by Joost Zabriskie in 1787 on River Road, Teaneck. (*Bergen County Historical Society Collections*)

inside of the roof. The ends of roof rafters were cutting into matching "tongues" and slits, one fitting snugly into the other and fastened with a wooden pin. The rafters were either thatched with river reeds or with white cedar shingles. Since glass was hand-blown (much like bubbles through a bubble-pipe or straw), windows had to be made up of many small panes fitted between wooden bars. Like many farmhouses of that time, its walls were built with blocks of sandstone, probably cut from an exposure of sandstone in the ridge below Hackensack and conveyed by water to the construction site. Clay from the riverbank was formed by hand into rectangular blocks and then baked into bricks. These old bricks, called "patties," often bear the marks of the fingers that shaped them. Requiring much work to shape a large number and much wood for fuel to bake them, bricks were usually used only in chimneys, although a very few people could afford to build a complete house of bricks. A diamond-shaped sandstone lozenge with carved mill wheel and the initials of Jan and Annetje Zabriskie, was placed in the south wall, identifying the date of construction: "*Anno* 1752."

In its original form, this house resembles the description of a contemporary house in Hackensack, which David W. Provost offered for sale in 1746. It was described as "Forty-Eight Foot in Length and Twenty-four Foot Broad, with a large

Cellar-Kitchen, a Dairy and Store Cellar all joyn'd together, the said Dwelling House has two large Rooms, and an Entry [hall], with a large flush Garret." According to this floor plan, the front door opened into a wide center-hall, which also served as a breezeway. The room on the north side of the hall was a parlor, holding the family's best bed, used only for wedding nights, births, and wakes. The large room on the south side of the hall was the Dwelling Room—here the family ate, worked and slept around the largest fireplace in the house. Three narrow rooms at the back of the house were used for a kitchen, a milk room and a root cellar, where food could be kept cold, much like in a modern refrigerator. A winding staircase led from the back of the hall into the garret.

Jan Zabriskie miller and wily middleman, had that proverbial "thumb of gold." By quick study (and perhaps by nature), he became profitably conversant with backcountry farmers, river boatmen, drovers, teamsters, ironmasters, and the polished upper strata of city merchants. Amidst general prosperity, Jan's twin children, Jan and Elizabeth, married into Manhattan's mercantile elite. John Zabriskie, Sr., married Jane (Jannetjen) Goelett at the Schraalenburgh Church on November 21, 1764. He and his bride resided at the Zabriskie-Steuben House. Jan and Jane had two children: Annetjen, born August 4, 1765, and Jan, Jr., born September 30, 1767. John took on senior and the third generation John became junior. They also started using John instead of the Dutch version "Jan" sometime before the American Revolution.

Jane's spinster sister, Mary, moved from New York to New Bridge and set up a shop in the former academy. Edmund Seaman purchased this property, located on the high bluff above the river, opposite Zabriskie's Mills. John's twin sister

Steuben House date stone with the tide mill paddlewheel. The lozenge is set on the south end of the state historic site. IZ and AZ for Jan and Annetje Zabriskie with a date of 1752 at the top of the diamond. D. Anderson Zabriskie carved his initials on the perimeter, DAZ 1892. (*Photo by Deborah Powell*)

Elizabeth Zabriskie married Edmond Seaman at Schraalenburgh on December 25, 1768. Edmund Seaman (1745–1828) was second son of Judge Benjamin Seaman (1719–1781), New York Assemblyman and merchant, and his wife, Elizabeth Mott. In the year of his marriage, Edmund became Clerk of the New York Assembly, a position he held until 1775. Three sons were born to Edmund and Elizabeth Seaman. On March 7, 1774, the New York papers announced:

> Friday Night, Mrs. Elizabeth Seaman, Wife of Edmund Seaman, Esq.; Clerk of the General Assembly of this Province, and Daughter of John Zabriskie, Esq.; of Hackinsack, in New-Jersey, died at her home in this City, in the 30th Year of her Age.

She died nine days after the birth of her third son, Edmund.

The Zabriskies grew wealthy from increased trade brought on by the French and Indian War (1756-1763) and doubled the size of their dwelling about 1767, expanding it from five to twelve rooms, warmed by seven fireplaces, and covering it with a fashionable gambrel roof. The enlarged house probably served as a two-family, intergenerational dwelling. It grew from a five-room house to its present size by a single enlargement, whereby the three-bay north block, 21 feet 3 inches by 35 feet 10 inches, and the second floor along the rear (or west elevation) were

Barn, tide mill, Steuben House, and Hackensack River in sketch believed to be by John Heaton. Mill experts from the Tide Mill Institute questioned why the gate needed to be pulled open as it should have opened with incoming tide. The worker on the left may be an enslaved person. (*Bergen County Historical Society Collections*)

added at the same time. We know that the Zabriskie mansion reached its present size by 1784, according to a compensation claim filed on January 24, 1784, by John J. Zabriskie, Sr., "now a refugee in the City of New York" for his former homestead at New-Bridge. Mr. Zabriskie described his estate as "One large Mansion House, seventy feet long and forty feet wide, containing twelve rooms built with stone, with Outhouses consisting of a bake House, Smoke House, Coach House, and two large Barns, and a Garden, situated at a place called New Bridge (value £850.)"

It is improbable that the Zabriskies undertook such a substantial construction project during the Revolutionary War. It is most likely that the house was enlarged after Jan Zabriskie's marriage to Jannetje Goelett on November 21, 1764, or about the time John's and Jane's son John Zabriskie, Jr.—third generation of that name to inhabit the sandstone mansion at New Bridge—was born September 30, 1767. This was to create a double house with separate quarters for two generations of the family, the older generation building and occupying the north addition with its own parlor, kitchen, and bedchambers, while the younger generation occupied the original house (albeit somewhat enlarged), taking over business operations.

This is (as its owner described it in 1784) a "mansion house." The use of dressed stone on the facade, architraves surrounding doors and windows, raised paneling and symmetrical arrangement of façade elements shows a deliberate aping of classical idioms. The gambrel roof, fairly new to Bergen County at the time of the Zabriskie-Steuben House's enlargement (*circa* 1767), is neither the perpetuation of a local folk tradition nor a local invention. Instead, it is part and parcel of the penetration of a Classical Renaissance into the older settled neighborhoods of the eastern seaboard. As economic expansion increased both the resources and aspirations of an entrepreneurial class for more comfortable standards of living, an educated Classicism appealed to a wider audience and influenced even the modest dwellings of merchants, lawyers, and well-to-do farmers. The Zabriskie-Steuben House can be counted among the five "great houses" of colonial Bergen County, built in the purest imitation of English country seats to spread the gospel of architectural refinement.

On September 19, 1774, *The New York Gazette and Weekly Mercury*, No. 1197, announced:

> New-York, September 19. At half-past ten o'clock in the evening on Tuesday night, died at Hackinsack, John Zabriski, Esq.; who, while in life, performed the several social duties in a manner becoming a rational being, and a good Christian.

Multiple spelling variations appear for Zabriskie, including Zabriski, Zebriskie, Zobriskie, Sabboresco, Saboroscoe, Saberasky, Zaborowsky, Zobrisco, and Sobrisco. Author Kevin Wright used the different spellings where referenced from the source documents.

Zabriskie's Pond and Van Orden's Mill

Each year, fewer among us remember a small pond near the southern boundary of River Edge, known as Zabriskie's Pond. This sheet of water resulted from

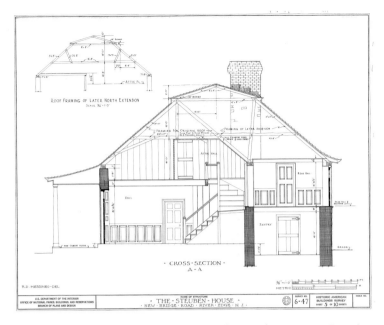

Historic American Buildings Survey of the Zabriskie-Steuben House. Drawing compiled after 1933. This view shows the 1752 gable roof line and the 1767 enlargement with the gambrel roof. The original 1752 roof line is exposed and visible in the Washington Room. (*Library of Congress*)

Only known image of the north room of the Steuben House prior to the removal of interior wall and jambless Dutch fireplace. The wall is partly pictured to the left of the photograph. The wall was the exterior wall of the original 1752 house. The north block and roof were raised to double the size of the house about 1767. In 1923, the owners decided to make one large room to use for a tea room. The pictured paneled wall and fireplace can still be seen today. (*Bergen County Historical Society Collections*)

the impoundment of the Cole's Brook below its conjunction with the Van Saun Millbrook. David Ackerman and his sons built a gristmill here between 1695 and 1710. On April 5, 1735, David Ackerman and his wife, Jannetje (Van Orden), sold the gristmill, millpond, and land covered with water, altogether about 9 acres, to John Van Orden, the eldest surviving son of Adam Janse Van Norden and his wife, Abeltie Slot. He married Theodosia Earle on August 3, 1729, at the Lutheran Church in Teaneck. They had seven children including John Van Orden, born March 2, 1732.[72]

John Van Norden married Rebecca Heaton, daughter of John Heaton, on June 23, 1754. He owned a stone house, a farm, a grist, and sawmill at New Bridge. Rebecca's father, John Heaton, was an Englishman who left home because of some family dissension and who lived with his daughter at New Bridge. John Heaton later fell heir to property in England, but supposedly was too proud to return and claim it. He was an artist and many family portraits painted by him were reportedly destroyed when the house burned in about 1800. Rebecca Heaton was born May 15, 1736, and died in 1816.[73] John Van Norden reportedly favored the rebels' cause but was too old to take an active part. When a skirmish occurred near his dwelling, the family offered help to the wounded of both sides "and were thoroughly robbed by the soldiers of both." His brother, Gabriel, was a loyalist who migrated to Nova Scotia after the war. Maps made of this neighborhood during the Revolution, however, indicate "Vrowe's" Mill at this location, confusing the neighboring Browers and perhaps "Brower's Hill." John's grandson, Theodore, claimed that he planted many trees about his property and loved the trout fishing, carefully preserving the stream that formed his millpond. He also stated that: "The last panther crossed the valley when my father was eight years old (1775), going toward the Palisades and returning." The last will and testament of John Van Orden, miller, was probated in Hackensack on June 28, 1810.

Theodorus William Van Norden moved to New York about 1785 and became a merchant banker at 16 Maiden Lane, later moving his counting house to Vesey Street. John's son and surviving executor, Theodorus Van Orden of New York City, sold the mill property at New Bridge to Andrew Zobriskie of New York in November 1813. The name appears as both Van Orden and Van Norden.

4

The Jersey Dutch

Before we get too far in our narrative, it may be worthwhile to contemplate (if only cursorily) the regional folk culture that once inhabited the Great Sandstone Valley of northeastern New Jersey and southeastern New York. For important reasons, we should refer to this community as Jersey Dutch and not simply as Dutch. While we are more familiar with the modern role of ethnic neighborhoods in perpetuating the distinctive cultural characteristics of immigrant communities, especially in urban settings, we have largely forgotten that agricultural communities, spread across much broader swathes of countryside, performed the same function before the rise of the industrial city. While much of our popular history has focused on stereotypes of the more ethnically homogenized New England Puritans and Virginia Cavaliers, the middle Atlantic colonies were a more mixed bag, due partly to the former Swedish and Dutch colonies. Today, perhaps the Pennsylvania *Deutsch* (Germans) are one of the most recognizable regional folk cultures. Yet the pivotal role of New Jersey in American history, progressing from the most culturally diverse colony to the most densely populated state, perhaps deserves greater study and appreciation. For while New York City shed most of the trappings of a Dutch colonial outpost in the early nineteenth century, it never lost the cosmopolitan flavor of its early settlement. The conservative agricultural community of northeastern New Jersey, however, retained its attachment to the blended folkways of its founding families for far longer, becoming at least superficially more "Dutch" than its ingredients might suggest. This became satirically and confusingly evident on January 10, 1863, when the following story appeared in the *New Jersey Herald and Sussex Democrat*, published in Newton, New Jersey:

A Dutch Yankee—Many years ago, when the "Know-Nothing" excitement was at its height, it so happened that a Dutchman, who could not speak a word of English plainly, was put up for constable by the American party at Paramus, New Jersey. This man kept a country tavern, and one day a gentleman from New York, of "Know-Nothing" politics, called there on his travels. He soon got into conversation with mine host, was surprised to learn that he was of the same politics as himself, and expressed astonishment that he was running for constable on the "American" ticket.

"Dat's just de fun!" said Hans, "pecause nobody can tell vat guntrymans I pe. Now, vat guntryman you takes me to pe?"

The gentleman replied, "A Dutchman, of course!"

"Ha! Ha! Ha!" exclaimed the landlord—"I spects I fools more as a hundred thousand bebles! I bees a Jerseyman!"

And he was a Jerseyman born, as was also his father before him. There are middle-aged men in the northern part of New Jersey who were born there, and have talked Dutch all their lives. Indeed, they speak the English language with much difficulty."[1]

So let us turn back the pages of time a century or more and see this mix in the making. Listen in for a moment to the Lutheran pietist preacher, Rev. Henry Melchior Muhlenberg, who inscribed this description of the congregation at New Bridge in his journal in October 1757:

> The inhabitants of Hackinsack are natives of this country. Most of them are descendants from three or four ancestors who came from Holland and purchased this tract (that is, the New Hackensack tract in northern Teaneck) from the Indians about 80 or 90 years ago and settled here. Hence, almost all of them are inter-related and bear the original family names, such as van Buskirk, van Horn, van Orden, etc. The old folks had a certain natural honesty and artlessness. They did not use documents, seals, signatures, bonds and other such contracts. A man's word and handshake was his bond. The older folks at the present times are shrewd; they are still good as their word; they are sociable and command great respect in their families. Like all other nationalities, they have a special love for their mother tongue. The young people are gradually degenerating because they receive no instruction in God's Word and are mixing with other nationalities.[2]

How revealing. After eighty to ninety years of enduring the hardships of pioneer life—surveying wilderness into farms, clearing the valleys for agriculture, establishing livestock on pastures, widening footpaths into cart ways and lanes, building bridges, wharves, boats, domiciles, and churches, establishing the rudiments of law and order, and marrying and multiplying on the frontier of settlement— Reverend Muhlenberg believes that these are "descendants from three or four ancestors who came from Holland" who "have a special love for their mother tongue." Yet, the Lutheran congregation's most prominent benefactors, the Van Buskirks, originated in the German state of Holstein on the border with Denmark. Of equal interest, perhaps, is the fact this is a Lutheran congregation and not Dutch Reformed, largely composed of the descendants of Swedes and Germans, rather than of Netherlanders. So some important distinctions seemed to have blurred through intermarriage over a generation or two.

Muhlenberg's observations and description also suggest the pioneer phase of frontier life was progressing into a more complicated stage of civilization. While we have all too few examples with good provenance to be able to say for sure, I think there is interesting evidence to suggest a greater diversity in furniture and tool styles, folk arts, architecture, and other elements of material culture the closer you approach the threshold of settlement in the seventeenth century, reflecting a once greater sense of ethnic diversity in the pioneer population. Cultural homogenization gradually stirred a new concoction, a distinctive folk mix that featured recognizable flavors and textures from its disparate ingredients. This process of cultural combination was probably richer in content than we might now detect since nation-states were only then emerging in parts of Western Europe and residual provincialism was probably far more controlling of loyalties, dialects, habits and costumes across a continent not far removed from the familial estates of kingdoms, duchies, and contrasting ethnic regions. The process of "creolization" is defined as the merging of two or more cultural identities so as to produce a distinct new cultural meld, different from its source contributors, though often containing recognizable elements of its antecedents. The process of creolization led first to the formation of regional folk patterns of culture that eventually nourished a slowly emerging American culture.

In plain fact, the proprietors of the Dutch West Indies Company never succeeded in convincing large numbers of their own countrymen to exchange comfortable abodes in the Low Countries for pioneer huts in a remote wilderness. Families seeking haven from religious intolerance throughout Western Europe made more willing adventurers to the New World. In my estimation, by the time of the American Revolution, only one-third of the population of Bergen County could claim Netherlandish descent. Africans comprised one-fifth of the population; Germans comprised another fifth; while English, French, Scotch-Irish, and Scandinavians comprised the remainder. Through intermarriage and the convenient adoption of a hybrid language rooted in Dutch, this varied stock blended to form the Jersey Dutch. Besides such distinctly Dutch surnames as Akkerman (Ackerman), De Groot, Blinkerhof, Hopper, Van Winkel, Brouwer and Blauvelt, the surnames of some founding families echo a diversity of origins: Zabriskie (Saborowski), Demarest (De Maree), Lozier (La Seur), Campbell, Christie, Stagg, Sandford, and Kingsland.

The process of creolization was particularly evident at New Bridge, which, as the gateway into the upper valley of the Hackensack, seems to have attracted certain ethnicities from among the general population of the former Dutch colony of New Netherland who wished to preserve their cultural identity: the Van Buskirks, who settled northern Teaneck, were Holstein (Danish) Lutherans; Cornelis Matthyszen, first owner of the lands in River Edge whereon the Steuben House stands, was a Swede and Lutheran; Albert Zabriskie, first owner of a neighboring tract in River Edge, was Polish Silesian and a Lutheran; and the Demarests, who established the French Patent (now New Milford), were French Huguenots, who established a French Reformed congregation.

In a journal of his travels through this vicinity in 1797–1799, Julian Ursyn Niemcewicz noted:

> The whole countryside is inhabited by old Dutch colonists. I recognized them by their favorite bent for navigation. They were all busy constructing or refitting boats. They are said to be ignorant, avaricious and inhospitable. They love to work and to

hoard. They have kept until now their mother tongue; however, nearly all speak and understand English.[3]

It is interesting to note how the genealogical entries in many Jersey Dutch Bibles change from Dutch to English after 1783, indicating the emergence of a larger and more nearly national sense of cultural identity.

Commercial fishing and boat-building were major industries in this neighborhood. "Their favorite bent for navigation" is understandable, given the land use practices of that age. The typical eighteenth-century farm in the Hackensack valley depended upon the river for transportation of bulk commodities and therefore would have to be conveniently situated near to a public dock. It might contain upwards of 150 acres, half of which would be cleared land "neatly divided into Tillage, Meadow, and Pasture." A domicile, preferably a good stone house, and a large barn serving as a granary would be situated on the upland or terraces above the river, close to the public highways that generally maintained a somewhat level gradient by following the contour of the ridges. Overland transportation was conducted by horseback, wagons and sleighs. This upland would have to provide a sufficiency of good water and a woodlot supplying enough timber for fuel and fences. Large apple orchards of about 120 trees, together with other fruit trees, would also occupy the well-drained slopes. Tidal flats bearing natural crops of salt grasses and reeds were called "*valayen*" by the Dutch. Though related to the English word "valley," the Dutch expression was defined by Jasper Danckaerts in 1680 as "low flat land which is overflowed at every tide—miry and muddy at the bottom, and which produces a species of hard salt grass or reed grass." The descriptive term survives locally in the toponyms, "Polifly" or "Polle Valaye" meaning "head of the tidal flats." Danckaerts also noted in his commentary that cattle preferred salt hay to "fresh hay or grass." Salt grass was therefore seasonally mown just before ripening and stored for animal-bedding and fodder. In some instances, lands were diked and drained to encourage the production of fresh hay made from grasses of European origin. It was reported "a good spot of very fine mowing Land ... commonly yields about 15 or 18 Loads of good English Hay yearly." Most Bergen Dutch farms were oriented to the production of cereal grains, respectively, rye, corn, buckwheat, wheat, and oats. Gristmills would have to be conveniently located for the conversion of kernel to flour and feed.

In August, many farmers went to city market, their produce carried in oxcarts and large market wagons over rutted, dirt roads. Most heavy goods were carried on sleds after snow and ice provided a smoother road surface. Those who waited for the early morning trade of the city grocers and hucksters went to a nearby lodging house and turned in for an hour or two before business commenced. Others attempted to make themselves as comfortable as possible on their wagons and sleep until daybreak.

The estuaries of the Hudson, Hackensack and Passaic Rivers harbored a diversity of fish, game, and wild plant foods. The sight of wild geese flying northward, especially in late January, was taken as an indication of approaching spring. Each February, fishermen speared eels through the ice. As February waned, immense flocks of blackbirds passed northwest over the valley, followed by the arrival of robins and bluebirds. Silvery smelt appeared in March. From the first week of April

Summer day along the Hackensack River, oil painting by David Arnot, *c.* 1850. Sloop docked at Anderson's wharf where present day Anderson Street Bridge is located. (*Artifact in the Bergen County Historical Society Collections, photo by Deborah Powell.*)

through the middle of May, fishermen hauled in seines of shad, working under moonlight when the tide was right. Sturgeon measuring 6–8 feet in length, and weighing 400 pounds, frequently became entangled in their nets. The catch also included herring, bass, and a great variety of other fish. At the beginning of May, large snapping turtles, some weighing 30 pounds, were caught in the meadows. Overhead, southern mudlarks migrated in noisy flocks. Yellow perch arrived between the end of June and the middle of August. Bass were taken toward the end of July, some weighing three and a half pounds. Large crabs were also found at this season. In late August, large flocks of reedbirds filled the meadows. When railbirds became plentiful in the first week of September, hunters poled shallow rail boats, or gunning skiffs, over the marshes at high tide. The southward flight of wild ducks in November signaled winter's approach. Wild geese returned southward as November concluded. Nineteenth-century newspaper accounts also mention otters, a rare yellow railbird, an immense crane, and very rare green heron.

Oysters and other shellfish were the chief food of coastal communities. The waters about New York City teemed with oysters of great size and exquisite taste. Pickled oysters were prepared not only for domestic consumption, but also for export, particularly to the West Indies. Oysters were commonly removed from the shell and cleaned, then boiled and dried on dishes. Nutmeg, allspice, black pepper, and enough vinegar to give "a sourish taste" were mixed with oysters and half the liquor in which they were boiled before thorough reheating. Boiling oysters were constantly skimmed to keep the liquid clean. Thus prepared, oysters were pickled in glass or earthenware containers with tightly fastened lids. Pickled oysters kept for years and could be shipped to distant markets. Lobsters were also caught in great numbers and pickled in the same manner. In 1748, botanist Peter Kalm noted, "a common rule … that oysters are best in those months which have an 'r' in their names, such as September, October, etc. but that they are not so good in other months."

The Hackensack River long remained the principal artery of commerce and travel through the cultivated heartland of Bergen County. By 1748, the river was considered "navigable for Vessels of about 50 Tons" as far inland as New Bridge. When visiting the Lutheran Church at New Bridge in October 1751, the Reverend Henry Muhlenberg noted that local farmers and merchants "bring the products they raise to the market in New York in little ships or vessels, and take back whatever is necessary for subsistence." The progress of such water craft was somewhat slowed "since the river has a tide." River traffic was also seasonal. Boats usually began making regular trips by the third week of March. Freezing weather generally closed the river to navigation by the end of December. Shallow draft boats were necessary to navigate the relatively shallow tidal channel. In 1759, John Zabriskie, of New Bridge, owned "a Boat carrying seven Cord, all in good Order to attend a Mill;

Fragment of pig iron with letters LON for Long Pond Iron Works. The pig iron was found in a 1967 archaeological dig of the wharf at New Bridge Landing by Roland Robbins. (*Artifact in the Bergen County Historical Society Collections, photo by Deborah Powell*)

when deeply loaded won't draw above four Feet, eight Inches Water; Sails and Rigging all in complete Order." Pig iron was shipped by ox cart from as far away as Long Pond Ironworks to New Bridge Landing. In 1773, letters published by Robert Erskine in the New York newspapers refer to the dock of John Zabriskie, Sr., of Hackensack as a transshipment point for Ringwood and Long Pond iron. River craft increased in size during the nineteenth century and two-masted sloop yachts and large, three-masted schooners became a common sight, especially carrying brick as well as agricultural commodities. In January 1868, a schooner belonging to Jacob Van Buskirk, of New Milford, burned while anchored near New Bridge. Its cargo consisted of 1,400 empty bags and thirty cords of wood.

New World Dutch Food Ways

Thanks largely to Swedish botanist Peter Kalm's account of his travels in northeastern North America between 1748 and 1751, we know something of the food ways of early New Jersey and the Hudson valley. Three home-cooked meals were the daily norm, featuring farm-fresh ingredients and orchard fruits, augmented by the once abundant wild game, fruits, and nuts of the primeval forest and stream, all thoughtfully prepared with potherbs from the household garden, honey from the hive, flavored with imported sugar and spices.

Rising with the sun, breakfast tea was poured over a lump of brown sugar placed in a cup. Slices of bread were toasted over hot coals, allowing butter to seep into every nook and cranny. Sips of tea alternated with bites of toast and radish slices. Shavings of small round cheeses might also be spread on buttered bread for a hearty start to the workday. In warm weather, tea and breakfast were served outdoors in the breezy shade of the overhanging front porch.

Served between noon and one o'clock, dinner was the most substantial meal of the day, featuring (as often as possible) a meat course, usually of roasted game, poultry, or fish in season, served with turnips, cabbage, and fruit for dessert. Without reliable refrigeration, rarely was more food served then a family might consume in a sitting. In summer, a weak punch of fruit and rum was most refreshing. Spiced wine, mixed with hot water and sugar, produced *Negus*. Tea, served again about three o'clock in the afternoon, provided a neighborly social hour. Chocolate, sweetmeats, preserved and dried fruits, plates of hickory and other nuts, cold pastry, and various cakes, consumed with cider or syllabub, were served as desserts.

A dish of cornmeal porridge, called *sappaan*, was almost invariably the centerpiece of evening supper. A spooned hollow made in the center of the porridge created a reservoir for fresh buttermilk. The porridge was eaten by the spoonful, each half porridge and half milk, with the buttermilk being replenished as needed. Leftover meat from the noonday meal, or more buttered bread with cheese, occasionally added variety to the menu. Leftover porridge was boiled with buttermilk the following morning into gruel, sweetened with sugar or syrup.

Large Dutch barns were granaries of a breadbasket economy. Alongside tobacco, local farms produced abundant harvests of corn, wheat, barley, rye, oats, and buckwheat for export as well as for domestic consumption. Late in the seventeenth century, Barbadian planters acquired the neck of land between the Passaic and Hackensack Rivers, forming the old precinct of New Barbadoes, to supply grain to the sugar plantations of the West Indies and also to ship white oak staves for coopering rum casks and sugar barrels. Sugar was received from the West Indies in exchange for farm exports.

Different cereals were successively harvested from May through November. Wheat and rye flour provided breadstuffs, the mainstay of the diet. Rye, corn, and malted barley were used in distilling and brewing. Oats, barley, and corn provided animal feeds. Scottish immigrants introduced oatmeal porridge. Tide mills along the Hackensack River featured the convenience of easy water transport to city markets. Inland gristmills harnessed the descent of the Saddle and Ramapo Rivers and their principal tributaries, most notably, Hohokus Creek, but farmers had to cope with poor roads, most easily passable in winter with sleds.

Buckwheat was sown in the middle of July and left standing until the first frost. Principally raised in hill country, its white blossoms made summer fields appear snow-clad. Buckwheat pancakes and pudding were locally esteemed as the most delectable breakfast dish on earth—the Dutch serving buckwheat cakes with country sausage and the English with maple syrup. In winter, cooks prepared buckwheat cakes either in a frying pan or on a hot stove. Devoured warm with butter, alongside tea or coffee, they often took the place of buttered toast, the breakfast fare most favored by English colonists. Buckwheat honey was darkly flavorful and nutritious, resembling molasses.

Fields of cabbages, potatoes, turnips, carrots, onions, leeks, parsnips, and a large variety of gourds, including squashes and pumpkins, were grown, commonly in rows among hills of corn, which shaded these crops from the hot summer sun. Boiled and mashed turnips, parsnips, and potatoes were common fare. Onions, leeks, carrots, spinach, and salsify flavored soups and stews. Boiled and mashed spinach combined with butter and hard-boiled eggs for a tasty repast.

An inventory of Jacob Van Waggener's property, taken or destroyed by British invaders in 1776, included "500 Cabbage heads." Testifying to its origin among Dutch settlers, cabbage salad is still known as "coleslaw." Its preparation entailed cutting long, thin strips from the inner leaves of a cabbage head. Oil (made from rendered fat), vinegar, salt, and pepper were added to the heaped platter and evenly distributed by tossing. Some preparers substituted melted butter for oil. Strangers who tasted coleslaw in a Dutch household avidly learned its preparation and spread its popularity. Other salad greens were similarly dressed.

Pumpkins were variously prepared for eating. In the style of native cooks, pumpkins were boiled whole or roasted in ashes. French and English colonists sprinkled sugar on hearth-roasted pumpkin slices. Otherwise, pumpkins were halved and the seeds removed for oven roasting. The roasted pulp was served warm with butter. Dutch colonists boiled pumpkin pulp before mashing and then boiled the mashed pumpkin in milk to make soup or gruel. They also made thick pumpkin pancakes by kneading pumpkin mash with cornmeal or other flour to make a batter that could be either boiled or fried. Some households baked pumpkin into pudding and tarts. Long slices of dried pumpkin were eaten with dried beef or other meat, especially on long journeys. To the far north, cooks peeled and quartered a whole pumpkin, boiling the pulp for four to six minutes. Left in a strainer overnight, the boiled pulp was mixed with cloves, cinnamon, and lemon peel and boiled again until the syrup was absorbed. The spiced pulp was thus preserved for future use. Otherwise, pumpkins were kept in a cool cellar until spring. As field pumpkins were generally stringy when cooked, the sweeter, denser flesh of cheese pumpkins was better suited for custards in pie making. Having learned their use and preparation from native communities, squashes were also eaten boiled, sometimes being served on the edge of the dish surrounding a serving of meat.

According to Peter Kalm, pudding or pie was the "Englishman's perpetual dish." An inventory of the Richard Ludlow's possessions, taken or destroyed in Bergen County during the British invasion of November 1776, included a brass pie pan and an iron pie pan. Milk, meat, or fruit pies were prepared according to the season. There is even record of pigeon pie. The popularity of pies quickly spread until it became everyone's "perpetual dish." Earthenware pie plates were soon counted among the most treasured heirlooms of the Jersey Dutch. They were part of a woman's outset or dowry—the basic set of household furnishings and equipment, which parents accumulated in preparation for a daughter's marriage. For this reason, many pie plates are decorated with a bride's name, initials, or possibly a wedding date. Others display political slogans, historic memorials, or simply bold, abstract designs. The decoration was done with liquid, buff-colored clay called slip that was applied from a cup through a goose-quill (much in the same manner that cakes are decorated). The body of the plate was formed from local clay, usually mixed with sand, rolled into a sheet, and then molded into a plate over a wooden template. Pie plates ranged from 5–15 inches in diameter and sold accordingly for five to fifteen cents apiece.

Henry Van Saun opened a pottery and brickyard along the Hackensack River in River Edge in 1811, buying land across the river in New Milford in 1813 for a kiln and clay pits. In 1829, Henry Van Saun's estate included brick, "pot-bakers ware" and "pottery machinery." Henry Van Saun is most noted for commemorative pie plates bearing stamped images of George Washington and Marquis de Lafayette. George Wolfkiel (1805–1867), of Pennsylvania, took over in 1830, buying the pottery in 1847. Some of his pie plates read: "Sally," "Molly," "Ginny," and "1848."

Only the wealthy could afford gardeners to supply their tables. In town and country, womenfolk, hooded in calashes for protection against the sun, appeared each spring with rakes and small painted baskets of seeds to set their kitchen gardens. Kidney beans, asparagus, celery, cucumbers, salad greens and culinary herbs were raised aplenty. According to J. C. Loudon's *Encyclopedia of Gardening* (1824), tender onion greens, turnip shoots, spinach, cold slices of boiled beets, radish leaves, cresses, mustard greens, and chopped chives were popular salad ingredients. Garden sorrel, tossed with patience dock and turnip tops, was a particular favorite of French and Dutch colonists. Artichoke hearts and beets were pickled.

Orchards supplied a cornucopia of fruit, including apples, peaches, cherries, plums, quinces, and pears. So seasonally abundant was orchard fruit that travelers were allowed to pluck and eat from trees overhanging roads and farm lanes. Apple cider was the common beverage, although children loved buttermilk ladled fresh from the churn. Those were also the days of pure applejack, considered the native

Teaneck farmer surrounded by his pumpkins, *c.* 1910. (*Bergen County Historical Society Collections*)

Redware pie plate made by George Wolfkiel, who had a pottery in the vicinity of the River Edge Swim Club. (*Artifact in the Bergen County Historical Society Collections, photo by Deborah Powell*)

drink, and most families kept a supply on hand. Peter A. I. Ackerman, of Saddle River, who kept a diary in the margins of his almanac, noted how farmers procured applejack: "Sold 405 bushels of apples to Benjamin Oldis at one shilling a bushel or 6 quarts of spirits for 10 bushels of apples." Mr. Oldis was widely admired for the excellent quality of the "Jersey Lightning" he distilled.

Strawberries and other wild fruits—especially, huckleberries, raspberries, blueberries, persimmons, grapes, and cranberries—so abounded in the woods that there was no need of cultivating them in gardens. Charles W. Idell, who resided in Hoboken, knowledgeably informed the Horticultural Society of London in 1826, "The first strawberries marketed in New York were wild ones from Bergen County, N. J." He noted African-Americans "were the first to pick this fruit for the New York market and invented those quaint old-fashioned splint baskets with handles. The baskets were strung on poles and thus peddled through the city." Demand created by rapid growth of the urban population, quickly outstripped the haphazard supply of wild fruit. Commercial cultivation of strawberries began about 1820 with farmers around Hackensack shipping berries grown in open fields and on hillsides by wagon and sloop twice weekly. Berries sold without their hulls or green caps, which were left on the vine. The half-pint splint baskets, called punnets, neatly nested atop one another in larger baskets called hampers. Strawberries sold for 3¢ to 8¢ per basket, earning farmers $30 to $40 per acre. The primitive handmade shipping containers were returned empty to the shipper. The *Crimson Cone*, a medium-sized cultivar of the *Early American Scarlet*, was variously known

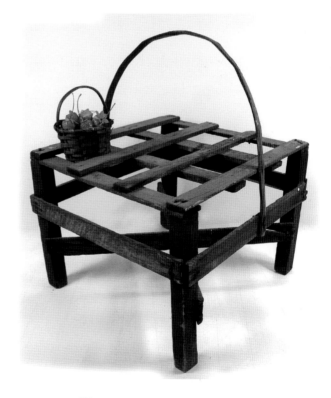

Strawberry basket in a wooden nine-slot basket holder. (*Artifacts in the Bergen County Historical Society Collections, photo by Deborah Powell*)

as the *Scotch Runner* or *Dutchberry*—New Yorkers, however, simply called them "Hackensacks," honoring their place of origin.

Most modern appetites would be disappointed with the relative paucity of meat in the colonial diet. Families reared swine and turkeys in great numbers. Those destined for winter market were fenced in an appropriate place at the lower end of the garden. Pork was preferred over beef, except among Jewish colonists whose religious observance proscribed its consumption. Pigs fattened on forest mast, field pumpkins, buckwheat, and a sweet mash of skimmed milk and bran. Fresh meat was most abundantly available in late November when farmers thinned their herds, determining what cattle might be sheltered and fed over winter. Surplus livestock either walked to market on hoof or were butchered. It was in late November, when mud roads were frozen into a hard surface, that farmers and drovers customarily made their "Big Trip" to city market, clogging highways and tavern yards along the route with their cattle. As much fresh meat as possible was consumed with the fruits of the harvest, explaining the timing of our traditional Thanksgiving feast.

With winter's onset, neighbors joined together in employing a "sticker" to expertly butcher fattened hogs. Families set to work before daylight, lighting fires to heat great caldrons of water for scalding "stuck" hogs to loosen the bristles. After scraping on a table, dressed carcasses were hung on a scaffold by the heels for butchering. Women generally prepared choice cuts for a community dinner. On this occasion, neighbors received liberal presents of pork, sausages, headcheese, or other products of the pig. The farmer who raised the heaviest porker remained the object of gossip over apple toddy for several days. As salting, pickling, smoking, or drying were the only available means of preservation, most cellars regularly stored barrels of salted, pickled or smoked pork as well as smoked beef.

Besides swine, beef cattle, sheep, chickens, and turkeys, geese, ducks, pigeons, and wild game supplied meat for the table. Clearing the forest cover for agriculture, however, rapidly diminished some game species, particularly deer, which became increasingly scarce near long-settled farmlands and villages. Before rails connected New York City and its rural hinterland, local farmers were only seasonally able to supply urban markets with poultry, venison, butter, eggs, pork, and other farm commodities. The supply of country produce dwindled with winter's arrival.

Publishing their *Historical Collections* in 1844, John Barber and Henry Howe noted how "the soil, particularly in the valleys, is fertile, and productive in early summer vegetables, apples, strawberries, & c., which find a market in the city of New York." They also reported, "several sloops ply, on the Hackensack, between here and New York, laden with the wood and produce of the country."

The official opening of the Erie Canal in 1825 brought the vast expanse of territory surrounding the Great Lakes into competition with seaboard producers, halving the cost of transporting goods between the Ohio and Hudson valleys. By 1850, the Erie Railroad, passing through the Southern Tier of New York counties, was conveying profuse quantities of farm exports year-round into city markets, contributing greatly to the comforts of city life and enriching rural producers. The opening of the Northern Railroad through Bergen County to Piermont in 1859 gave impetus to the truck farming, carrying 400,000 baskets of strawberries to Manhattan in its first year of operation. The tapering hickory-splint baskets were used to prevent the berries at the bottom from being crushed in transport. Farmers crudely painted their initials on the baskets, so that they could retrieve them from the heap of empty baskets dumped alongside railroad depots.

The Jersey tomato now began its rise to fame. Bergen County farmers raised and shipped vast quantities of asparagus, eggplants, lima beans, potatoes, cabbage, sweet corn, muskmelons, watermelons, and orchard fruits. Scores of small truck farms and gardens prospered around Moonachie and on the borders of the Meadowlands. Toward the end of July, melons and corn—the two chief products of Bergen County—were carted in a constant stream to Paterson and New York. Three farms straddling the present boundary between New Milford and Teaneck counted 21,000 hills or mounds where melons were cultivated. Herring, smelt, striped bass, perch, and shad from the river were caught and sold at the Fulton Market in New York for twenty cents per pound. Poultry farms grew to meet the increasing demands of urban markets. Bergen County cider mills ground the produce of local farms and received train carloads of cider apples from northwestern New Jersey and the western part of New York State. In October 1882, Warren Cluss' cider mill at New Bridge alone boasted orders for 12,000 gallons of cider from four New York firms.

Many gentleman farmers turned to livestock breeding, introducing new breeds of horses and dairy cattle. Theodore A. Havemeyer's beautiful Mountainside Farm was home to more than 300 head of Jersey cattle. He spent $2,500 a mile to level and macadamize the local roads leading to the Mahwah station on the Erie Railroad, easing the transit of the great amount of freight carted to and from his farm. In February 1895, ex-Mayor Hugh Grant of New York City purchased the David Zabriskie farm in the Flats section of Oradell for conversion to a stock farm.

On August 11, 1899, the *Bergen Democrat* duly reported: "Slowly but surely farms are disappearing, to be cut into building lots or made into thriving suburbs for greater New York, especially along the ridge running from Hackensack to Carlstadt and Rutherford."

Bergen County farmers persisted in marketing great quantities of melons, corn, tomatoes, and lima beans. One eyewitness in August 1900 said, "It is a sight to stand at the foot of Kelly's hill, Fairview, during the afternoon and evening, and see the heavily loaded trucks towed up by extra teams provided by residents in that vicinity." Yet, by 1904, the *Hackensack Republican* lamented:

> Our old brand of Hackensack melons are gone. This county, which was once the banner county for melons, finds that the seed does not produce the delicious melon which gave the Hackensack variety the top record and Colorado and other Western States out ranks it. Here and there a farmer will be found marketing Hackensack melons, but in only a few instances can they be relied upon.

Land in farms peaked in 1860 at 123,160 acres and declined to 15,889 acres by 1940. In 1958, the New Jersey Department of Agriculture counted 5,000 acres of cropland, 1,500 acres of pasture, and 30,000 acres of forested lands in Bergen County. Urban and built-up areas covered 103,700 acres. By this time, only 5 percent of Bergen County land was devoted to agriculture. The number of farms declined from 547 in 1954 to 384 in 1959, the average size of a Bergen County farm then being 19.5 acres. By 1962, Bergen County only led the other counties of New Jersey in the sale of nursery stock and florist products. In 2017, 335 acres of farmland are listed as preserved through the New Jersey Farmland Preservation Program.

Early Homesteads

Converting the land into farms made the seemingly inexhaustible harvest of timber and loose cobbles an obvious source of building material. The great oak and chestnut forest impressed the Dutch with its potential for building materials. Utilizing the native harvest of timber, New Netherlanders continued transferring an ancient Germanic technology of post and beam construction to the shores of the Hudson River. Some of the earliest farmhouses of New Netherland might open wide our eyes with amazement, but to the medieval homemaker, these sturdy (though often highly combustible) shelters provided a thick skin against the elements where man and his domestic beasts could huddle under a common roof, separated only by a thin partition. A landlocked Noah's Ark of just this type was erected within the present bounds of Bogota, Bergen County, by Johannes Winkelman, manager of the van Nederhorst Colony, in the spring of 1642. We have specific knowledge of this primitive residence thanks to the insightful research of Reginald McMahon of River Edge.[4] Central to our understanding of this New Netherlandish *bouwhuys* was Mr. McMahon's discovery of part of the original contract for Winkelman's house dated February 21, 1642, whereby the colony manager employed two house carpenters in the construction of this barn-domicile. Overall, the building measured 43 feet wide by 90 feet long and resembled the Dutch barns that later became a common feature of the landscape. Massive wooden timbers formed the skeleton of the structure: the spanning beams were to be 24 feet in length, 9 inches × 14 inches thick, spaced 9 feet apart, and so raised by the posts and girts as to form a 12.5-foot story beneath them. These heavy hand-hewn members framed a central enclosure, 24 feet wide and 90 feet long, that was subdivided into residential quarters and a barn. The garret was correspondingly divided between living space and hay storage. The dwelling-end of the building had a hip-and-gable roof typical of Old World structures and perhaps a center door with small garret windows. The barn end was entered through a pair of double-leaf Dutch doors. Small square windows were set on either side of these barn doors, while another door into the loft was used for pitching hay and straw. Storage space was increased by inclusion of side aisles called *uytlaten* running the full length of the building on either side of the central nave: one to be 9' wide and the other to be 10' wide. Thus, the *bouwhuys* had an overall width of 43'. There was a door into each of the aisles, centered in the sidewalls of the building, and aisle doors on both gable-ends.

The Winkelman House was probably sheathed with wide weatherboards of the type found in northern Holland.[5]

New Netherlanders continued their ancient habit of assembling a framework of heavy timbers, joining the constituent parts by mortise and tenon, then securing the joints with wooden pegs. The H-frame was a hallmark of the Continental style of framing (differing somewhat from English methods). There are incidental references to this technology in the ancient records, as when Nicholas Varlett applied to the Council of New Netherland on March 28, 1656, "for leave to remove the Frame of a house from Hoboocken [to New Amsterdam], which he had sold to Michiel Jansen for 230 florins."[6]

Worthy of note, the town records for New Harlem in New York record expenses incurred during construction of a frame dwelling for Hendrick J. Vander Vin, the *voorleser* (religious teacher) of this Hudson River community, about the year 1680. Adolph Pietersen De Groot, a New York house carpenter, was paid 250 guilders ($100) "for building the town's house."[7] According to the contract, De Groot would construct a house 22-feet long and 20-feet wide. The townspeople also paid the carpenter's board (forty guilders) and supplied labor for processing and hoisting the heavy framing timbers into place. Eight local citizens were paid for "Riding shingles, clapboards, etc"[8] The peculiar expression "Riding shingles, clapboards, etc." is explained by a reference in the writings of Cornelis van Tienhoven when in 1650 he states that "One pair of draft horses or a yoke of oxen only is necessary, to ride the planks for buildings, or palisades or rails from the land to the place where they are to be set." "Information relative to taking up land in New Netherland, in the form of Colonies or private bouweries. Delivered in by Secretary van Tienhoven, on the 4th of March, 1650."[9]

The Jersey Dutch Sandstone Cottage Style

Before departing our overview, let's visit the iconic sandstone cottages that yet persist in our midst, despite a rising tide of architectural vulgarity. What we casually call the "Dutch Colonial Style" actually has no precedent in Holland, but rather is a regional folk expression of Georgian architectural models, adapted to a rising middle class's aspirations and means. Mansions and farmhouses were executed in wood, but sandstone examples have garnered greater attention because of their seeming durability and charm. To best understand the Jersey Dutch sandstone cottage, we must first consider its basic building blocks—the native red sandstone.

In 1896, state geologist Henry Kummel divided this sedimentary wedge into three depositional series: "An often pebbly, brown-red sandstone (a freestone much used for building) and soft red shales" prevail near the top of the basal Stockton Series. Besides a large outcrop between Trenton and Rocky Hill, the Palisades are enclosed by the Stockton Series. There is considerable inter-bedding, however, and individual beds often appear as thin lenses of sediment. Cross-bedding of the sandstone and ripple-marks, mud-cracks and raindrop impressions in the shale indicate deposition upon a near-shore platform, delta front and intertidal zone.

The most obvious source would be glacially deposited cobbles and blocks found in surficial deposits. Sampson's Rock, perched atop the Palisades behind William B. Dana's residence in Englewood, is a red sandstone boulder measuring 10 × 7 × 9 feet.[10] Otherwise, the glacial drift is so thickly and uniformly spread along the base of the western slope of the Palisades and on the sandstone ridges of the stream valleys "as to conceal the sandstone, excepting in a few very small outcrops."

Given the northwest dip of the formations, the most likely outcrops, suitable for quarrying, would be exposed along the southeast faces of the sandstone ridges. The best-known sandstone quarries were worked at Garret Mountain near Paterson, at Beattie's quarry at Little Falls and Belleville. Captain John Anderson also opened a sandstone quarry along High Mountain Road, 1 mile north of Haledon, by 1815, later owned by the New Jersey Brownstone Company.[11]

William Nelson thought it improbable that any quarry of sandstone was worked in the region of Paterson before the Revolution. The earliest stone dwellings were therefore "built of the red sandstone of the country, usually taken out of some outcropping ledge, supplemented by weather-worn fieldstone of the same material, or the Green Pond conglomerate scattered by prehistoric glaciers far and wide over the land." At first, the walls were laid in clay and pointed with lime, possibly derived from aboriginal shell middens. The interior walls were also crudely plastered with mud, binding materials and a thick finish coat. Lime was eventually imported from Albany, New York City, and Newark.

The Dey Mansion is two stories in height, below a gambrel roof, and measures 52 feet long and 30 feet deep. It has a brick front with doors and window openings trimmed with polished brownstone, "squared and set in the most accurate manner." The sides and rear are composed of coursed rubble with the windows and doors trimmed in brick. Brick was also used in the end walls above the eaves. The masonry was laid up in yellow clay and pointed with mortar. A 12-foot-wide center hall runs north-to-south flanked on each side by two rooms and fireplaces faced with rubbed red sandstone. The ceilings on the first floor are 9 feet in height, and on the second floor, about 8 feet in height. Nelson believed the house was not built more than twenty years before the Revolution by Colonel Theunis Dey (1726–1787), who was married to Hester Dey.

On July 5, 1780, while at Preakness, surgeon Thatcher dined with the wealthy Dutch family of George Doremus, who lived "in a style superior to the Low Dutch in general; the table was amply furnished with cherries, raspberries and other fruits, which abound in this country." Five days later, he and his fellow officers noted:

> [They] erected a large arbor, with the boughs of trees, under which we enjoyed an elegant dinner, and spent the afternoon in social glee, with some of the wine which was taken from the enemy when they retreated from Elizabethtown. Our drums and fifes afforded us a favorite music till evening, when we were delighted with the song composed by Mr. Hopkinson, called the 'Battle of the Kegs,' sung in the best style by a number of gentlemen. [12]

Two mentions of quarries appear in *The New-York Evening Post*, one on April 11, 1812, a real estate advertisement offers the sale of a large stone house, a sawmill, other out-buildings, and "a quarry of Free Stone" at Little Falls on the Passaic River, situated 3 miles from Paterson and 6 miles from Paterson Landing, "where boats ply to the City of New York, and a road is contemplated to be opened, which will bring it within fifteen miles of the City of New York." A second is listed on May 9, 1815; J. P. Durand, of New York, advertised small farm and house, situated on the old Bloomfield Road, about 2.5 miles from Newark and 1.5 miles from Belleville and

Gambrel roof sandstone house with dormers in Closter. (*Bergen County Historical Society Collections*)

the Passaic River, whereon "quarries of excellent free stone, which probably extends to a great distance on the farm," were located "by the side of the Second River."

The beautiful low-pitched gambrel roof of the Jersey Dutch sandstone cottage are associated with many examples in northeastern New Jersey and Rockland County, New York.

English settlers in southwestern New Jersey introduced the use of the gambrel roof on their patterned brickwork houses by 1690. While two early examples combine the gambrel with a two-and-a-half story brick house, the gambrel was commonly associated with one-and-a-half story brick houses built in Salem County between 1727 and 1746 with isolated examples dating as late as 1764. This source of diffusion explains why the gambrel roof spread throughout the lower Hudson valley, while it occurs infrequently at an early date in the northern reaches of Anglo-Dutch settlement. The distinctive slope of the Bergen Dutch gambrel is not so much a consequence of conscious art as of practical application—the steep slope of early English examples are found on houses only one room deep, whereas the Bergen Dutch used them to span houses one-and-a-half to two rooms deep. This allowed the Bergen Dutch to increase the depth of their stone houses, built low to the ground, and thus expand their living space without building taller buildings. Gambrel or hipped roofs provided an additional floor within the roof. In most farmhouses, the commodious garrets were generally stored with dry goods; seed grain, feathers, wool, flax; agricultural implements, fish seines, pigeon nets, smoked provisions and seasonal textile equipment such as wool cards, hatchels, spinning wheels, looms and reels. Middle-class homesteads also included "dormitories within the slopes of the roof" as evidenced by the Brinkerhoff-Demarest Homestead on

Teaneck Road. Hendrick H. Brinkerhoff probably erected his center-hall sandstone dwelling about 1784. In March 1828, two years after his death, an advertisement of sale in the *Paterson Intelligencer* describes his "Dwelling House, one story high, four rooms and an entry on the lower floor, with two bedrooms in the garret, and a convenient garret ¼" Bedsteads and chairs were counted among garret furnishings in Bergen Dutch household inventories. Children, farm laborers, and travelers would sleep in such quarters on low bedsteads, slawbanks (literally, "sleep benches," or folding beds), or mattresses. Finished bedchambers with dormers were obvious status symbols and any "well finished house, fit for a gentleman," would have second-story living quarters in part of its garret.

Sandstone is a name applied to a kind of freestone which is made up chiefly of grains of sand loosely cohering. It exhibits various degrees of hardness, but is usually hard enough for a building-stone, and frequently when very soft in the quarry, becomes hard by exposure to the air. Being very easily shaped by the hammer alone it forms a cheap and commodious material for walls, chimneys, and even for the main body of a building; and when farther wrought by the chisel it is susceptible of no small degree of elegance ... The finer grained varieties are even capable of being wrought into mouldings, entablatures, and other delicate and ornamental parts of a building, a beautiful example of which is afforded in the northern side of the City-Hall in New-York, one of the most superb buildings in the world. [13]

"Washington House, Paramus Road. Photographed 1897, torn down 1908" (Aycrigg family home). This is a very compelling photograph. (*Bergen County Historical Society Collections*)

Two houses and lots for sale describe the Bergen County homes in *The Evening-Post* on March 6, 1806:

> To be sold at private sale, or exchanged for a House and Lot in an eligible art of the city of New-York. An elegant Country Seat, adjoining the Hackensack River at the New-Bridge, about 3 miles above the Town of Hackensack. The house is finished in the modern style, with five rooms, five fire places, a good cellar and kitchen. The out-houses and fences are in complete order, and neatly constructed. The lot on which the buildings are erected contains about 14 acres, in a rich state for cultivation, handsomely ornamented with grafted trees, producing every species of the best of fruits. There is a valuable fishing place appurtenant to the premises, where shad may be caught in abundance, in the season.

A second ad appears in the spring of 1819, trustees offered to sell the estate of John A. Schuyler, Esquire, deceased, lying in the counties of Bergen and Essex. The Schuyler farm fronted the Passaic River for nearly a mile and contained about 500 acres of upland, fit for grain, grazing, and meadow, and about 600 acres of salt meadow, of which 500 acres were enclosed and drained by sluices to exclude salt water and drain freshwater, a part of which had been planted with English grasses. The premises included:

> An elegant and well-built stone house, with a brick front, sixty-six by fifty feet, and finished in an elegant and substantial manor, and several smaller dwelling and a variety of out-houses, well calculated for the accommodation of farmers. The situation of the mansion is one of the most elegant on the river, distant eight miles from the city of New-York, and about two and a half from Newark. The garden is extensive and elegant. It has a large quantity of wood-land—and the whole offers one of the most eligible purchases for a gentleman of fortune and enterprise of any in the state of New Jersey.

The successful blend of freestone with Classical forms and ornament made the Jersey Dutch cottage form. By 1834, Thomas Gordon would admire its distinctive aspects and describe it as "ancient," though its oldest examples had barely stood for eighty years:

> There are few spots in New Jersey presenting more pleasing attractions than this country above the Hackensack, and on the highlands on each side of the river. The houses, built in the ancient Dutch cottage form, of one full story, with its projecting pent houses, and dormitories within the slopes of the roof, are sometimes large, always painted white, and surrounded with verdant lawns, shrubbery, and well-cultivated gardens. And we may here remark, that the taste for horticulture and ornamental shrubberies, appears more general in the central and northern parts of New Jersey, than in the southern parts, or in the state of Pennsylvania. [14]

The Blackhorse Inn: Good Entertainment for Travelers

The origins of an old stone tavernhouse, denominated on one map of Revolutionary War vintage as the Blackhorse Inn, is lost in the proverbial mists of time. Lawrence

Glass plate photograph of the Steuben Houses from the Sons of the American Revolution, *c.* 1940.

Pieterse Van Buskirk resided near the river, south of French Creek, before 1738. The first inn probably opened in Lawrence P. Van Buskirk's house soon after a "new bridge" was built at the narrows of the Hackensack River in 1744. The farm of the late Lawrence P. Van Buskirk was divided among his children: Jacobus, Abraham, Andrew, and Elizabeth Vroom, wife of Isaac Vroom.

On September 17, 1768, Andrew Van Buskirk began to drive a stage wagon from New Bridge to Paulus Hook, setting out twice weekly on Tuesdays and Saturdays. With the onset of winter, he reduced his trips to one every Tuesday, "after the Holy Days, till the Severity of the Season is over."[15] Andrew Van Buskirk advertised the sale of his stagecoach tavern at New Bridge in February 1771, describing it as a stone dwelling house with a good shingle-roofed barn on about an acre of ground. The house had three good rooms on a floor with two small back rooms. It stood at the New Bridge, opposite to John Zabriskie's residence, a location "very convenient for fishing and fowling." He also advertised the sale of 25 acres of mowing ground and woodlot, located within half a mile of the dwelling house. He noted, "there has been a tavern kept for many years;" with the inn being near to the Latin School, it was "very convenient to keep boarders." He was willing to sell very cheap and offered easy payments "as the owner has no use for it."[16] Despite this assertion, Andrew Van Buskirk resumed running his "Stage betwixt Hackinsack New-Bridge and Powles-Hook" twice weekly in April 1771.[17]

On account of relocating his stage line from the New Bridge to Hackensack, Andrew Van Buskirk was obliged "to discontinue his driving a stage-wagon." On June 9, 1767, Peter P. Demarest, Jr., applied to the Court of the General Quarter Session of the Peace for a tavern license. Exactly where the Demarest tavern was located is something of a mystery, though it likely stood near the present intersection of New Bridge and Old New Bridge Roads. Peter Demarest started "to drive a covered WAGGON from that Place to Powles-Hook, twice every week, viz., on Monday and Friday" in May 1772. His wagon was "new and well fitted, with Curtains and the Horses in excellent Heart."[18] On April 6, 1773, Van Buskirk returned to his old route, reassuring his clientele:

> As there were so many stage-wagons set up, he expected that the public would have been regularly attended on the stage days, but as those stage-wagons, like fair weather birds, have kept at home, and given no attendance during the last winter, he now informs the public that he has now erected a NEW STAGE WAGGON, on a plan more commodious than any others; and proposes to drive his wagon from the New Bridge and Hackinsack Town, to Powles-Hook and back again, on the days he formerly used, viz. Tuesday and Saturdays." As always, Van Buskirk kept "good entertainment for travelers.[19]

In May 1775, Andrew Van Buskirk informed the public that "the flying machine" he formerly drove between Hackensack and Paulus Hook would take "a better and shorter road" between Hackensack and the Hoboken Ferry. Verdine Ellsworth began driving the "New Caravan from Powles-Hook to the New Bridge above Hackensack." At about this time, Cornelius Hoogland acquired the stone tavern at New Bridge. Eyewitness accounts of the retreat from Fort Lee on November 20, 1776, state that an American rear guard used the stone dwellings on opposite sides of the New Bridge as forts, while American engineers tried to dismantle the bridge. In 1782, Cornelius Hoogland submitted a compensation claim for twelve gills of rum destroyed or lost to the enemy in 1776.

New Bridge Latin School

There has been considerable speculation as to the location of the New Bridge Latin School. Advertisements indicate that the School was located "on an Eminence," near unto "the little River at that Place" and "near the Landing." The school opened in 1766 "under the Inspection and Direction of the Rev. Mr. Goetschius." While French Creek may have been a more-ample stream in days bygone, it is doubtful that it ever was described as a "Little River" or that any landing was located along its banks. The so-called "Little River" is actually a small inlet or cove of the Hackensack River, set apart from the main stream by a mud island. This cove or inlet partly survives within Brett Park, near the intersection of Old New Bridge Road and Riverview Avenue. Early deeds mention a dock or landing along this channel, adjacent to the house of Doctor Abraham Van Buskirk, which stood nearly opposite the present New Bridge Inn. A lot of 6.75 acres ("about seven acres of land") abutted this landing and the Little River. Revolutionary War maps show a dwelling stood upon a steep bluff or "eminence" above the Hackensack River, facing River Road, within the bounds of this tract. This was the New Bridge Latin School.

Stephanus Voorhees opened the New Bridge Latin School "under the Inspection and Direction of the Rev. Mr. Goetschius" in April 1766. Francis Barber was Voorhees' "Able Assistant." An English teacher competent in penmanship, was available to teach "the Latin Scholars, Writing, and Arithmetic two Hours a Day" for a small additional charge.[20] A number of young men from prominent New York City families attended the academy and the teachers advertised "many respectable Families will take in Youths to Board, on the most reasonable Terms, to encourage the said School." In late April 1768, a New York newspaper reported that Philip French Livingston, the eight-year-old son of William Livingston and a student at the New Bridge Latin School, recently took a Sunday sail "in a Canoe on the little River at that Place." He was found drowned in about two feet of water near the Landing.[21] Francis Barber assumed management of the school in September 1769. Terence Reilly taught bookkeeping, mercantile accounting, and mathematics.[22] John Wright, a graduate of New Jersey College at Princeton, succeeded Barber in September 1771.[23] On December 30, 1772, Theobald Burke offered instruction in reading, writing, arithmetic, book-keeping, surveying, mensuration, and navigation at the New Bridge Schoolhouse. He described the academy as "situate on an Eminence, in a fine Air, and exceeding commodious; a good Entertainment for Boarders, from 14 to 16 l. per Annum, quite convenient to the School-House."[24]

On February 3, 1775, Albert Banta, David B. Demarest and Hendrick Kuyper, acting as executors of "the estate of the late Rev. Johannes Henricus Goetcheus, of Hackensack, and Scrallenburgh," advertised the sale of a property "at New Bridge, about seven acres of land, whereon is a good dwelling-house, orchard and other conveniences, wherein Mrs. Goelett now lives." This is likely the property, which the New Bridge Latin School occupied.[25] By the time of the American Revolution, the relative of John Zabriskie, Jr., Edmund Seaman, the son of a wealthy New York merchant, owned this same property, probably having purchased it from the estate of Reverend Goetschius in 1775. He and his father were later accused of loyalist sympathies and their property confiscated. Cornelius Haring, agent for Forfeited Estates in Bergen County, sold Edmund Seaman's property at New Bridge to Captain Gyles Mead, who was a tanner, on March 25, 1779.[26, 27]

The stone building that originally housed New Bridge Latin School survived until 1881. On March 15, 1881, Barney and Jane Cole sold the ten-acre lot where it stood to Martial G. Jouffret, of New York City, for $6,000.[28] Martial Jouffret, an entrepreneur with considerable hotel experience, purchased the John A. Cole residence and "fitted up the building for a hotel and restaurant where wayfarers can always be accommodated." He immediately rented all his rooms to summer boarders and found it necessary to rent an adjoining house. The opening hop at Jouffret's villa, situated only a few minutes' walk from Cherry Hill depot, with dancing in an open pavilion was held June 6, 1881. Jouffret's villa quickly became a popular resort for New Yorkers with the Sunday train bringing new arrivals weekly.

Select School.

MISS E. WINFIELD

RESPECTFULLY informs the inhabitants of Hackensack, and its vicinity, that she has opened a SELECT SCHOOL, at Mrs. *Maria Earle's*, three doors north of Mrs. Campbell's Hotel. The following branches will be taught, viz :—

Spelling, Reading, Writing, Arithmetic, English Grammar and Definitions,—Geography, with the use of the Globes—History—Fancy and Fine Needlework,—Drawing, and Velvet Painting.

Miss W. flatters herself, that by diligent attention to the improvement of her pupils, to be enabled to give general satisfaction, and obtain a share of public patronage.

Terms of Tuition as low as any in the village.

Hackensack, Jan 12, 1825.

There were schools for girls too. Miss E. Winfield advertises a well-rounded education in 1825. Winfield opened "a SELECT SCHOOL at Mrs. Maria Earle's, three doors north of Mrs. Campbell's Hotel" in Hackensack. "The following branches will be taught, viz: Spelling, Reading, Writing, Arithmetic, English Grammar and Definitions, Geography, with the use of the Globes, History, Fancy and Fine Needlework, Drawing, and Velvet Painting." (*Unrecorded newspaper*)

Unfortunately, the villa burned to the ground on June 28, 1881, with Mr. Jouffret and family narrowly escaping in their nightclothes. Fittingly, a new school for New Bridge District No. 10 was built on a little rise of ground affording a fine view of the Hackensack River and overlooking the villages of New Bridge, Cherry Hill, River Edge and Schraalenburgh. It opened on January 23, 1891. It occupied nearly the same site as the old stone schoolhouse, standing near the present intersection of Riverview Avenue and River Road in Teaneck.[29]

5

An Incomplete Record:
Free Africans, Enslavement, and
Indentured Servants

The odd mix of surnames associated with the old stone houses at New Bridge Landing—Ackerman, Zabriskie, Demarest, Campbell, and Christie—invites the question, how Dutch were the Jersey Dutch? A survey of early church records, where individuals often listed their place of origin, tempered with information from census reports, provides a prismatic breakdown of ethnic diversity in Bergen County during its pioneer settlement: Netherlanders, 28 percent; Africans (probably Angolans), 19.6 percent; Germans, 19.6 percent; English, 10.6 percent; French, 9 percent; Irish and Scots-Irish, 5.7 percent; Scots, 4 percent; and Barbadians (English?), 2.4 percent. The long use of Dutch as a common language, albeit much extended by English, French, German, and Minsi vocabulary, largely disguises significant cultural diversity among the Jersey Dutch, where true Netherlanders comprised less than a third of the population. In fact, "Jersey Dutch" is probably best used to describe a multi-ethnic community bonded by a hybrid dialect and material culture, rather than a community of singular national stock.

Pioneers of African descent comprised the second largest ethnic group among the Bergen Dutch. In 1834, Thomas Gordon explained the circumstances of this migration:

> The vice of slavery was early introduced into the State, and took deep root, particularly in the eastern portion. In the county of Bergen, in 1790, the slaves amounted to near one-fifth of the population; and in Essex, Middlesex, and Monmouth, they were very numerous, the counties having the most Dutch population being most infected.[1]

The first African-Americans in New Netherland came from a broad stretch of coastal lowland and plateau, watered by the Congo and Cunene Rivers, along the west coast of Africa. Bantu-speaking peoples of such diverse dialects as Luganda, Zulu, and Swahili inhabited this territory. The principal ethnic communities included Matabele, Mashona, Zulu, and Basuto. The evidence is slim but rather consistent. A letter written by Domine Jonas Michaelius on August 11, 1628, mentions "the Angola slaves."[2] One of the Africans who signed a petition requesting manumission from servitude in 1644 was named Paul D'Angola. A letter written by the Reverend Henricus Selyns to the Classis of Amsterdam on October 4, 1660, speaks of Stuyvesant's Bowery (in the present vicinity of Third Avenue and Tenth Street in Manhattan), where "there are forty negroes, from the region of the Negro Coast, besides household families."[3]

A Dutch slave ship brought the first Africans, comprising ten men and an unrecorded number of women, to New Amsterdam in 1626. At the time, the concept of slavery did not exist in English or Dutch law, but originated in the New World as a form of indentured servitude without predetermined tenure. Consequently, in New Netherland, Africans were freed—by their own initiative—after eighteen years of servitude, although their children remained company laborers. Thus, the first Africans in the Dutch colony, kidnapped from the homelands, remained servants of the Dutch West India Company until their liberation on February 25, 1644, when they were placed "on the same footing as other free people here in New Netherland"—provided that they make an annual payment of some produce and a fat hog to the Company and that they were agreeable to the stipulation "that their children at present born or yet to be born, shall be bound and obligated to serve the Hon'ble West India Company as Slaves."[4] This unfortunate provision apparently troubled some, for Junker Adriaen Van Der Donk, in describing the African population of New Netherlands in 1650, noted that, besides those Africans brought to New Amsterdam on the slave ship *Tamandare* in June 1626:

> There are also various other negroes in this country, some of whom have been made free for their long service, but their children have remained slaves, though it is contrary to the laws of every people that any one born of a Christian mother should be a slave and be compelled to remain in servitude ...[5, 6]

Nevertheless, a small but growing community of free Africans was established.

Surrender of New Netherland to the English in 1664 freed the remaining Dutch West India Company's slaves. Traveling down Broadway in 1679, Jasper Dankers and Peter Sluyter described:

> Many habitations of Negroes, mulattoes and whites. These Negroes were formerly the proper slaves of the (Dutch West India) company, but in consequence of the frequent changes and conquests of the country, they have obtained their freedom and settled down where they have thought proper, and thus on this road, where they have ground enough to live on with their families.[7]

Free Africans are counted among the earliest settlers of Bergen County. In 1696, Anthony Robertse, a free African, purchased several hundred acres of land in present-day Hackensack from Captain John Berry, including the neighborhood where the Bergen County Courthouse now stands.[8] He was also known as Anthony Anthonyseen. He may be the same Jochem Anthony Robbert from New York who married Mary Jeems, widow of James Benson, in the presence of the Court of Bergen on April 26, 1686.[9]

Agents of the East Jersey Proprietors, reporting on various leasees and squatters upon the contested Romopock Tract in May 1740, referred to "a parcel of free Negroes, as Solomon Peterse, James Peterse, also without leases ..."[10] On June 14, 1742, proprietary land agents reported, "Francis Francisco Bastion and John Crumble, free Negroes, settled on the land near Pascack River, came and requested leases of the Proprietors, the one for 200 acres and the other for 400 acres ..."[11] Their leases were issued in August 1742.[12]

These free Africans had trouble defending their improvements against claims:

> One Francis Francisco Bastian, a free Negro, under the color of a lease from this Board (of East Jersey Proprietors) to him as possessed himself of a part of a tract of land formerly surveyed for Peter Sonmans near Pascack and which said Sonmans had conveyed to one John Durie ...

The Board of Proprietors asked Bastian to resettle within the bounds of the Romopock Tract, where they would defend his title.[13]

John Crumble also had difficulties defending his leasehold. On April 4, 1743, the Board received notice:

> Caspar Sille, a free Negro partner with John Crumble, to whom a lease was made of part of the land claimed by Vanderlinda complaining that Vanderlinda had caused him to be arrested at Tappan by a warrant from Judge Herring & obliged him to give a note for six pounds to one John Perdun, Clerk to the judge for rent and court charges, otherwise the judge threatened to put him in prison.[14]

John Crumble came personally before the Board of East Jersey Proprietors to complain of mistreatment:

> [He] repeated many tales, which he said Vanderlinda gave out of his having agreed with the Proprietors & that they had given him orders to turn all the seed of Cain off the land & by which they were extremely discouraged.[15]

James Alexander, president of the Board, assured him that there was "no foundation for these tales." The Board agreed to defend John Crumble against Vanderlinda's claims and to intercede on Bastian's behalf to delay his removal until he had time to harvest his crop from land he had mistakenly settled and cultivated. Both men, however, continued to suffer injury to their property and threats to their safety. The Proprietors, however, were willing and able to indemnify these "free Negroes" against losses incurred as a result of disputed surveys and land titles.

Thus, the pioneer population of Bergen County (then including present Passaic and Hudson Counties) included not only Africans held in slavery, but also an enterprising number of free Africans who endured despite legal and cultural impediments placed in their path. According to the 1737 census, "Whites" in Bergen County numbered 3,289 while "slaves and other Negroes" numbered 806 (or 19.6 percent). The more questionable returns of the 1745 census indicate that African-Americans constituted 20.4 percent of the total population of the county. In

1790, African-Americans constituted 19.7 percent of the population of the county. In the census returns for 1790, the category of "all other free persons" included 192 persons, whereas "slaves" numbered 2,301. Thus only 7.7 percent of the total African-American population in Bergen County was listed as "free persons" at that time. In 1810, African-Americans comprised 15 percent of the total population. By this date, 38 percent were enumerated as "free coloured persons."[16]

Slavery is an ancient evil, inhabiting most parts of the world in one form or another at one time or another. Its victims are deprived not only of the fruits of their talents and labor, but of basic human rights. On the seventeenth-century frontiers of settlement, slaves and indentured servants were exploited as a means to circumvent the scarcity and high cost of labor in a resource-rich land. When Judge William Pinhorne purchased a half-interest in the Secaucus Patent from Edward Earle in 1679, the island contained a farmstead with "five tobacco houses ... between thirty and forty hogs," which "four Negro men (and) five Christian servants" operated. Across the Hackensack River, William Sandford purchased and named New Barbadoes Neck in trust for his uncle, Nathaniel Kingsland, of the island of Barbados, on July 4, 1668. This peninsula was partitioned in 1671 and Isaac Kingsland settled the northern portion in about 1682. Major Kingsland subsequently claimed headrights to land for the settlement of "himself, wife, one child, four white servants and eight Negroes." Captain John Berry, another Barbadian immigrant, was issued a grant for lands on New Barbadoes Neck, extending 6 miles northward of Sandford's Spring (Boiling Spring in Rutherford) in 1669. He applied for headrights to land in 1675, claiming the settlement of himself, his wife, "two daughters, one son, one maid servant and thirty-two Africans."

In 1694, the East Jersey Assembly responded to numerous complaints about slaves killing swine on private plantations under the pretense of hunting by requiring owners or their proxies to accompany such hunters.[17] This legislation implies that at least some enslaved people had a certain freedom of movement and possession of firearms. The Assembly also required slaves to earmark their own swine. Such enactments indicate that slaves were enterprising on their own behalf, probably raising and selling produce and livestock to procure such private possessions as hunting weapons. Estate inventories, however, commonly counted furnishings used by slaves as the slaveholder's possessions. Obviously, legislation promulgated exclusively to regulate the conduct of slaves was exclusionary in intent as well as in effect, regulating enslaved people to a status decidedly apart from free citizens.

In 1710, Colonel Edmund Kingsland sold a large tract on New Barbadoes Neck, adjoining the Passaic River, to Arent Schuyler. A copper deposit on Schuyler's estate was first mined about 1712. John Schuyler inherited his father's mansion and copper mine. A notice of sale, published August 29, 1746, offers "two Negro Men, who understand Mining; as also the Utensils belonging to the Mine, in Kingsland's lands" at Joseph Johnson's house in Newark. In 1768, fire destroyed the steam engine that pumped water from the mine and operations were suspended until 1793. Colonel (Arent) John Schuyler inherited the Schuyler estate in 1773.

Describing Colonel Schuyler's elegant estate on June 29, 1776, Lieutenant Isaac Bangs of the Continental Army noted the following of the workforce:

Daguerreotype of a woman with a fragment of newspaper clipping. "Another Revolutionary Relic Gone. On the 21st last, a colored woman living in the family of James Paulison, at New Bridge, died at the advanced age of ninety-eight years. She was born a slave in the Paulison family, at the old homestead below the village of Hackensack, where she lived until emancipated in 1840, after which she resided in the family of James Paulison. She retained a vigorous mind until near her death, and her recollections of Revolutionary times were very vivid." *The Bergen Democrat*, March 24, 1871. Note, the article does not give her name. (*Artifact in the Bergen County Historical Society Collections, photo by Deborah Powell*)

About 50 or 60 Blacks, all of whom, except those who are necessary for domestic Service, live in a large, convenient House built for that Purpose without the Gate; in the House every servant their particular Sphere to act in. I never saw more than 2 in the House otherwise than in the Kitchen & those were waiters. Those who live in the Out House each have their particular Department & regular Hours to Work in; their Victual is cooked at certain Hours by their own Cooks, to which they are regularly called by a Bell, which Rings in the morning for the Servants to turn out to their Work, and at 7 for Breakfast, at 12 for Dinner, at a proper time for them to leave their Work, & again at 8 in the evening for each to repair to their House, after which no Noise is heard. Notwithstanding they have so large a Family to regulate, Mrs. Schuyler also sees to the Manufacturing of suitable clothing for all the Servants, all of which is the Produce of their own Plantation ...[18]

The bell-tolled schedule of labor, described by Lieutenant Bangs, suggests an agricultural regimen. As Schuyler's mine was abandoned in 1768, these workers were probably not engaged in digging or hauling ore. Colonel Schuyler must have employed them in the construction and maintenance of a 3-mile "Causeway of Cedar Logs" running through the great cedar swamp and across the Hackensack meadows. He built this road at his own expense in 1766 but sought the proceeds from a public lottery to defray the expense of spreading gravel bed over the plank roadbed. By his last will and testament, probated in 1807, Schuyler provided freedom for all his slaves when they reached twenty-eight years of age. This seeming act of generosity did nothing more than unnecessarily ratify the Gradual Abolition Act of 1804.

Schuyler's plantation system of slavery was an anomaly in Bergen County—as rare as the wealth that most citizens might earn from a copper mine. Slavery persisted locally on a far more limited scale. Complete tax returns from 1784 for Hackensack Township offer some insight. Out of 285 individuals listed, thirty-five persons (12 percent) claimed a total of fifty-seven slaves. There were 18,662.8 improved acres of land held in 208 separate parcels, making the average holding in improved land 89.7 acres. Parcels of improved acreage ranged in size from 1.3 to 500 acres. The average holding of improved land for slaveholders equaled 126.6 acres. Two slaveholders claimed no improved acreage, implying that their two slaves (representing 3.5 percent of the total) were engaged primarily in occupations other than agriculture. This data shows most slaves (96.5 percent) engaged in agriculture on comparatively larger farms. Jacob and John Degroot each claimed seven slaves and, together with Peter Degroot, claimed a total of 325 acres of improved land. All other slaveholding households only claimed one or two slaves.

Out of 125 estate inventories filed between 1803 and 1808 in Bergen County, twenty-eight households (22 percent) contained enslaved people. Thus, African-Americans, comprising one-fifth of the population, resided in one-fifth of the county's households. The number of slaves per household ranged from one to seven persons. Seven households had but one slave; seven households had four slaves; two households had five slaves; one household had six slaves; one household had seven slaves; and two households simply recorded the presence of slaves without enumeration. In every instance where description is sufficient to make a determination, these slaves resided within the kitchen of the homestead and not in separate slave quarters or out buildings (as on the Schuyler plantation). Under such a close arrangement, it would be easy to "represent" some slaves as "family," although the reality of the unequal relationship is too obvious to permit such a superficial representation.

At the time of his death in 1804, Peter Tibow, of Franklin Township, kept seven slaves and operated a storeroom, workshop and blacksmith shop. The occupations of other slaveholders included twelve farmers, three weavers, two blacksmiths, two carpenters, a turner/carpenter, a sawyer, a cooper, a chair maker, a farmer/brewer, a saddler, miller, a potter, and a judge. Households primarily or exclusively engaged in agriculture account for half of the households where slaves were resident. Remembering that most craftsmen and professionals also engaged in farming, the presence of slaves in their households suggests agricultural employment, although some slaves were craft workers such as blacksmiths, chair makers, carpenters and sawyers. It is impossible to tell in such trades as weaving whether slaves were employed in raising and processing wool and linen or weaving cloth. In some documents, shared skills are suggested. For example, a "Negro boy" assisted John Capple, a turner and carpenter, and chair maker Daniel Demarest worked beside a "Negro slave named Tone (Anthony)."

In some instances, the number of slaves in a household suggests family relationships, and even multi-generational families, although the absence of surnames makes this speculative. The estate inventory of Peter Tibow mentions two males, two females, a boy, a girl, and a male child. The inventory of Ryneer Earle, of Secaucus, mentions an older man named Har, an older woman named Dana, a young man named Bol, two boys named Sezer (Caesar) and Jack, and a girl named Sal. The household of Jacobus D. Demarest, a cooper, included an older man, a young man, a young woman, and a boy.

Other estate inventories indicate the presence of African-American workers only in the prime of their working life. The estate inventory of Isaac Nichol, of Hackensack Township, notes, "1 Negro woman named Dolly, aged 25; 1 Negro Man named Peter, aged 26 years, very infirm; 1 Negro Man named Cuff, aged 21; 1 Negro Man named Adam, aged 18." Bonds of marriage or kinship are sometimes suggested. "A Negro woman, child and boy" listed in one household and a man named Jack and a woman named Tiny in another.

Despite limited options and rare opportunities for economic independence, reinforced by the oppressive attitudes of racism, the value of labor provided slaves with some leverage. On August 20, 1790, James Jay paid Richard Ryerson of Pompton £81 to secure the services of "Claus, a negro man." Their agreement states that Claus had resided with James Jay "four weeks on trial, and is so well satisfied with the usage he has received, that he declares that were he sure to be always treated in the same way, he would like to live with me all his life." Reportedly, certain "mischievous people" informed Claus that he would "be treated with unmerited severity," so Jay promised "that if the said Claus shall within a year from the date hereof show just and sufficient cause to complain of ill-usage, I will sell him within six months after such complaint ..."[19] Of course, we may assume that Claus would have preferred his freedom to any such pledges of kind usage with the option of being sold.

The longing for personal liberty and preservation of family ties among slaves is well illustrated by a petition to Jacobus Demarest, Justice of the Peace, by "a Negro man slave named Sam, aged about thirty-three years, belonging to and residing with Peter Christie, of the Township of Hackensack," on August 10, 1801. Therein, Sam "declared his consent and desire to have his residence or place of abode changed to the City of New York ... first because his wife resides there and secondly because an opportunity will thereby be afforded him of obtaining his Freedom after eight years' servitude."

By the advent of the nineteenth century, slavery survived principally in the rural northern townships of Bergen County. Of estate inventories recorded between 1803 and 1808, households with slaves were numerically clustered in the following townships: nine in Harrington Township; four in Franklin Township; four in

The 1790 document, signed by James Jay, is about an enslaved man named Claus. (*Artifact in the Bergen County Historical Society Collections, photo by Deborah Powell*)

Hackensack Township; two in Saddle River Township; two in Pompton Township (now Passaic County); two in Bergen Township (now Hudson County); and one in New Barbados Township. By comparison, the abstract of tax returns for Bergen County in 1783 indicate that New Barbados Township had the largest slave population with seventy-two, followed by Harrington (fifty-eight), Hackensack (fifty-five), Saddle River (fifty), Bergen (now Hudson County) (forty-nine), and Franklin (twenty-one).

When Helen Bogert, widow of Cornelius Bogert, died in 1803, her household included "1 Negro Male Slave named will, aged 63 years," "1 Negro female Slave named Sock, 1 Negro male Slave named Will, aged 19 years, 1 Negro Female Slave named Yaan." Mention of an elderly man is unusual as most slaves appear to have been of working age and manumission prevailed after long years of servitude. A law prohibited traffic in slaves between New Jersey and other states in 1798. Slavery in New Jersey began to decline after passage on February 14, 1804, of an Act for the Gradual Abolition of Slavery. Its provisions were extended on February 24, 1820, so that every child, born of a slave after July 4, 1804, should be free but would remain a servant of the owner of the mother, if a male until the age of twenty-five years, and if a female until the age of twenty-one years. Each of these acts also regulated the manumission of enslaved people.[20]

The 1860 census for Hackensack Township lists three enslaved people born before 1804: Jack Sisco (eighty), Susan Brown (seventy), and Betty Brown (eighty).

An advertisement appeared in the *New York Gazette Revived in the Weekly Post Boy* on July 3, 1749:

> Run away on the 26th of June last, from Mr. John Zabriskie, at Hackinsack, a Negro Man named Robin, about 20 Years of Age, and of a yellow Complexion: had on when he went away, a Linen jacket, short Trousers, and Leather Hat: This is therefore to forewarn all Masters of Vessels to take the said Fellow on board. And if any Person takes said Negro, and brings him to the Work House, they shall have Twenty Shillings Reward, and all reasonable Charges paid, by John Zabriskie.

Only six years later on January 27, 1755, Jan Zabriskie placed an advertisement in the same paper seeking return of indentured servant Paulus Smith, aged thirty years, a miller by trade, who had escaped five days earlier. It reads:

> Absented from his Master's Service on the Twenty Second Day at Night, a High Dutchman (German), named Paulus Smith, about 30 Years of age, of middle Stature, has brown bushy Hair; Had on when he went away, a Castor Hat, a whitish Cloth Coat, a Cloth Pair of Breeches, a brown Cloth Jacket, almost new, and speaks very short: He had other Clothes with him. Whoever takes up and secures the said Servant, so that his Master may have him again, shall have forty Shillings reward, and all reasonable Charges paid by John Zabriski, at Hackinsack, East-Jersey. He is a Miller by Trade. If he returns back, all faults will be forgiven.

It is not known how common runaways were in Bergen County.

6

A Bridge That Saved a Nation

New Bridge and the American Revolution

Strategically located at the narrows of the Hackensack River, New Bridge is steeped in Revolutionary War legend and lore. Set in a no man's land between the two opposing armies, it served as a fort, military headquarters, intelligence-gathering post, encampment ground, and battleground throughout the long war. The first recorded visit by a tourist came in the summer of 1888, when a granddaughter of Hackensack's Revolutionary War tavern keeper, Archibald Campbell, drove up in her carriage and asked to be shown the vaulted root-cellar where her grandfather had hidden to escape his British captors in 1780. Writing about the old Zabriskie-Steuben House in 1909, one correspondent noted:

> It is certain that one or more skirmishes occurred around this house during the War for Independence, for when the roof was removed some years ago, to be replaced with a new one, the rafters were found with bullets imbedded in them, and there were marks of many others. There is a dungeon in the cellar and any number of old nooks and passages which might have been useful in those times, when it was unsafe to venture abroad much or when the possession of valuables might have worked injury to the owner. The front side of the building is of dressed stone, but the back is rough and appears like the original buildings. The gables are of brick, but whether these bricks were made on the place it is impossible to say.

Much has changed and evidence of the past is much harder to come by these days. It is possible, however, with a careful search of the historic record and some imagination to revisit New Bridge in the times that tried men's souls.

A Rising Tide

King Frederick the Great of Prussia touched off the Seven Years' War in August 1756 by invading the German kingdom of Saxony, an ally of the Austrian Empire, thus threatening the balance of power in central Europe. Though long hereditary enemies, France and Austria formed an alliance in 1756. Only England, whose King George was a Hanoverian prince, sided with the Prussians.

The North American phase of the war, known as the French and Indian War, began when Colonel George Washington led Virginian troops into the Ohio Country in 1753 to dispute French claims to this important tributary of the Mississippi. The resulting skirmish triggered a full-scale war. Although the French and their Indian allies massacred English General Braddock's army when they attempted to capture French Fort Duquesne (Pittsburgh, Pennsylvania) in 1755, the British were able to seize French Canada in a series of military campaigns that resulted in the fall of the French capital of Quebec in 1759. Except for frontier skirmishes, the war ended with the French surrender of Montreal in 1760. Through the Treaty of Paris, signed in 1763, the French gave up Canada to the British. In so doing, England removed the only European power opposed to the British colonies, lying between the Atlantic seaboard and the Appalachian Mountains.

New Jersey became a theatre of war when King Teedyuscung organized a confederation of Minisinks, Unami Delawares, and Mohicans, allied with the French, to retaliate against the proprietors of Pennsylvania and New Jersey for fraudulently depriving them of their homelands. Captain Armstrong, a war captain of the Delaware Indians, led a raiding party across the Delaware River into New Jersey in May 1755, which resulted in the massacre of Anthony Swartwout and his family near Swartswood Lake. In response, New Jersey Governor Jonathan Belcher declared war against the Delaware Indians and ordered blockhouses to be built and defended at strategic locations along the upper Delaware River. Fighting continued, with brutalities on both sides, until New Jersey Governor Francis Bernard negotiated an end to hostilities at a conference held in Easton, Pennsylvania, in October 1758, where he met with King Teedyuscung and resolved all outstanding native claims to land in New Jersey.

As we have learned all too well over the centuries, war is good for business. Beginning in 1764, Peter Hansenclever supervised a major expansion of the iron industry in the Jersey Highlands and New Bridge Landing bustled with an increase in trade. As a miller and merchant in the New York market, Jan Zabriskie prospered. Of this period, newspaper advertisements provide rare glimpses of an increasingly busy inland port and mill landing, where commerce pulsed with every tide and where overland traffic by foot, hoof and wheel, passing between Manhattan island and the interior of North America, funneled across the strategic bridge.

The names "New Bridge" and "Old Bridge" did not come into common use until Michael Cornelisse established the Paulus Hook Ferry in July 1764, making the overland route via New Bridge of considerable use to travelers going to and from Manhattan. At that time, New Bridge was the nearest river crossing to Newark Bay. A "New road or highway, which leads from New Bridge Easterly to Teaneck"—in other words, present-day New Bridge Road—was laid out on the line dividing the farms

The 1861 map showing New Bridge along the Hackensack River, close-up section. (Philadelphia: G. H. Corey, Publisher, *Map of the Counties of Bergen and Passaic, New Jersey: From Actual Surveys, Bergen County Historical Society Collections*)

of Peter Demarest, deceased, to the north and Lawrence P. Van Buskirk, deceased, in 1767. On June 9, 1767, Peter P. Demarest, Jr., applied to the Court of the General Quarter Session of the Peace and was granted a license to keep Tavern for the term of one year. The stage stop, therefore, was popularly designated "New Bridge."

Wooden drawbridges were vulnerable to spring freshets and ice floes. On January 1, 1764, the Board of Chosen Freeholders "ordered that Johannes Demarest and John Zabriskie shall procure iron chains and fix the Same to the Draw Bridge over Hackensack River instead of ropes and after so done receive their pay from the County Collector." This experiment with hand-forged chains proved unsatisfactory, leading to the events of May 22, 1765:

> [The Freeholders] further ordered that Laurence Van Buskirk, Esq., and John Zabriskie do take the chains that are now on the New Bridge and dispose of them to the best advantage & for the benefit of the County and it is further ordered that they shall buy a good pitch'd rope and fix it on the Draw Bridge and also have the said bridge put in good Repair.

Repairs were again ordered to the New Bridge on May 11, 1768 and on May 12, 1773. On November 3, 1773, the winch needed fixing and the Freeholders ordered, "the wheel belonging to the Draw Bridge at the New Bridge" to be repaired ¼" On May 15, 1776, "The County Collector produced the account relative to the repair of the New Bridge amounting to 65 Pounds 3 Shillings," which was a considerable expense for the time.

The Bridge That Saved a Nation

I have stood at the Alpine Lookout on the Palisades Interstate Parkway and contemplated the remarkable and for many years unmarked place where British troops landed and scaled the mountain on November 20, 1776, with the intent to capture the Continental garrison at Fort Lee. This daring maneuver precipitated the American Crisis and darkest hour in the American War of Independence. To help fill in the void in our understanding of the places where history was made that fateful day, I have compiled the following account:

Fort Washington (Fort Tyron) commanded the highest point on Manhattan island and, in companionship with Fort Lee on the opposite heights, was positioned to obstruct British naval operations on the Hudson River. When British men-of-war passed the guns of these forts and avoided sunken obstacles in the river, General George Washington concluded that Fort Washington should be abandoned and ordered General Nathanael Greene to evacuate "Mount Washington as you judge best, and so far revoking the order given to Col. Magaw to defend it to the last." When Washington arrived at Fort Lee, however, he did not press the matter against the objections of Generals Greene, Putnam, and Mercer as well as Colonel Magaw. He did however forbid General Nathanael Greene from sending further reinforcements across the river. As he later admitted to his inner circle of friends, Washington hesitated against his better instinct.

Fort Washington fell to a British assault on November 16, 1776, when Colonel Robert Magaw surrendered 2,700–3,000 Continental defenders, who crowded its inner works. Its loss not only greatly embarrassed the American cause, but also its namesake commander, General George Washington, who now added this latest fiasco to a stinging string of defeats and harrowing escapes in New York. Without an American navy to contest British command of the seas and waterways, New York City was lost. Fort Lee was rendered useless and a greatly humbled General Greene immediately began evacuating military stores as fast as wagons became available, starting with gunpowder and ammunition but received no boats from Newark despite several urgent requests.

Most fortuitously for the fledgling nation, Generals Washington, Putnam, Mercer, and Greene narrowly escaped capture, having ill-advisedly crossed the river in a small boat as the enemy advanced upon Fort Washington. Returning to the safety of the Jersey shore, Washington reportedly watched from a vantage atop the crest of the Palisades as the hapless American garrison, betrayed and besieged, surrendered an hour later. Unable by itself to close the Hudson River to the British Navy, Fort Lee and its outlying artillery batteries atop the Palisades, situated uncomfortably on a narrow neck of land between the Hackensack and Hudson Rivers, were ordered abandoned.

Fort Lee was a square earthwork with four bastions, occupying the neighborhood now defined by Parker Avenue, Cedar Street, and English Street in Fort Lee. The often separately named Fort Constitution comprised "several batteries facing the North River in which several 32 pounders in addition to two middle-sized and one extraordinarily heavy iron mortar are located." These heavy guns were positioned on Bluff Point, east of Hudson Terrace Street, overlooking the river. The narrow road rising from Bourdet's (Burdett) ferry in Edgewater passed through a ravine between these works.

On October 8, 1776, General Greene ordered soldiers' barracks to be built no closer than fifty rods (825 feet) to the fort, or south and west of Dead Bridge Brook (now Lemoine Avenue). As Hessian Colonel Colonel Earl Emilius von Donop later reported, "At the summit of the forts themselves (which is to say, on the high ground southwest of these fortifications) there were huts and tents for more than 6,000 men and quantities of all sorts of provisions and a large amount of ammunition." Thomas Sullivan of the 49th Regiment of Foot, described "very artificial and convenient huts, at Fort Lee, (made) of timber lined with a kind of mortar, each held four men commodiously, and had large ovens and other necessaries made there for their winter quarters." He was probably describing what Lt. Joseph Hodgkins (Massachusetts) referred to as a "Log House with a stone Chimney" on September 30, 1776. After the fall of Fort Washington, the garrison at Fort Lee grew to about 2,700 men, many being five-month enlistees in General Heard's Brigade from New Jersey, General Beal's Brigade from Maryland, and part of General Ewing's Brigade of Pennsylvanians, whose term of service was nearing expiration. They were sent to remove military supplies from Fort Lee to Ackquackanonck (Passaic), Springfield, Bound Brook, and Princeton.

Even though winter was fast approaching, the weather was still mild enough for the British to build on their momentum and conclude their campaign around New

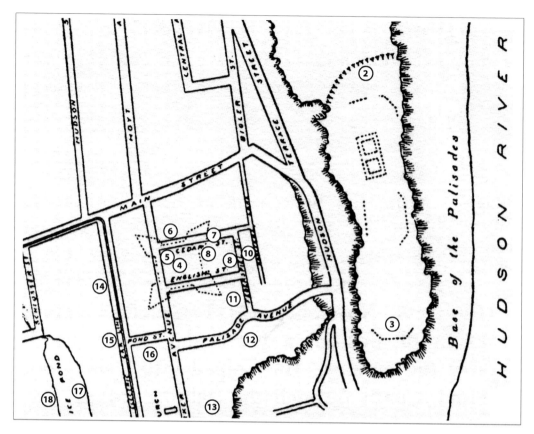

Drawing of the fort at Fort Lee. Location of artifacts found noted in circled numbers. "Reference: 1. Site of the Redoubt which commanded the sunken obstructions between Fort Lee and Fort Washington. 2. Site of the abattis enclosing the works on Bluff Point. 2 and 3. Site of works on Bluff Point. 4. Site of the main fortification of Fort Lee. 5. House here stands on site of old butcher shop. Just south of house a few years ago, there was about twenty-five feet of the embankment of the fort. 6. Here George Beucler dug up a dozen cannon balls. 7. George Hook dug up nine bullets in a cluster in June, 1901. 8. C. W. Dubois dug up bullets and bullet moulds when he excavated a cellar and well about 1898. 9. Mrs. Mary Federspiel dug up part of exploded shell. 10. Mrs. Federspiel dug up cannon ball in 1861. 11. James Sullivan dug up three cannon balls in 1885. 12. Site of army oven. 13. Washington's well. 14. Michael Tierney dug up three cannon balls in in 1875. 15. Site of old pine tree which sheltered the platform for the celebration July 4, 1873. The late James F. Tracey said that four or five soldiers' graves were once pointed out to him in that vicinity. 16. Site of old pond, known as Parker's Pond Lot. The Fort Lee Monument was erected here in 1908. 17. When Hook's Ice Pond was widened in 1898, the workmen dug up along the east side quantities of lead, bullets, bullet moulds, cannon balls, a sabre, bayonets, bombshells, shoebuckles, a saddle pommel and stirrups, shovels a pickaxe and other tools. 18. On west side of the soldiers' huts. Here in 1875–6, George Hook dug up bars of lead, bullet moulds, cannon balls, bayonets, etc. In the remains of a camp fire he found guns with their stocks burned. 19. Traces of breastworks visible as late as 1901. They probably extended north of Whiteman Street. 20. Heaps of stone, the remains of the fireplaces in the soldiers' huts, some still recognizable." (*E. Hagaman Hall, L.H.D for the American Scenic and Historic Preservation Society, 1909*)

York City, perhaps to even end the rebellion. The moon shone half full and faded to blue as November 19, 1776, dawned sunny but cold, melting away a dewy frost. At eventide, a heavy rain drenched Manhattan and fog curtained the daybreak. Under command of Lieutenant-General Lord Cornwallis and his deputy, Major-General John Vaughan, two divisions of British troops were to set out across the Hudson River on a daring expedition into New Jersey.

The first division, composed of about 2,500 British and German troops, clambered aboard about fifty flatboats and *bateaux* at Kingsbridge (West 230th Street in the Bronx) on what was then the northernmost tip of Manhattan, awaiting orders to row out of the Spuyten Duyvil and to land "about 5 miles further up the River" at a carefully chosen spot at the base of the Palisades. These troops passed "a very disagreeable night in the Flat boats, under a thick heavy Rain." Starting out at 9 p.m., a second division of approximately 2,500 troops marched up Broadway from Kingsbridge to "Colonel Cortland's House," where they waited until 3 a.m., when they began marching to a landing point (near what is now Ludlow Metro-North Railroad Station) on the river for embarkation.

Undoubtedly accompanied by at least one of several loyalist guides (who knew the highways and byways of Bergen County well enough), Lord Cornwallis sailed under the rainy half-moon to inspect the narrow pass up the steep Palisades that his army was to scale at daybreak. Given low visibility, especially in a constant downpour, it seems probable (to me) that loyalist guides with lanterns would have had to pinpoint the proposed landing site from the shore. In any event, arriving at midnight, the British commander stared in utter disbelief at the half-mile ascent up the steep escarpment that was pointed out to him, where his troops would have to climb a stony path scarcely four feet wide to overcome a nearly vertical rise of 420 feet in elevation.

Unconvinced an ascent of the cliff at the Closter New Dock (also known as Lower Closter Landing and later as Huyler's Landing) was feasible, he explored about 2.5 miles further north along the river, probably viewing Closter Dock (Alpine Boat Basin), which he found even more unpromising; the ascent was equally daunting, but its choice would have added several more miles and hours to the march on Fort Lee, thus costing the invaders the element of surprise. Moreover, the proximity of 5,000 American troops in the Highlands under Major General William Heath would pose a threat to the British rear as they advanced southward. Another 7,000 American troops under Major-General Charles Lee were stationed at North Castle in Westchester County, NY, posing an additional threat to the defense of Manhattan, now depleted by the troops who would make the crossing.

With daylight approaching, Cornwallis returned to the Lower Closter Landing and ordered an advance guard of two companies of light infantry to scramble to the top of the Palisades and form a defensive perimeter, which would be enlarged as soon as the first division, composed mainly of light infantry and chasseurs, began landing at daybreak (6.48 a.m.) on November 20, 1776, passing out of the Spuyten Duyvil and into the Hudson River. According to Colonel Earl Emilius von Donop, the landing point and upward climb seemed "dreadful and impractical." He noted, "All the troops had to pass one at a time up a steep path that was hardly 4 feet wide."

A water color copy of the British Invasion up the Palisades; the original is by Captain Thomas Davies. (*Artifact in the Bergen County Historical Society Collections, photo by Deborah Powell*)

All this did not pass unnoticed. Thanks to the pioneering research of military historian and author Todd Braisted, we may finally dispense with legend and appreciate the facts of history. Braisted has found evidence that American guards were placed at Bergen (Jersey City), Hoboken, Bull's Ferry, Hackensack, and, most critically, on or near Clinton Point, about 3 miles above Fort Lee and directly opposite Spuyten Duyvil. It was this latter outpost of American sentinels who spied British transports on the river and fired warning shots to alert the garrison. Its officer commandeered a horse and headed south to warn Fort Lee and its breakfasting garrison. Given the distance, it would have taken at least an hour for this officer to reach the fort and appraise its commander of the developing situation.

Most importantly, Braisted has identified Lieutenant John Clifford, of Heard's Brigade of New Jersey State Troops, as the "officer" whom eyewitness Thomas Paine described in *The American Crisis* as arriving "with information that the enemy with 200 boats had landed about seven miles above." Thus informed, General Greene immediately ordered the garrison to assemble under arms and sent word to General Washington in Hackensack by way of Little Ferry (moving at 4 mph, a horse and rider would have taken about an hour and a half to complete the 6-mile journey.) Yet, according to Washington's secretary, Lieutenant-Colonel Robert H. Harrison, an express rider from Orangetown, New York, arrived at Washington's headquarters in Hackensack at 10 a.m., bringing the first news of the British landing above Fort Lee. According to Thomas Paine, "General Washington arrived in about three-quarters of an hour, and marched at the head of the troops towards the bridge," but arrived where? Did Washington meet the advance troops of the retreating garrison of Fort Lee at Liberty Pole (Englewood) as is commonly told?

Maybe not. *Aide-de-camp* Major William Grayson's report to General Mercer, dated November 20, 1776, noted:

> An advanced party of them (i.e., the British) proceeded as far as a Hill, two miles above the Liberty Pole, at the crossroads, where I left his Excellency. The Road leading from thence to Hackensack (New) Bridge as well as the Bridge is open for our people to retreat & from present Appearances it is expected they may be got off without Loss of many of them.[1]

Sending a similar report to General Charles Lee, Grayson again noted the British troops were halted on "a Hill two miles above the Liberty Pole, about a mile and a half above General Greene's Quarters, where I left his Excellency."

It seems Washington and his staff road out to General Greene's headquarters somewhere in the English neighborhood, although it is not clear from Grayson's statement whether Greene's headquarters was half a mile above the Liberty Pole or 1.5 miles below it (in Leonia?). In any event, this was the decisive "crossroads" at the intersection of Tenafly Road and West Palisade Avenue, where two roads led from Liberty Pole towards New Bridge, the only span across the Hackensack River that might carry the Fort Lee garrison to safety: Liberty Road, described as a "bye-road to New Bridge", veered northwest and thus closer to the assembling enemy force; whereas Lafayette Place departs southwest to Genesee Avenue,

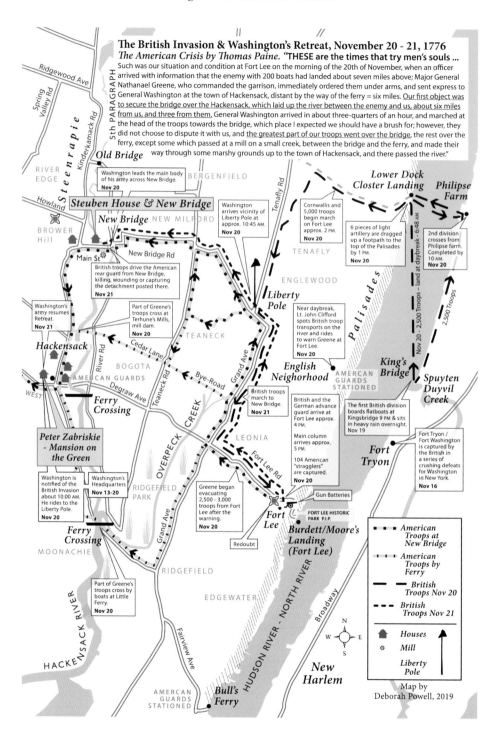

The British Invasion & Washington's Retreat, November 20 - 21, 1776
The American Crisis by Thomas Paine. "THESE are the times that try men's souls ... Such was our situation and condition at Fort Lee on the morning of the 20th of November, when an officer arrived with information that the enemy with 200 boats had landed about seven miles above; Major General Nathanael Greene, who commanded the garrison, immediately ordered them under arms, and sent express to General Washington at the town of Hackensack, distant by the way of the ferry = six miles. Our first object was to secure the bridge over the Hackensack, which laid up the river between the enemy and us, about six miles from us, and three from them. General Washington arrived in about three-quarters of an hour, and marched at the head of the troops towards the bridge, which place I expected we should have a brush for; however, they did not choose to dispute it with us, and the greatest part of our troops went over the bridge, the rest over the ferry, except some which passed at a mill on a small creek, between the bridge and the ferry, and made their way through some marshy grounds up to the town of Hackensack, and there passed the river."

Invasion and Retreat map shows movements and timing of events on November 20 and 21, 1776, in Bergen County. (*Created by Deborah Powell based on the Claire K. Tholl map*) continuing southwest on Loraine Avenue to Forest Avenue, and thence to Teaneck Road, which turns north to its junction with New Bridge Road.

Reinforced by lead elements of the first division, the British atop the mountain advanced westward ("to the right"), reaching the nearest houses, firing a few shots, and taking a few prisoners. They advanced "about 2 miles into the country," reaching the intersection of East Madison Avenue and Engle Street in Cresskill, where they halted as the second division began crossing the river from the vicinity of Mount St. Vincent—the highest point on Tetard's Hill—at about 8 a.m., completing their passage by about 10 a.m. Once the second division was atop the cliff, there was further delay as seamen from the transports helped drag eight light artillery pieces up the steep path, a task they completed at about 1 p.m. Captain Johann Ewald, having landed with the second division, noted:

> We climbed ashore along a steep bluff and scaled the rocky and bushy height as quickly as possible. At the top, we found several plantations in a district called Dunne fly (Tenafly) where the jaguars and light infantry deployed in a semicircle behind the stone walls and posted sentries by platoon at distances of three hundred paces. Fort Lee lay two hours away from us on the left. [2]

In my humble estimation, it was there and then—standing in Greene's headquarters and facing a crisis potentially fatal to his cause—that Washington truly assumed decisive command of the Continental Army, willing to act upon his best appraisal of the military situation, even if it meant overriding his generals' opinions. It was a two-way street as his generals had also learned from the humbling loss of Fort Washington and now offered advice but ultimately deferred to their commander-in-chief's judgement.

Upon reaching the vicinity of Liberty Pole, Washington perceived the enemy's "intent evidently was to form a line across from the place of their landing to Hackensack (New) Bridge and thereby hem in the whole Garrison between the North (Hudson) and Hackensack Rivers." He knew he had "not above 3000 Men, & they much broken & dispirited not only with our ill Success, but the loss of their Tents & Baggage." He quickly realized that defense of the fort was untenable and that his immediate task was to preserve the army under his command. Hence, he immediately ordered the hurriedly assembled garrison to cross to the west side of the Hackensack River at New Bridge and personally led his troops towards that vital crossing. With a loud explosion, mistaken by some for cannon fire, the fort's powder magazine was blown up. As Washington stated later in his correspondence, "we were lucky enough to gain the Bridge before them, by which Means we passed all our Men, but were obliged to leave some hundred Barrels of Flour, most of our Cannon and a considerable parcel of Tents & Baggage." About two hours after its garrison marched off, General Greene returned to the huts and tents outside Fort Lee to round up several hundred more men. It was this last body of retreating Americans that an advance guard of the invaders spied on the road. Lord Cornwallis formed his men into two columns, with his reserve on the left, and began marching south down Tenafly Road at about 2 p.m. At the outset of the march, he was about 7 miles from Fort Lee. Captain Ewald later recorded the following in his journal:

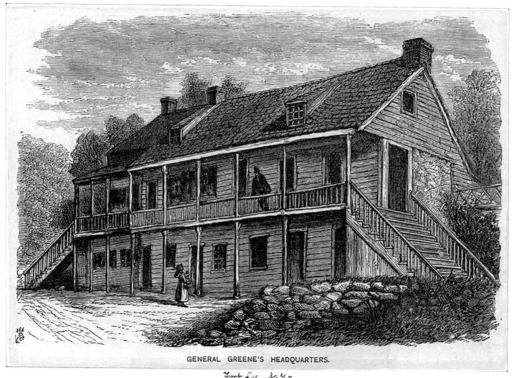

GENERAL GREENE'S HEADQUARTERS.

Fort Lee - N. Y.

Sketch of what is thought to be Greene's Headquarters at Fort Lee. (*Bergen County Historical Society Collections*)

As soon as the grenadiers joined us, the corps advanced a half an hour farther into the country, and both Jager companies were posted on the highway (presumably Tenafly Road) somewhat forward toward New Bridge. I saw a plantation lying at a distance of a thousand to twelve hundred paces, whither I proceeded with several jaguars to learn from the inhabitants just where I was. The owner of the house approached and informed me that this highway (Liberty Road?) ran to New Bridge, a small place where there was a bridge over the Second River (i.e., Hackensack River), which joined another road [presumably West Palisade Avenue] from (the English) Neighborhood that one must take to get to Fort Lee.

During this conversation I discovered a great glitter of bayonets and a cloud of dust in the distance—Who is that?—That must be the garrison of Fort Lee!—Can't we cut them off from the bridge?—Yes, you have only two English miles from here to there!—I ran back to Captain Wreden and told him of my discovery. He believed that these people were the second column of our army. I wanted to know the truth and took several jaguars with me to draw near this column in the flank, crawling from stone wall to stone wall, and discovered that it was American. I began to skirmish with them and sent back a jager to fetch more men, but instead of jaguars, I received an order from Lord Cornwallis to return at once. I had to obey, and informed him what I had discovered.

"Let them go, my dear Ewald, and stay here. We do not want to lose any men. One jager is worth more than ten rebels." [3]

There is no other recorded account yet discovered of any skirmish along the route of the American retreat. Instead, the British columns continued towards Fort Lee, abandoned by all but 100 stragglers and drunks. Completing a 9.5-mile march from their landing point on the Hudson River, the advance guard of British and German troops reached Fort Lee at about 4 p.m. The main columns ("after making a large detour") arrived at Fort Lee at about 5 p.m. By then, it was dark.

Captain Thomas Glyn later reported, "Lord Cornwallis' Corps took possession of the Fort and Redoubt, where we found great Magazines, several pieces of Cannon, a very convenient Block House for the protection of our troops." An important storehouse full of corn (wheat) was found at the foot of the mountain in Edgewater and large quantities of provisions were stored in almost every house. Echoing Lord Cornwallis' assessment, Johann Emanual Wagner, of the Von Minnegerode grenadier battalion, wrote, "The hope is now indulged in that most of the Rebels will return to their homes because they had pinned their faith on Forts Washington and Lee." British troops would demolish Fort Lee and the "Rock Redoubt and Batteries depending" on December 10, 1776.

Without a single entrenching tool, however, Washington perceived the level country between the Hackensack and Passaic Rivers would be equally unsuitable to making a stand against a superior enemy force. Thus, on November 21, he continued the retreat across the Passaic River at Acquackanonk Bridge, where he paused awaiting three regiments left to defend the crossings on the Hackensack River. Looking over his shoulder at the well-tended farms of the Jersey Dutch, he greatly regretted leaving "a very fine country open to their Ravages, or a plentiful Store House from which they will draw voluntary supplies."

At 9 a.m. on November 21, 1776, Major-General Vaughan set out from Fort Lee with the 2nd Battalion Light Infantry, the 2nd Battalion Grenadiers, one company of Chasseurs and the Donop Jager Company to secure New Bridge. Captain Johann Ewald noted:

> Toward morning on the 21st the 1st battalion of Light Infantry under Colonel Abercromby, and the Donop Jager Company under Captain Wreden, occupied New Bridge where there was a bridge over the Hackensack River, which cannot be detoured. The Americans had occupied the houses on both sides of the bridge and defended themselves very well, but in spite of this the post was forced and the greater part were killed, wounded or captured. [4]

General Washington summarized the timely escape in a letter to Governor Livingston: "We were lucky enough to gain the Bridge before them; by which means we saved all our men."

Ensign Henry Strike, of the 10th Regiment of Foot, also participated in the advance to the strategic river crossing, and left his account for posterity:

Our Charleville musket was pulled out of the Hackensack River by an eight-year-old boy fishing from the bridge in front of the Steuben House in 1915. (*Artifact of the American Revolution is in the Bergen County Historical Society Collections, photo by Deborah Powell*)

> We push'd on New-Bridge, where the Rebels (on our appearance) began to set fire to their Stores, and some Houses; but on Our advancing to the bridge, they fled without effecting as much Mischief as intended; as a good part of the Stores fell into Our hands. On the March one of our flanking parties fell in with a Rebel advanced Guard and kill'd 2, or three of them. This day a body of Light Dragoons landed and joined us. At night we took post at Old Bridge (River Edge-New Milford) which ye Dastardly Rebels had broke down to stop the pursuit, 22 miles from New-York.

British engineers hastily reconstructed the bridge, enabling troops to cross on November 22, 1776, and move on to Hackensack. Lord Cornwallis advanced the main body of his troops on November 25 and established headquarters at New Bridge (probably in the Steuben House). The British Fourth Brigade encamped at New Bridge on November 29, 1776. General von Mirbach's Brigade, under command of Colonel Johann Gottlieb Rall, crossed the New Bridge into Hackensack on November 29, 1776.

John Zabriskie, Jr., the third generation of that name to inhabit the sandstone mansion at New Bridge, was born September 30, 1767, the son of John and Jane (Goelet) Zabriskie. When his grandfather, John the first, died in September 1774, he assumed the title of "junior." We can imagine the wide eyes of this nine-year-old boy, face pressed against the pane, as he counted the ragtag garrison of Fort Lee, General Washington at their head, passing his threshold and vanishing southward in a cold drizzle. Continental troops used his home as a fort to defend their passage.

Political philosopher, writer, and abolitionist Thomas Paine was with the troops on November 20, 1776 and wrote about the retreat in the *American Crisis* to garner public support for the American Cause:

> These are the times that try men's souls. The summer soldier and the sunshine patriot will, in this crisis, shrink from the service of their country; but he that stands it now, deserves the love and thanks of man and woman. Tyranny, like hell, is not easily conquered; yet we have this consolation with us, that the harder the conflict, the more glorious the triumph. [5]

The fifth paragraph read:

> As I was with the troops at Fort Lee, and marched with them to the edge of Pennsylvania, I am well acquainted with many circumstances, which those who live at a distance know but little or nothing of. Our situation there was exceedingly cramped, the place being

a narrow neck of land between the North River and the Hackensack. Our force was inconsiderable, being not one-fourth so great as Howe could bring against us. We had no army at hand to have relieved the garrison, had we shut ourselves up and stood on our defence. Our ammunition, light artillery, and the best part of our stores, had been removed, on the apprehension that Howe would endeavor to penetrate the Jerseys, in which case Fort Lee could be of no use to us; for it must occur to every thinking man, whether in the army or not, that these kind of field forts are only for temporary purposes, and last in use no longer than the enemy directs his force against the particular object which such forts are raised to defend. Such was our situation and condition at Fort Lee on the morning of the 20th of November, when an officer arrived with information that the enemy with 200 boats had landed about seven miles above; Major General (Nathaniel) Green, who commanded the garrison, immediately ordered them under arms, and sent express to General Washington at the town of Hackensack, distant by the way of the ferry = six miles. Our first object was to secure the bridge over the Hackensack, which laid up the river between the enemy and us, about six miles from us, and three from them. General Washington arrived in about three-quarters of an hour, and marched at the head of the troops towards the bridge, which place I expected we should have a brush for; however, they did not choose to dispute it with us, and the greatest part of our troops went over the bridge, the rest over the ferry, except some which passed at a mill on a small creek, between the bridge and the ferry, and made their way through some marshy grounds up to the town of Hackensack, and there passed the river. We brought off as much baggage as the wagons could contain, the rest was lost. The simple object was to bring off the garrison, and march them on till they could be strengthened by the Jersey or Pennsylvania militia, so as to be enabled to make a stand. We staid four days at Newark, collected our outposts with some of the Jersey militia, and marched out twice to meet the enemy, on being informed that they were advancing, though our numbers were greatly inferior to theirs.[6]

Of the capture of Fort Lee, Thomas Glyn noted in his *Journal*:

Such was the confusion of the enemy that not only all their tents were standing, their meat at the fire, but all their sick fell into our hands; had not a countryman early in the morning apprised them of our landing the whole might have been prisoners.

Cornwallis himself attributed a timely warning and fast retreat to a quick-witted "countryman." In any event, the British failure to capture the American garrison at Fort Lee, and perhaps defeat the American rebellion, was a consequence of self-confident British officers not realizing, despite reminders from local loyalists, that "New Bridge was the key to the peninsula between the Hackensack and the Hudson."

On November 21, 1776, Lord Cornwallis finally ordered:

The 2nd Battalion of Light Infantry, the 2nd Battalion of Grenadiers, with one company of Chasseurs, to be in readiness to march at nine this morning under the command of Major General Vaughan ... to secure the New Bridge on the Hackensack River from being destroyed by the enemy in their precipitate retreat.

As part of a reinforcement of the British army then sweeping across New Jersey toward the Delaware River, the 4th Brigade camped at New Bridge on November 25, 1776.

1777 at New Bridge

On December 14, 1776, Major-General William Heath led 600 American troops on a forced march of 12 miles from Tappan to occupy the village of Hackensack. He seized fifty Tories and captured several vessels at the dock laden with household furnishings and supplies. Fifty barrels of flour, a number of hogsheads of rum, and other provisions were found at Colonel Abraham Van Buskirk's house at New Bridge. Later intelligence reports of the incident noted:

> Mrs. Brinkerhoff, now the wife of Johannes Duryee of Hackensack, said that John Zabriskie ¼ came to Peter Zabriskie's home (in Hackensack) some time in January 1777 and related that he had taken a list of the Militia officers who had carried off the stores of Dr. Van Buskirk's, etc., near the New Bridge at the retreat of the enemy from thence, etc. A young man student living at Mr. Isaac Van Giesen's in Hackensack, was at New York on the day that the above stores were conveyed off by the Militia and in the evening saw John Zabriskie's Negro deliver a letter to a gentleman containing the detail of what had happened respecting the stores, and a list of the officers who had commanded the militia above.[7]

The son of William Christie's neighbor at Schraalenburgh estimated the strength of British forces at New Bridge on December 23, 1776, at "six companies of Regulars and three of late enlisted Tories at the New Bridge." The 7th Regiment of British Regulars was stationed at New Bridge at this time.[8]

We do not know what Jan Zabriskie, Jr., overheard of his father's political whisperings, but on July 14, 1777, he may have watched approaching *bateaux*, loaded with soldiers under command of Major Samuel Hayes, as they landed alongside the gristmill. They arrested his father as a "disaffected person" and imprisoned him at Morristown. His own uncle, Joost Zabriskie, testified against him at trial on August 6, 1777. Once on parole, John, Sr., abandoned the family homestead, fleeing to New York City where his family found refuge with their cousins, the Seamans. Whatever bitterness the Zabriskies felt at the British evacuation of Manhattan was compounded when the victorious revolutionary officers of the State of New Jersey confiscated their properties.

In the spring of 1777, an American prisoner who pretended to enlist in the British service in order to escape, traveled from New York City to Hackensack and later reported "there was a small guard at the (New) Bridge and to the north ¼"[9] By this time, Captain Elias Romeyn's company of the Bergen militia was "stationed at New Bridge, Brouwer's Hill, the Liberty Pole, marching ¼ from place to place as necessity required ¼"[10] John Zabriskie of New Bridge was included on a list drawn up by the New Jersey Committee of Safety on July 11, 1777, of forty-eight men suspected of enemy sympathies. This list included several local persons: John Zabriskie, Esq., New Bridge; Gabriel Van Orden, Steen Rapie; Cornelius Banta, Sluckup; and John

Van Buskirk, Esq., Kinderkamack. On July 14, 1777, Major Samuel Hayes of Newark led a small force of Americans who arrested all but three of these loyalists, including John Zabriskie.[11]

In anticipation of a British movement from New York, General Washington ordered Lieutenant Daniel Morgan and his riflemen to advance to positions along the Hackensack, warning them to "keep your guards advanced to Hackensack (Little) Ferry and the (New) Bridge above, (so that) patrolling parties may safely lay by day at Fort Lee."[12]

According to a letter addressed by Lieutenant General Sir Henry Clinton to General William Howe on September 23, 1777, a corps landed at Fort Lee and marched "by Newbridge, Hackinsack and Slaterdam." Clinton "ordered General Vaughan to leave one battalion and two pieces of cannon at Newbridge, to cover that very important pass."[13] After a day's fighting along the Passaic River, General Vaughan withdrew his entire force to New Bridge.

1778 at New Bridge

In late summer of 1778, Washington stationed his chief of intelligence, Major Alexander Clough, at New Bridge, "a place from which he could intercept and question every traveler who had been in New York City, and even more important, a place from which he could send spies of his own into the city." Major Clough's mission was concealed and protected by Colonel George Baylor's Regiment of Light Horse. General Washington addressed a letter "to the officer commanding the militia at Hackensack New Bridge," explaining that "Major Clough, who commands at Hackensack, is under the necessity of sometimes allowing persons to carry small matters into New York, and to bring a few goods out, that he may the better obtain intelligence." Militiamen were asked not to detain any person showing a pass from Major Clough, despite their appearance as contrabanders.

On September 22, 1778, 6,000 British and Hessian soldiers waded ashore at Paulus Hook and swiftly advanced to New Bridge, where they threw up earthworks on Brower's Hill to secure the left flank of a defensive line strung across the peninsula.[14]

From reedy marshes only a few feet above sea level along the Hackensack River, Cherry Hill in River Edge suddenly rises 113 feet in elevation, offering a commanding view of the countryside for many miles around. In order to attract suburban buyers, the old name of Brower's Hill was changed when the railroad came to this neighborhood in 1873. The shallow swale (where Van Saun Park is now found) is bounded east by Cherry Hill and west by "the hill commonly called the *Cacel Rugh* at the road (now Howland Avenue) which leads from the New Bridge to Sluckup."

Several living springs feed brooks that descend the narrow vale between ridges, concentrating in Van Saun Mill Pond before contributing their commingled waters to Cole's Brook and finally the Hackensack River. This hollow between the hills was anciently known as Sluckup, but changed to the more poetic Spring Valley in 1832.

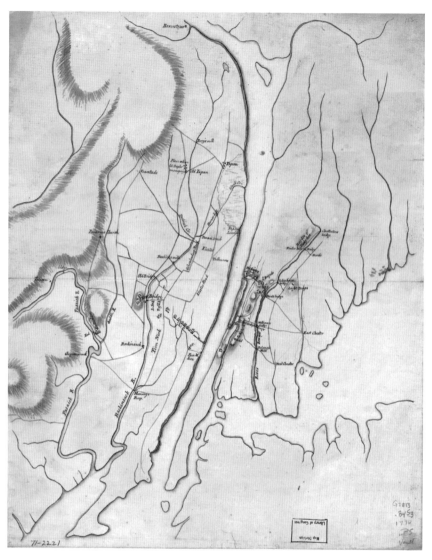

On September 23, 1778, approximately 6,000 British and loyalist troops under Sir Henry Clinton and Lord Cornwallis entered Bergen County via Paulus Hook (Jersey City) for the purpose of obtaining forage for the winter and operations elsewhere. This map shows the troops extending from the Hudson River to Brouwer's Hill on the west side of the Hackensack River. Of note are the two forts or redoubts on Brouwer's Hill, which Captain John Peebles of the 42nd Regiment describes as being "on the high ground about ½ mile north side of Newbridge." The forts were begun on September 25 and finished on October 1, being described by the same officer as "Squares with a platform for 1 Gun in each." These forts were occupied by the 15th Regiment of Foot when they were attacked by several hundred militia under General Lord Stirling on September 29, which resulted in no casualties on either side. The map also notes the location in River Vale where Major General Charles Grey surprised Colonel George Baylor and his 3rd Light Dragoons, killing, wounding and capturing most of the regiment. The foraging completed, the British retired to the area around Fort Lee on October 13, and back to their original stations around New York two days later. (*Grand Forage 1778 by Todd W. Braisted, 2016*)

According to Abram D. Banta, the Bergen Militia under Captain Outwater were "watching to counteract the movement of the enemy near New Bridge and Schrawlenburg, seeking opportunities for foraging incursions, and to attack the Fort on Brower's Hill, now New Bridge." Abram Banta and "his company marched within three or four hundred yards when the enemy fired cannon upon them while they were going into the Fort, and Gen. Wayne, on account of the inequality of his force, retreated to where his brigade remained three or four weeks." It was likely during this brief encounter that a cannonball struck the hill west of the Van Saun millpond; it was dug out of the earth and displayed in the mill until about 1888. On September 27, 1778, sixty of Van Buskirk's Volunteers were on guard at New Bridge.

The Invasion of September 1778: Atrocity at Overkill

When Sir Henry Clinton's army, 6,000 strong, waded ashore at Paulus Hook on September 22, 1778, friends of American independence were wise to puzzle over his intentions, apprehending a decisive march northward along the Hudson River to "cut off the communication between the Southern and Eastern states." The Continental Army, reinforced by a large body of Jersey militia, kept just beyond reach of their deadly opponent and alert for any sign of determined motion. The British swiftly advanced to New Bridge, dug in at Brower's Hill and stretched a defensive line across the peninsula, eastward through Liberty Pole to the Palisades. By this means, "they confined themselves to a small portion of country, between two navigable rivers, exposing only a small front, impenetrable by its situation, and by works thrown up for its further security." The invaders then set about stripping the countryside of its fresh harvest and fattened cattle, engaging a fleet of about 100 small vessels to haul plunder down the Hackensack River. Some farmers thought that the devouring host seemed "much fonder of forage than of fighting."

Major Alexander Clough, stationed at New Bridge with the Third Regiment of Light Dragoons, engaged in the shadowy world of military intelligence where distinctions between friend and foe often blurred. The regiment retreated to Paramus with the sudden appearance of the British army. After four days assisting Bergen militiamen in driving cattle out of reach of British foragers, Colonel George Baylor moved his Light Dragoons from Paramus to a spot where he might best gain immediate intelligence of any northward invasion. Accordingly, on September 27, 1778, Quartermaster Benjamin Hart secured quarters for the six troops of Baylor's Dragoons in six different barns along the Overkill road (in what is now River Vale), while Colonel Baylor made his headquarters at the dwelling of Cornelius A. Haring, about a half a mile above a bridge over the Hackensack River. The Dragoons drove some cattle with them and privates in the Third and Fifth Troops were posted as forage guards that night. The remainder of the men bedded down in barns near their unsaddled horses. Although the Overkill neighborhood was infected with loyalists, the position seemed sensible and secure, provided the usual precautions against surprise attack were taken.

Despite its ominous sound, the name Overkill derived innocently enough from a small bridge and hamlet lying "Over de kill" where several farmhouses, barns,

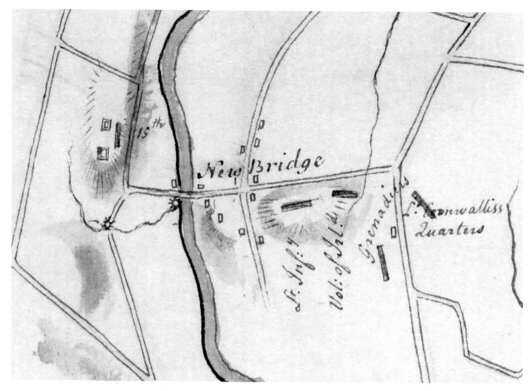

Map by John André, 1778. Besides showing Cornwallis' headquarters, the map notes the Brower Hill fort/earthworks, the tide mill, the Steuben House, and British forces. In the accompanying journal, André notes what we know as Baylor's Massacre and records other events: September 23 (1778), at 5 a.m., the troops under Lord Cornwallis, consisting of the light infantry, grenadiers, volunteers of Ireland, 3rd and 4th Brigades, and a detachment of Dragoons under Major Gwynn moved from Bergen to English Neighborhood, where they were encamped with their left to Newbridge. About sixty militia who were posted at the Liberty Pole at the head of English Neighborhood Creek were surprised by Captain Needham of the Dragoons. A few were killed and twenty-seven taken. On the 24th, the position of the grenadiers was changed. On the 25th, a redoubt was begun on the heights beyond Newbridge. One battalion of the guards was moved to the wood between the North River at the right of the line. (*Journal of John André. HM 626. The Huntington Library, San Marino, CA*)

and stables edged the main road to Middletown, New York. Several lateral roads (presently called Piermont Avenue, River Vale, and Old Tappan Roads) joined above the Overkill bridge, interlacing the Kinderkamack, Schraalenburgh, and Tappan roads. The site was clearly strategic and presently exposed to danger, for the British left was anchored on Brower's Hill at New Bridge, only 9 miles south of the Overkill bridge.

The Dragoons needed to keep their ears to the ground. To secure their position in proximity to the enemy, Colonel Baylor personally "fixed a guard, of a sergeant and twelve men" at the bridge to provide sufficient alarm of any approach of the enemy. This guard was posted with orders "to Patrole a Mile below the Bridge, & at some

Redrawn Robert Erskine map, No. 113, of the Hackensack Valley; the original is in the New York Historical Society. (*created by Deborah Powell*)

Distance from the Roads—the Patroles were to be relieved every hour." A significant addition to the historic record, provided by the Blauvelt tradition, is indication that this American guard was stationed at the Blauvelt farm, just above the bridge; the men being quartered in the barn and several officers in the house. The Blauvelts recalled:

> Those placed on the bridge a little to the south of the house left their positions early on the evening of the massacre and joined their companions in the (Blauvelt) barn saying it was useless for them to keep watch as the night was so dark that the enemy could never find their way about. The American captain hearing their return ordered them back to their places and they reluctantly obeyed his command. In a short time, however, they returned using their former arguments about the darkness of the night and the difficulty of troops traveling.

The return of the patrols at seemingly short intervals (as remembered by the Blauvelts) may not reflect any fatal dereliction of duty, but only that the patrol was relieved hourly as ordered.

Waiting for cover of darkness, the 2d Light Infantry, 2d Grenadiers, 33d and 64th Regiments of Foot and fifty Dragoons, under command of Major-General Charles Grey, stepped onto Kinderkamack road at New Bridge about 10 p.m. on Sunday, September 27. At about midnight, a second force under command of Lord Cornwallis marched northward on the Closter Road. This pincer movement was described as "a preconcerted plan with Sir Henry Clinton," who intended "to surprise some Light Horse and Militia lying in or near Tapaan."

As the British troops advanced northward on Kinderkamack road, they received "certain intelligence of the situation of the Dragoons, a whole regiment of which lay at Old Tapaan, ten miles from Newbridge." Precise information on the American cantonments and patrols permitted the British "to come unperceived within a mile of the place." Guided by local Tories who knew the ground, six companies of Light Infantry under Major Turner Staubenzie passed to the rear of the American guard near the bridge, quartered on Cornelius Blauvelt's farm, "by going through Fields & bye-ways a great way about." They approached their target between 1 and 2 a.m. The remaining six companies under Major John Maitland halted for a time, allowing the others to get around behind the house and barn, then marched by the road, completing the encirclement, "by which manuvres the Enemy's Patroll, consisting of a Sergeant and about a Dozen Men, was entirely cut off." By this stratagem and "without the slightest difficulty," the encircling British Light Infantry "took or killed the whole guard without giving any alarm to the Regiment." The American guard was attacked with bayonets rather than musket fire, since the success of the British attack depended upon overwhelming the sergeant's guard "without any noise or alarm." At least one American sentry, however, escaped. The American officers staying at Blauvelt's house were captured without injury. Five Dragoons quartered in Blauvelt's barn were mortally wounded and, the next morning, these fatalities "were buried under the shade of a large tree in the vale opposite the house, near an old tannery which was in operation at that time."

Having destroyed the American sentries without raising any alarm, Major Staubenzie moved the 71st Light Infantry Company forward to surprise "a Party of Virginia Cavalry, stiled Mrs. Washington's Guards, consisting of more than a Hundred, commanded by Lieut.-Col. Baylor ¼" Private Samuel Brooking's account is indicative of the confusion and cruelty experienced by the startled Americans. He was bedded down in a barn with nineteen other Dragoons. Realizing that they were surrounded, they attempted to escape but were driven back by repeated stabbing. Those who then surrendered and marched out of the barn as prisoners were also bayoneted. Sam Brooking escaped through another door with a bayonet stuck through his arm and raced through the darkness to warn headquarters. Along the way, he repeatedly heard British soldiers shouting "skiver them, & give no quarters." He saw Colonel Baylor's headquarters surrounded by the enemy and so continued onward into the night, covering 4 miles to Paramus. Major Staubenzie's troops attacked Baylor's headquarters in the Haring house, seriously wounding Major Clough and Colonel Baylor with bayonet thrusts as they "attempted to get up a large Dutch Chimney ¼" Baylor's adjutant, Lieutenant Robert Morrow, was stabbed seven times and knocked in the head with musket butts. Captain Sir James Baird's Company of 2d Light Infantry was then "detached to a barn where 16 Privates were lodged, who discharged 10 or 12 Pistols, and striking at the (British) Troops sans effect with their Broad Swords, Nine of them were instantly bayoneted and seven received quarter." In 1876, one historian reported that the barn on the Haring farm "was standing until a few years ago, and it is said some of the posts and beams still retained the bloody evidence of British inhumanity." Major Maitland's troops, arriving at that time, proceeded to attack "the Remainder of the Rebel Detachment, lodged in several other Barns, with such Alertness as prevented all but three Privates from making their Escape."

As noted above, the six troops of American Dragoons were quartered in six different barns. Depositions from American survivors show that the barn where First Troop slept was surrounded and taken by the 2d Light Infantry. Southward Cullency of First Troop reported that five or six of the wounded were clubbed in the head with muskets upon Captain Ball's orders to "take no Prisoners." Cullency received twelve stab wounds.

The Dragoons of Second Troop, sleeping in a neighboring barn, were suddenly awakened by the cries of First Troop so that some of them managed to dress. Reaching the barn door, however, they realized that they too were surrounded by British soldiers and asked for quarters. Told to come out of the barn, they were stripped and robbed of their clothing and valuables. The British soldiers sent to Captain Ball in a neighboring house for orders; when the messenger returned, the Americans were herded back into the barn and bayoneted. Private Thomas Bensen was one of those awakened when he heard the Dragoons of First Troop cry out that they were surrounded by the enemy. He was stabbed twelve times with bayonets, but managed to escape by jumping over the barnyard fence. Five men in his troop were killed. Private Julian King suffered sixteen wounds and Private George Willis suffered nine wounds. They heard the British soldiers send for Captain Ball to learn "what they were to do with the Prisoners, who returned for answer that they were to kill every one of them." After Thomas Talley of Second Troop was taken prisoner, he was stripped of his breeches and then ordered back into the barn, where he was bayoneted six times and left for dead.

Some privates of Third Troop were standing forage guard when they were surrounded by the enemy. After asking for quarters, they too were bayoneted. A corporal and three privates were left for dead. Corporal Henry Rhore managed to crawl back into the barn but died of his wounds the next day. Sergeant Thomas Hutchinson escaped unhurt. Except for two guards on duty, the whole of Fourth Troop survived their capture without injury, owing entirely to "the Honour of Humanity" felt by an unnamed captain of the British Light Infantry who disobeyed orders and spared the captured Dragoons.

James Arney of Fifth Troop was standing forage guard when his troop was surprised. Sergeant Sudduth of Fifth Troop commented:

> [Sudduth was] awaked from his sleep by a noise among the men, and the first words he heard were kill them! kill them! upon which our men cried for quarters, and the enemy told them to turn out, and as they did turn towards the door of the barn the enemy bayoneted them, and five of them were killed after they came out of the barn, unarmed, and with intent to surrender themselves prisoners of war. [15]

Bartolet Hawkins, a private in Fifth Troop, was also awakened when "alarmed by the Enemy." Unarmed and hopelessly surrounded by four British soldiers, he

An archaeological excavation in 1967 discovered the burial site of Continental Dragoons. They were slain Sept. 28, 1778 and then buried in tanning vats. In the 1970s, the remains were reinterred at this site. The excavation was cosponsored by the Bergen County Board of Chosen Freeholders and the Bergen County Historical Society. (*Bergen County Historical Society Collections*)

asked for quarters. One of their officers, however, ordered them to stab him. After bayonet thrusts from two British soldiers, he was left for dead on the ground near the barn door. According to Dr. Griffith, Barlett Hawkins of Fifth Troop suffered three wounds, two of them in his breast. Hawkins told Griffith:

> After he got out of the Barn where he lay he asked for quarter, and the Officer called out to the Soldiers to Stab him which they immediately did.—That he heard the British Soldiers say they could give no quarters as it was contrary to their Orders.

Private Joseph Carrol of Sixth Troop, alarmed by the call of his sergeant, got up and quickly dressed. Surrounded by British soldiers as he went to saddle his horse, he asked for quarters but was stabbed with bayonets. The British soldiers, however, allowed four men of this troop, who tried to hide themselves in the straw, to surrender without subsequent harm. The rest of the troop escaped.

By tally of American surgeon David Griffith (as reported to Lord Stirling on October 20, 1778), the Third Regiment of Dragoons comprised 104 privates, "out of which Eleven were killed outright, 17 were left behind wounded, 4 of whom are since dead, 33 are Prisoners in N York, 8 of them wounded, the rest made their escape."[16] The British soldiers lay upon their arms until daybreak, then marched onward via the Kakiat road, turning east and crossing the Hackensack River at Perry's Mills, thereby making their way to Tappan.

Which troop of American Dragoons was stationed in Blauvelt's barn? Contemporary evidence indicates that the guard consisted of thirteen men (not including officers stationed in the house). Cornelius D. Blauvelt related:

> On reaching the stable he found five men lying dead on the ground from wounds and many more seriously wounded. It appears only a portion of the English soldiers entered the house, the remainder being detailed for the bloody tragedy in the barn. The wounded ones received immediate attention and at night the others were buried under the shade of a large tree in the vale opposite the house, near an old tannery which was in operation at that time.

James Southward of Fifth Troop reported:

> He escaped unhurt by concealing himself in the Barn which the Enemy entered—that there were 13 Men of his Regiment in the Barn, 5 of whom were killed outright, all the rest, except himself, were Bayoneted.—that he heard the British Officer order his Men to put all to Death, & afterwards, ask if they had finished all? That they offered quarters to some who, on surrendering themselves were bayoneted.[17]

James Sudduth of Fifth Troop also reported that five of his comrades were killed after they came out of the barn with intent to surrender. The correspondence of these numbers suggests that Fifth Troop comprised the thirteen-man sergeant's guard quartered in Cornelius Blauvelt's barn that night and that the five fatalities of this troop were subsequently buried across the road at the tannery. The sixth burial at this place, evidently a sergeant, was likely posted on or near the bridge when he was killed. The other sentry escaped and reportedly reached the Haring House where Baylor and Clough were quartered.

The tradition handed down from Cornelius Blauvelt tells of an "American captain and doctor and other officers" who were captured in his house that night, none of whom were wounded or killed in the attack. A count of those taken prisoners to New York, compiled by Dr. Griffith in October 1778, includes Captain John Swan, Lieutenant Robert Randolph, Cornet Francis Dade, Cadet John Kelly, and Surgeon's Mate Thomas Evans. Captain Swan and Surgeon's Mate Thomas Evans were probably captured at the Blauvelt dwelling as were some or all of the remaining subalterns listed as prisoners.

David C. Blauvelt died in January 1835, aged sixty-two years, outliving his father by only three years. The inventory of David Blauvelt's possessions gives a general description of his house and outbuildings, presumably the same "large stone house" where he and his family resided in September 1778. His dwelling consisted of a garret for storing grain, flour, meal, and feed; the "upper Room" outfitted with beds, cupboard, floor cloths, table and tea service; the "Lower Room" with brass clock, mirror, beds, chairs, tables, closet and other furniture; a cellar with barrels and casks for storing lard, butter, cider, vinegar, soap, apples, and potatoes; and the kitchen with its meat casks, iron pots, lye cask, and farming tools. David Blauvelt had a blacksmith shop on the premises (probably located on the east side of the road near the old tannery), two barns and a saw mill (which apparently sawed both lumber and basket splints). The barn and barnyard contained horses, cows, calves, sheep, hogs, fowls, corn in the ear, harness, fodder, wagon, sleighs, sawed timber, and a windmill. The other barn stored hay.

Lastly, we must recognize that there is a mystery to the Blauvelt narrative. In 1776, Cornelius D. Blauvelt was listed as a first lieutenant in the Bergen Militia. Yet, he was neither attacked nor taken prisoner on the night in question. An important part of the Blauvelt narrative tries to explain why "not a single cent's worth of property" was plundered from Cornelius' house, despite the fact that American officers were found quartered there. The initial encounter between Mr. Blauvelt and General Grey almost sounds like an exchange of passwords; according to the narrative, when the British forced entry into his home and asked who he was, Lieutenant Blauvelt "coolly replied 'I am a man for my country and will fight for it till I die.' Grey said he also was a man for his country and complimented Mr. Blauvelt for his patriotism." One wonders who it was that subsequently attempted to murder Cornelius D. Blauvelt, but the answer to this and to other questions have gone to the grave with the participants. Captain Abraham Blauvelt of the First Regiment of Orange County Militia, who was surrounded by British troopers later that night and bayoneted, was Cornelius' older brother. His younger brother, Theunis, a loyalist, was commissioned captain in the Third New Jersey Volunteers and joined the Tory exodus to Nova Scotia at the war's end.

Other Events in 1778

In 1778, Joost Zabriskie, a weaver of Hackensack Township, had his house burnt to the ground (18-foot square, a cellar under the whole), his loom destroyed, his fishing nets stolen. Moreover, he was taken prisoner to New York and had to pay "the doctor for curing may body when wounded by the robbers."

A report published in *The New York Gazette and Weekly Mercury* on October 19, 1778, stated: "When the British troops withdrew from the New Bridge, near Hackinsack, the Continentals and Militia that were in that Neighborhood, marched directly towards Newark, Elizabeth-Town, &c." [18]

1779 at New Bridge

On May 18, 1779, Captain Patrick Fergusen of the 70th Regiment led three detachments from the 71st and 57th Regiments across the Hudson River to attack an American outpost at Paramus Church. The 63rd Regiment landed at Fort Lee to cover Fergusen's flank. Logistical failures deflected Fergusen's men from their primary objective, but the 63rd Regiment marched toward New Bridge where "a party of about forty rebels attempted to take up the planks of the bridge, which they could not effect. Several shots were exchanged without damage I believe on either side." Fifty of Van Buskirk's Volunteers and two companies of the 63rd Regiment were stationed at New Bridge. On the following day, Captain Fergusen's detachments and the remainder of the 63rd Regiment joined at New Bridge and occupied the heights a quarter mile to the west. In May 1779, Samuel Demarest, of Hackensack Township, lost nearly all of his earthly possessions, as the enemy burnt a large house, fifty by twenty-one feet, together with a large Dutch barn, 44 feet wide by 45 feet, a wagon house "according to the Dutch construction", and his corn crib long, plundering his livestock, grain, provender and farming utensils. [19]

The summer had been quiet, except for occasionally raiding parties from the small British redoubts along the Hudson River. On June 9, 1779, Captain Allen McLane's company was assigned to the command of Major Lee, of the Light Dragoons, who was then stationed two miles beyond Paramus Church. In July and the first two weeks of August, he and his men spent their nights at Old Bridge, New Bridge, Closter Dock, Liberty Pole, Schraalenburgh Church, Hackensack, Fort Lee, Bergen Woods, and Paulus Hook, scouting enemy movements across the Hudson River, picking up deserters from the British army and gathering intelligence. Foraging parties were sent into Teaneck and the English Neighborhood. On Wednesday, August 4, 1779, he and his troop moved to New Bridge where the men were employed cooking three days' provisions. On Sunday, August 8th, heavy rains fed a great freshet in the Hackensack River. On the next two days, farmers in the English Neighborhood were employed in cutting down trees and placing obstructions in the roads leading from Fort Lee and Bull's Ferry, as well as in the different passes leading up the Palisades from the Hudson River, opposite Spuyten Duyvil Creek southward to Bull's Ferry. American cavalry officer Major Henry Lee conceived a daring plan to capture the earthworks at Paulus Hook, which, according to intelligence provided by a deserter, was garrisoned by "Van Buskirk's regiment, 200 strong, invalids 200 strong, a lieutenant commandant of artillery, the whole under Major (William) Sutherland." On August 19, 1779, Major Henry Lee surprised and captured the earthen fort and blockhouse at Paulus Hook. The watchword was

"Stony Point." According to his own account, "the troops moved from the vicinity of New-Bridge about four o'clock." on August 18, 1779. During a march through dark woods, prolonged to almost three hours by either the "timidity or treachery of the principal guide," nearly 200 men of the 1st Battalion became separated from Major Lee and the main body. The attacking column had to struggle 2 miles through marsh and then ford several ditches with water breast-deep. At about 3.30 a.m., hand-picked troops stormed over the abatis and into the earthworks before any piece of artillery could be fired. They seized two blockhouses, the principal fort, and the barracks, together with their defenders. The Americans lost two killed and five wounded; British losses amounted to about fifty killed and 159 taken prisoners, including nine officers. At the time of the attack, a party of 130 from Van Buskirk's New Jersey Volunteers were out on a marauding expedition to the English Neighborhood. They proceeded according to plan to Douw's Ferry on the Hackensack River, where Captain Henry Peyton and a rear guard was supposed to have boats ready for their evacuation. Through mistaken intelligence, however, these boats had prematurely returned to Newark. The retreat up the roads to New Bridge, a march of 22 miles, was covered by a reinforcement of Virginians sent forward by Major-General Stirling. Major Lee's troops "arrived safe at the New-Bridge with all prisoners about one o'clock p. m. on the nineteenth."[20] That night was spent at New Bridge and the following day, the Americans took up the bridge, in expectation of a retaliatory raid.

Captain Jacob Van Buskirk of the Third Battalion of New Jersey Volunteers, a son of Lt. Col. Abraham Van Buskirk, was severely wounded in the battle of Eutaw Springs, South Carolina, on September 9.[21]

An article in the Royal Gazette on September 4, 1779, reported, "Young Col. Fell has a hundred men at Hackinsack with guards at New-Bridge, &c."[22]

On November 2, 1779, General Wayne collected between sixty and a hundred wagons from farmers in the vicinity of Paramus and marched about 1,500 troops "from New Bridge up along by Liberty Pole and Schraalenburgh Church to Closter" to gather grain, forage, and livestock.[23]

1780 at New Bridge

On March 22, 1780, two detachments of the British Army crossed the Hudson River into Bergen County. Some 300 men from the Brigade of Guards commanded by Lieutenant-Colonel John Howard landed at Closter for an attack on the American outpost at Hoppertown (now Ho-Ho-Kus) while about 300 British and Hessian troops from New York City, commanded by Lieutenant-Colonel Duncan MacPherson, landed at Weehawken to attack the town of Hackensack. The invaders entered the lower part of town at about 3 a.m. One half of the enemy column reportedly marched through the village but the rear guard, "consisting

Rare 1776 cartridge box. (*Artifact of the American Revolution is in the Bergen County Historical Society Collections, photo by Deborah Powell*)

mostly of Hessians", made considerable mischief. MacPherson's troops burned the Court House (destroying the Town Clock), (In seeking compensation, the County of Bergen estimated the value of the Court House at £500 and the Town Clock at £57 12*s* 0) broke into houses, mashed furniture, and plundered every Whig home in the village of clothing, bedding and currency, taken about fifty or sixty patriots as prisoners. John Chapple, a shoemaker, had his house burnt to the ground (His house "contained two Rooms and an entry and a Milk House on the Lower floor and on the Upper Story was Convenience for two Rooms more, the one being furnished and the other not and a Good Convenient Garret"). John Banta, a gunsmith, was taken prisoner. At about 4 a.m., raiders broke into the tavern house of Archibald Campbell, taking silverware, twenty-two Spanish milled dollars, 4,000 Continental Dollars, china tea service, and a mahogany tea chest filled with Hysan tea. Sparks and flames from the burning Court House supposedly flew across the Green and Archibald Campbell's tavern was "saved by the family throwing water on the roof." They broke the doors and smashed the windows of William Provoost, carrying him a prisoner to New York. Blacksmith John Brower, at New Bridge, had his shop looted. After reaching their objectives, the two detachments rendezvoused at Zabriskie's Mills (at Arcola, in Paramus), and with their prisoners, "the troops retired by New-Bridge and the English Neighborhood ¼"[24] The militia and the Continental troops at Paramus were alarmed and aroused to action. According to one account, the enemy, retiring from Red Mills and Hackensack, found the planks torn up from the New Bridge and were delayed "two hours replacing them, during which time skirmishing was going on with those in pursuit."

British Major Christopher Stuart reported that about 100 American soldiers, joined by about thirty Bergen militiamen, kept "a continual fire on their rear."

[Stuart was] induced to believe the friendly inhabitants would have assembled and endeavored to obstruct their retreat by hoisting or cutting away the bridge, but on my arrival finding that the militia had not collected according to my expectations, and the enemy having taken up the bridge and posted themselves on an eminence on the other side, I thought it prudent to retire to my station, the men having received no refreshment during the day.[25]

One prisoner who escaped from the British after their raid on Hackensack was tavern keeper Archibald Campbell. "This gentleman they forced from his bed, where he had been confined ¼ with rheumatism, and obliged him to follow them. He is said to have escaped at New Bridge by hiding under the bridge and standin ¼ in two feet of water."[26] A more entertaining version of Archibald Campbell's ordeal was recorded in 1844 by John Barber and Henry Howe in their *Historical Collections of the State of New Jersey*:

In the latter part of March, 1780, a party of about 400 British, Hessians, and refugees, passed through Hackensack on their way to attack some Pennsylvania troops at Paramus. It was about 3 o'clock in the night when they entered the lower part of the town. All was quiet. A small company of 20 or 30 militia, under Capt. John Outwater, had retired for the night to the barracks, barns, and out-houses, where those friendly to the American cause generally resorted to rest. One half of the enemy marched quietly through. When the rear, consisting mostly of Hessians, arrived, they broke open the doors and windows, robbed and plundered, and took prisoners a few peaceable inhabitants, among whom was Mr. Archibald Campbell. This gentleman, who had been for several weeks confined to his bed with the rheumatism, they forced into the street and compelled to follow them. Often in their rear, they threatened to shoot him if he did not hasten his pace. In the subsequent confusion, he escaped and hid in the cellar of a house opposite the New Bridge. He lived until 1798, and never experienced a return of the rheumatism.[27]

A young man of the town was said to have been wounded by a spent ball, which cut his upper lip, knocked out four front teeth, and was caught in his mouth. Captain Outwater received a ball below the knee, which he carried with him to his grave.[28]

On April 15, 1780, a cavalry detachment of about one hundred and twenty men, together with a body of 312 infantry, composed of the 17th Dragoons, Queen's Rangers, Diemar's Hussars and Lieutenant Stuart's Volunteers, commanded by Major Du Buy of the Regiment of Bose, landed at Bergen Point and Fort Lee. According to an account published in *The Royal Gazette* on April 19, 1780, these troops met at the English Neighborhood:

The whole detachment proceeded to the New Bridge upon Hackinsac, which they reached between 2 and three o'clock in the morning of the 16th, having fallen in with

Above: This may be where Archibald Campbell hid after escaping the British, 'he escaped and hid in the cellar of a house opposite the New Bridge.' Currently the root cellar in the Steuben House is not restored. (*Photo by Deborah Powell*)

Right: John Outwater's grave at the Outwater Family Cemetery in Carlstadt, NJ. After the war he went on to serve as a judge and assemblyman. With Joseph Cooper, he drafted the 1797 reform election law including women as potential voters. (*Photo by Deborah Powell*)

a rebel patrole at that place, under the command of an officer who was taken prisoner with three of his men, the others making their escape.[29]

Leaving about fifty men to defend the New Bridge, British troops marched on to Paramus and to Hoppertown, where they attacked "a superior body of infantry in connected cantonments, [and] carried several houses." Some 250 American troops were then stationed at Hoppertown under command of Major Thomas Langhorne Byles. The British retreat, however, was slowed by snipers:

In retiring, small parties of militia, with a few of their troops, who had been upon out duties, kept hovering round the detachment in different directions, and altho' unable to make any impression, they incommoded the march of the troops by a constant scattered fire from different quarters, but with little effect, altho' they continued their attempts to the place of embarkation viz. Fort Lee.

The defense of New Bridge by Lieutenant Bryson and about thirty American soldiers was described in the Chatham newspaper on May 17, 1780:

Lieutenant Bryson being a few days before detached by Major Byles with a small party to the New Bridge, defended that post for some time with great gallantry and coolness, he sustaining in person, with his espontoon, the attack of four horsemen, and received several wounds; but being overpowered with numbers, surrendered to one of their officers. It is said he received marks of politeness from them, on account of his bravery and deliberate courage displayed by him during the skirmish.[30]

Zabriskie House Massacre, 1780

The following account—an extract of a latter from New-Barbados, Bergen County, dated May 30, 1780—was published in the *New-Jersey Journal* on June 14, 1780:

This morning a detachment of about 300 of the enemy, under the command of Col. Buskirk, made a descent into this county. Their object was professedly to murder and carry off militia. They divided themselves into two parties, each going upon a scout. They met at the house of J. Zabriskie at about one o'clock, a. m. and mistaking each other for the rebel guard, (as they call it) fell upon each other in a most furious manner, and by the discharge of their muskets and use of the bayonet, they appear to have made a dreadful slaughter; the ground round the house being in a measure covered with blood, and in someplaces, the clotted gore remained in heaps when I arrived at the spot, which was at five o'clock.—After this they finding their mistake, retreated over and took up the bridge to prevent our men pursuing them. 'Tis said they had seven or eight killed on the spot, besides wounded—All were carried off.[31]

Mary Frances Bogert Secor related the recollections of Reverend Mr. James D. Demarest, a son of David Peterse Demarest:

Impact-flattened musket ball from a 2001 archaeological dig under the Steuben House front porch. (*Artifact of the American Revolution is in the Bergen County Historical Society Collections, photo by Deborah Powell*)

The following incidents were related to me by my grandfather, the Rev. James D. Demarest, on the ninth of March, 1868, that being his eighty-eighth birthday, and are given as nearly as possible in his own words, which were entered in my note-book as he proceeded:

The house now occupied by James Ely, at the crossroads at New Bridge, in Bergen County, New Jersey, was formerly the homestead of Peter des Marest, who was the father of eighteen children, David. P., my father, being one of that number. [32]

When, in 1778, the British held possession of that portion of New Jersey, bordering on the Hudson, and the redcoats made their first appearance at New Bridge, my father was lying ill with a fever, and unable to flee or protect his family, which at that time comprised my mother and five children. Warned in time of their approach, Peter the eldest son, then thirteen, was dispatched with the horses and a wagon load of such household effects as could be most readily and hastily collected and loaded, without order or care, and was told to drive with all possible speed, in an opposite and safe direction, and not spare the horses. In his flight, the goods were falling off, but there was no time to be lost in their recovery, and Peter plied the whip while his tears fell thick and fast.

Meanwhile, two neighbors, David Demarest, better known as Fytjes Daff (Sophia's Dave), and John Van Buskirk, familiarly known as 'Jockey John,' notorious Tories, both of them!—had gone to meet the enemy, carrying with them, as a present, several loaves of bread, which they presented with demonstrations and expressions of welcome, and in return for this favor, sought protection for their homes and property. They also sought to dissuade the invaders from their purpose of sacking those of their neighbors who were loyalists, but were active in pointing out the homes of those whom they designated as rebels, my father being described as 'one of the worst of them.' So grovelling was their demeanor, that instead of having the effect intended, it reacted unfavorably and they were threatened with the bayonet. This so intimidated them, that instead of returning by the highway, they skulked off, and making a wide detour, gained their homes.

When the British reached my father's house, an officer and several men entered, and seeing my father in bed, turned to my mother, who was wringing her hands in anguish, and asked 'What is the matter with that rebel?' 'He is very sick' she replied. 'No, he is not!' they shouted, 'He is a rebel, and has been shot.' Whereupon, with oaths and imprecations, several of them roughly turned and otherwise maltreated my poor sick father, in search of bullet wounds. Satisfying themselves that was really ill, and not wounded, they finally desisted and then proceeded to demolish the furniture.

The dresser was thrown forward and its contents rendered worthless. The milk was poured from the pans, and by using the few remaining chairs as bludgeons, the rest of the effects were broken, thus wantonly destroying everything too heavy or cumbrous to be carried away. Among the articles taken was the lid which they wrenched from the silver cream pitcher. The pitcher is now in our closet. Why they left it and took only the lid, I am at a loss to know, but presume it was laid aside and forgotten. After their departure, may parents, grateful for their personal safety, united in rendering fervent praise to God.

For a number of weeks after this event, and after my father had recovered from his illness, those who were capable of bearing arms in the defense of liberty, feared to sleep at home; and consequently father, and my brother Peter, with a few of their neighbors, secreted themselves nightly in various places, not daring to occupy any of their lodgings two nights in succession.

On one occasion, the old stone house, then owned by Mr. Zabriskie, which stood a short distance from the Hackensack River, near the site of the present 'New Bridge,' which at that time was a fording place, had been agreed upon as their place of refuge for the night. By some providential means the supposed secret reached the ears of the Tories, and the marauders who infested that locality, one of whom, a neighbor, not yet wholly depraved, fearing the awful consequences certain to follow this exposure, apprised them of their danger, and cautioned them to seek other and safer quarters for the night.

A barrack located not far from this house was accordingly occupied, whence the movements of the local enemy could be watched. Shortly after midnight they were heard cautiously approaching the house in two divisions; one having forded the river, and the other made a circuit intended to prevent escape. Their plan was to surround the house and then deliberately begin the work of slaughter. The night was intensely dark, and not being able to recognize each other, both divisions supposed they had encountered the 'rebels' and with a desperation and determination worthy of a better cause, opened and continued a fatal discharge of musketry, killing and wounding several of their own number. Daybreak revealed to them their mistake and terminated the conflict.

At a later hour the bodies were quietly removed, and were probably buried the following night, for there were no ceremonies or demonstrations of any kind that were publicly known.

In 1779, at the age of fourteen, Peter enlisted under his father, then Captain des Marest, as a private.

Father and sons were blacksmiths, and as occasion required, shod the horses of the American army, for which extra service they were paid in Continental currency. I have in my possession some of the currency which they then received.[33]

In 1780, while on parole, Jan Zabriskie abandoned his mansion at New Bridge and fled to the protection of the British lines in Manhattan.

On the night of July 20, 1780, Brigadier General Anthony Wayne assembled the 1st and 2nd Pennsylvania Brigades and Colonel Moylan's regiment at New Bridge, together with militia reinforcements, for a daybreak raid on Bull's Ferry Blockhouse (in present-day Guttenburg). Frustrated in his attempt to reduce the small fortress, he later justified his withdrawal on the verge of victory, claiming the risk of a British force crossing the Hudson River induced him "to withdraw in time to secure our passage over New Bridge and to drive off the cattle, after burning the boats at the landing."[34]

Major John Andre composed a satirical poem called *Cow Chace*, mocking General Wayne's unsuccessful attempt to capture the blockhouse. Published in The Royal Gazette on August 16, 1780, Andre's poem included the verse:

> *For many Heroes bold and brave*
> *From New-Bridge and Tapaan*
> *And those that drink Passaick's wave,*
> *And those that eat Soupaan.*[35]

In the middle of August 1780, the Continental troops were engaged in erecting a blockhouse and batteries at Dobb's ferry, to defend the passage at the ferry-way, where the Hudson River at this point is about 3 miles wide. On August 25, 1780,

Major André's profile, cut by John André for Miss Rebecca Redman, 1778. (*Redrawn from original silhouette owned by The Library Company of Philadelphia, PA*)

the army decamped and marched south on a three-day expedition to collect forage and provisions "from the disaffected inhabitants on the lines."

Camp Steenrapie, Bergen County

To prevent British interference with the landing of allied French troops in Rhode Island, General Washington moved his troops into a position to challenge the British military stronghold on Manhattan. Washington's Grand Army marched into Bergen County from Orangetown, New York, on August 23, 1780. The right wing of the army moved south along Schraalenburgh Road, Washington Avenue, and Liberty Road to the Liberty Pole in Englewood, while the left wing marched along a route roughly approximated by Piermont Road and Tenafly Road. The soldiers occupied a wide arc, extending from the Hudson River at Fort Lee and Englewood. Four brigades foraged as far south as Hoboken, Paulus Hook in Jersey City, and Bergen Point in Bayonne, destroying whatever wood and forage they could not bring off in wagons. Washington's headquarters was originally given as "Teaneck" in his general orders. The weather was extremely hot and the countryside suffered from an unprecedented drought that killed the tobacco crop. Farmers were "obliged to feed their cattle with hay and water them from wells, as the creeks and rivulets were dry." A terrific thunderstorm, accompanied by lightning, brought some relief on August 31, 1780.

The purpose of the expedition was to forage the countryside for provisions, which were desperately wanted in the army, and to await the arrival of the French Expeditionary Force. According to Dr. James Thatcher, a surgeon in the Massachusetts 16th Regiment, Washington's troops had nearly exhausted their provisions and "the soldiers have for several days drawn nothing but one pound of flour a man." According to the transcripts of the council of war, held at Camp Steenrapie on September 6, 1780, Washington and a majority of his generals thought nothing could be done against the British in New York City without French cooperation, due to British naval superiority.

On September 4, 1780, the Continental Army crossed the Hackensack River on the New Bridge, "turned to the Right up the River towards Tappan and encamped on a high Ridge of land in a place called Steenrapie." According to noted military historian, Todd Braisted, "there were approximately 14,000 infantry, artillery and cavalry at Steenrapie and environs." Since detachments and regiments were posted in numerous locales, it is difficult (if not impossible) to pin down how many troops were in camp on any given day. Thirteen brigades, comprised Continental troops from Pennsylvania, Delaware, New Jersey, New York, Connecticut, Massachusetts, New Hampshire, and Rhode Island, encamped in two lines west of Kinderkamack Road, one atop the ridge and one below. The main body of the camp extended from River Edge Avenue, 2 miles north to the vicinity of Soldier Hill Road. Three artillery regiments, having strength of about thirty cannon, were with the army. The artillery park was located near their center along Ridgewood Avenue. Light infantry were posted on the heights behind New Bridge (Brower's Hill, later named Cherry Hill) and Van Saun Park in River Edge.

One day, Kevin rattled off the well-known people at New Bridge and I created this image to show this stunning information graphically. The portraits are all in the public domain. (*Created by Deborah Powell*)

At least 3,377 militiamen, who were enlisted for six months or less, added to the strength of Washington's army. Lafayette had his headquarters at the north end of the encampment, near Soldier Hill Road, perhaps in a stone house that was torn down to make way for the Atwood-Blauvelt mansion on Kinderkamack Road. General Washington established headquarters in the Zabriskie-Steuben House, issuing orders and correspondence from either "near New Bridge," or simply at "New Bridge."

Lieutenant William S. Pennington described Steenrapie as "a little village on the west side of Hackensack River, and four miles above the town of Hackensack. It is a very delightful country. Milton's delineation of *Paradise Lost* does not exceed the beauties of it." During the Steenrapie encampment, Hendrick C. Banta, who resided on what is now Howland Avenue in Paramus, sold a barrel of cider from his mill to the troops "every other day." His son Cornelius Banta, then ten years old, reportedly "saugh [*sic.*] Washington three times on his hors [*sic.*]." The commander-in-chief's presence hereabout gave rise to the name of the Washington Spring.

The period of time Washington's army spent in Bergen County in late summer 1780 was extremely difficult upon all concerned. Records of damages suffered by inhabitants indicate considerable plundering and marauding by the soldiers. David Hall, a soldier in Colonel Stewart's Battalion of Light Infantry, Second Pennsylvania Regiment, assigned to Lafayette's Light Corps, was executed by hanging in camp on September 12, 1780, one of five soldiers convicted of "plundering money and plate" from local inhabitants.

Distressing news of Major General Horatio Gates' defeat at Camden, South Carolina, on August 16, 1780, reached the army on the evening of September 5. This was the second Continental Army to be nearly wiped out in South Carolina within three months. Desertion to the British was rampant from the camp, as

View from Brower Hill, the Steuben House is top center in the photograph. Unfortunately smoke from the train's steam engine obscures some of the view. Taken the first half of the twentieth century. (*Photo by Elizabeth Benedict Timpson née Zobriskie, Bergen County Historical Society Collections*)

signified by troop returns and British intelligence records, which indicate the British took two prisoners and 157 deserters during the Continental Army's stay in Bergen County. Indeed, the British were as well informed as to Washington's strength and disposition as he himself could have been.

During these weeks, the army also lost no fewer than twenty-three soldiers to disease, including General Enoch Poor, who died "after a short illness of putrid fever" on September 8, 1780. His body was brought to the Brower House on Main Street, River Edge (where the New Bridge Landing Shopping Center is now located) and placed in a mahogany coffin for burial in the churchyard of the Hackensack Dutch Reformed Church (the Church on the Green). General Washington led the guard of honor attending the burial. According to legend, other casualties, attributed to disease, were buried near the famed Spook Bridge on Howland Avenue in River Edge.

The beautiful countryside, however, did afford moments of leisure and relaxation as Lieutenant William S. Pennington, of the Second Regiment of Continental Artillery, spent the afternoon of August 29, 1780, "very agreeably with a number of gentlemen of our battalion, on the banks of the Hackensack River, drinking milk punch." Major General Baron von Steuben entertained a number of officers at his dining table on September 8, 1780. According to surgeon James Thatcher, "Notwithstanding the scarcity of provisions in camp, the Baron's table continues to be well supplied; his generosity is unbounded."

The 1920s graveside memorial service in Hackensack for General Enoch Poor by BCHS members. (*Bergen County Historical Society Collections*)

On September 13, 1780, General Washington, French officers and six allied Oneida chiefs rode in front of the Continental Army on parade review. When they reached the artillery park, thirteen cannons fired a salute. News of the arrival of the French fleet reached camp on September 15, 1780. General Washington, the Marquis de Lafayette, and General Henry Knox departed for Hartford, Connecticut, on September 17 to meet with Count de Rochambeau and Admiral de Jarnay, the newly arrived commanders of the French Army and fleet. The army was left under the command of Major General Nathanael Greene. The Continental Army decamped from Steenrapie on September 20, 1780, returning to Orangetown, New York.

Alexander Hamilton at New Bridge in 1780

Alexander Hamilton, an artillery captain from New York City, was promoted to lieutenant-colonel and appointed an *aide-de-camp* and secretary to General Washington in 1777. Hamilton was well aware of the precarious condition of the Continental Army and already considered the Continental Congress, acting under the weak central authority imposed by the Articles of Confederation, to be ineffectual in its efforts to sustain its troops. This letter, written from the Zabriskie-Steuben House at Historic New Bridge Landing in River Edge, is addressed to Lieutenant-Colonel John Laurens, who had also served in Washington's official "family" as an *aide-de-camp* (1777–79) with Hamilton, where they formed a very close friendship. Laurens was in Philadelphia on parole, having been captured in the fall of Charleston in May 1780. The letter offers insight into its writer's gloomy outlook on the war effort and his growing disdain for weak and indecisive government. It highlights New Bridge's complex involvement in the American Revolution as a battleground, military headquarters, and intelligence post, repeatedly occupied and contested by both armies. Two years later, Laurens was killed at the battle of the Combahee River in South Carolina on August 27, 1782, only twenty-seven years of age.

Letter to [Lieutenant] Colonel John Laurens

We ought both my Dear Laurens to beg pardon of our friendship for mutual neglect in our correspondence, though I believe you are a good deal in arrears to me, and I am sure one of my letters might have miscarried—I informed you that the application, in favor of (Brigadier General Du) Portail (also captured at Charleston) and yourself, had been referred to a general exchange as respected.

When the general exchange will take place is precarious, but it may happen in two or three months. The enemy have offered to exchange all the officers and men on Long Island and in New York for an equivalent in our hands. They have above four hundred private men. The offer has been heretofore evaded in hope of offensive operations— four hundred men you in garrison would have been equal to twice their number out of it—and might have made a critical difference in the event. But unhappily for us our prospects of offensive operations, and that of a genuine exchange becomes probable in proportion. Two months will explain the business; and I counsel you to defer your plan; you then will have time enough to execute it against next Campaign or to ruin yourself in a rash attempt. If we are able to act offensively, we shall do it on good grounds, and you may look with certainty for relief—if we are not able to do this, I believe the enemy's offer will be accepted; and I think there will be no difficulty in including you.

I am angry with you for having 'taken the liberty' to introduce (Arnoldus) VanDerhorst and Mr. (Richard Keith) Call. If you had simply introduced them (without taking such a liberty with me) I should have been obliged to you. They will tell you however, that we have done all we could to make their stay in Camp agreeable.

I have conveyed your reproof to the lads. They have considered me as the Secretary of the family and fancied me a partnership which did not exist—Writing or not writing to you, you know they love you, and sympathize in all that concerns you. Indeed my Laurens, I often realize your situation.

But play the Philosopher if you can, and improve your captivation improving your mind. Tell me not of the difficulty— I expect you will surmount difficulties which would bear down other men with your sensibility and without your fortitude. I was told you were going to explore the caverns of the blue mountains in quest of knowledge— enterprises of this kind are worthy of you, not fruitless repinings at your fate.

Hamilton, miniature portrait.
(*Attributed to Charles Shirreff, c. 1790. R. W. Norton Art Foundation*)

I give you in a former letter my ideas of the situation of your country and the proper remedies to her disorders. You told me, my remedies were good, but you were afraid would not go down at this time. I tell you necessity must force them down. And that if they are not speedily taken the patient will die. She is in a galloping consumption and her case will soon become desperate. Indeed, my dear friend, to drop allegory, you can hardly conceive in how dreadful a situation we are. The army, in the course of the present month, has received only four or five day's rations of meal, and we really know not of any adequate relief in future. This distress at just a stage of the campaign sours the soldiery. Tis in vain you make apologies to them. The officers are out of humor, and the worst of evils seem stop be coming upon us. A loss of our virtue. Tis in vain you attempt to appease; you are almost detested as an accomplice with the administration. I am losing character, my friend, because I am not over complaisant to the spirit of clamor. So that I am in a fair way to be out with everybody. With one set, I am considered as a friend to military pretensions, however exorbitant, with another as a man, who secured by my situation from having the distress of the army, am inclined to treat it lightly. The truth is I am an unlucky honest man that speaks my sentiments to all, and with emphasis. I say this to you because you know it and will not charge me with vanity—I hate Congress—I hate the army—I hate the world—I hate myself. The whole is a mass of fools and knaves: I could almost except you and Meade. Adieu.

A. Hamilton

My ravings are for your own bosom.
The General and family send you their love.
New Bridge
Sept. 12, 1780 [36]

1781 at New Bridge

On March 14, 1781, about fifty militiamen were stationed at New Bridge.

New Bridge Restored

Even before a formal cessation of hostilities in September 1783, the Freeholders were again ordering repair of New Bridge. On May 18, 1782, the Board appointed a Committee "to View and put in repair the Bridge commonly called the New Bridge." On May 12, 1784, more comprehensive improvements were required and the Freeholders authorized payment of "13 Pounds 4 Shillings and 10 pence to John Demarest ¼ for Building the New Bridge." Again on October 9, 1786, the Board ordered the Committee to "View the New Bridge to see what repairs are Necessary & Get Persons to Do it by Days' Wages & Likewise to Get a Tackle and runner fixed to the Draw Bridge." This record suggests that the bridge operated by means of a sliding draw. One source claims that the sliding draw was converted to a lift bridge in 1812 but offers no citation from contemporary sources.

   After a thriving contraband trade with both sides, Bergen Dutch farmers rebuilt damaged dwellings.

Hamilton letter to Colonel John Laurens, written from New Bridge, N.J. on September 12, 1780, during the Steenrapie Encampment. *(From the New York Public Library. digitalcollections.nypl.org/ items/b917eb3b-decb-ad32- e040-e00a18060e3e)*

7

Post American Revolution at New Bridge, Baron Steuben's Jersey Estate

Discouraged in his hopes of returning to a profitable station in Europe, Major-General Frederick Wm. Baron von Steuben informed the New Jersey legislature that he was "anxiously desirous to become a citizen of the State of New Jersey." In recognition of his "many and signal services to the United States of America," state legislators responded on December 23, 1783, by presenting him with the use and emoluments of the confiscated estate of Jan Zabriskie at New Bridge, provided that the Baron would "hold, occupy and enjoy the said estate in person, and not by tenant." Accordingly, General Philemon Dickinson of the New Jersey Militia, informed the Baron of this legislative gift and related his knowledge of the estate based upon recent inquiries:

> There are on the premises an exceeding good House, an excellent barn, together with many useful outbuildings, all of which I am told, want some repairs ¼ there is ¼ a Grist-mill; a good Orchard, some meadow Ground, & plenty of Wood. The distance from N York by land 15 miles, but you may keep a boat & go from your own door to N York by water—Oysters, Fish & wild fowl in abundance—Possession will be given to you in the Spring, when you will take a view of the premises.

General Dickinson regretted that the legislature had only vested Steuben with life-rights and not outright title to the property:

> This not, my dear Baron, equal either to my wishes & your mind, but 'tis the best I could probably obtain—You'll observe by the Act, that you are to possess it, but not tenant it out, I am ashamed of this clause but it could not be avoided—This may easily be obviated, by keeping a bed & Servants there & visiting the premises now & then— but I flatter myself, from the representation which has been made to me, that it will be your permanent residence; its vicinity to N York, must render it agreeable to you.

Major General Baron von Steuben. Steuben was at the Steenrapie Encampment at New Bridge in the same year this was painted. (*Charles Willson Peale, 1780. Pennsylvania Academy of the Fine Arts*)

Under these terms, it is likely that the Prussian Inspector-General contemplated taking up residence at New Bridge. His biographer, Friedrich Kapp, writing in 1859, says only, "Steuben, when informed that Zabriskie, in consequence of that confiscation, was left without means, did not accept the gift, and interposed in behalf of Zabriskie." Unfortunately, the documented facts do not square with this kindly interpretation. On January 24, 1784, John J. Zabriskie, "now a refugee in the City of New York," filed a claim for compensation from the British government for the loss of his former homestead at New-Bridge, which had been "possessed under this Confiscation Law." Zabriskie's 1784 account clearly describes the well-known sandstone mansion, which yet stands at this location. Whatever the conflicting sentiments of the Revolutionary War mercenary and dispossessed loyalist may have been, one fact was equally evident to both: The Zabriskie mansion was not some sleepy country-estate that needed only the fires stoked and the slip-covers lifted to make it cozy. It had served repeatedly as a fort, military headquarters, an intelligence-gathering post, an encampment-ground, and the scene of numerous skirmishes. Undoubtedly, the abuses of war had rendered the dwelling house uninhabitable, stripped of its furnishings. The old and impecunious Saxon soldier was hardly able to restore its former grandeur. Besides, the legislature had not given him title to the property, but only a right to life-tenancy. It would hardly have been worthwhile for him to invest a large sum in the renovation of a property he did not own.

Before investing in his estate at New-Bridge, General Steuben first intended to acquire title to the property in fee simple. On December 24, 1784, the New Jersey legislature responded to his overtures by passing a supplement to its previous act, which authorized the agent for forfeited estates to sell the property to the highest bidder and to deposit the money in the State treasury. Interest upon the sum was to be paid to the Baron during his lifetime. Accordingly, the Zabriskie estate at New Bridge was sold on April 1, 1785, but its purchaser was none other than the Baron himself, acting through his agent, Captain Benjamin Walker. The purchase price was £1,500. The general's personal interest and familiarity with his Jersey estate was outlined in a letter addressed from New York to Governor Livingston on November 13, 1785, wherein he noted:

[He had] become the purchaser of that part of the estate of John Zabriskie, lying at the New-Bridge, near Hackensack, and the term of payment being arrived, an order from the commissioners of the continental treasury on the treasury of New Jersey lies ready for the agent whenever he shall please to call for it.

Before I take the deeds for this place, I have to request the favor of your Excellency to represent to the legislature, that the only lot of wood belonging to the place was withheld by the agent at the sale on a doubt of its being included in the law because it is at the distance of three quarters of a mile from the house, and therefore could not, he supposed, be considered as 'lying at the New-Bridge,' though on enquiry I find it was an appendage to the estate, and indeed is the only part of it on which there is a stick of wood; and it was bequeathed to J. Zabriskie by his father along with the house and mill; the lot consists of about 13 acres, it was left unsold with the house and mill, though every other part of J. Zabriskie's estate was sold some years since, and being now unpossessed, great part of the wood is cut off, and the destruction daily increases. If the legislature meant to include it in the law, I must request that directions may be given to the agent to include it in the deed. If otherwise, as it is essential to the other part of the estate, I have to request that I may be permitted to purchase it at such valuation as may be thought just.[1]

Between 1783 and 1785, General Steuben withdrew $26,000 from the national treasury, including the sum that he used to purchase the former Zabriskie homestead. He apparently spent considerable money to renovate both his leased farmhouse on Manhattan as well as his prized Jersey estate. Yet his improvident lifestyle and poor management of personal finances outstripped his income and the number of his creditors daily increased. On February 28, 1786, New Jersey legislature ordered that if payments on the property were not met by the following March (1787), then the Baron should have the use and benefit of the estate even though he resided in another state. Thus it was not until 1786—three years after the initial presentation of the property to Steuben—that the legislature abandoned its stipulation that he should occupy the property in order to receive its profits. With this encouragement, Steuben apparently leased the mansion and mill back to Jan Zabriskie and so enjoyed the rental fees. There is evidence to suggest that Captain Walker, as Steuben's business agent, and perhaps the Baron himself, occupied rooms in the house while managing the domestic renovation and commercial renaissance of this valuable site. The tax assessments for 1786 list Walker & Zabriskie as merchants at New Bridge. Arndt Von Steuben (his father was a cousin to Steuben) claimed that Steuben spent winters in New York, but he retired to his country home in summer. Receipts from New Bridge Landing have survived, which were issued

Frederick the Great medal commemorating the Battle of Rossbach, 1757. Twenty-seven-year-old Steuben was at the Battle of Rossbach, although anyone could have dropped the 1.75-inch bronze medal. The donor reported it was found at Old Bridge, New Milford, in modern times (1 mile north of New Bridge.) (*Artifact in the Bergen County Historical Society Collections, photo by Deborah Powell*)

under the style of the partnership of Walker & Zabriskie. There is also at least one letter (*circa* 1788) addressed by Senator William North to Benjamin Walker at Hackensack. On July 4, 1786, Jan Zabriskie hosted General Steuben and his entourage at New Bridge. Unawares, the Baron paid for his own entertainment as Mr. Zabriskie's servants charged refreshments obtained from the New Bridge Inn to the general's account.

In 1786, Steuben's sights turned northward to a grant of 16,000 acres in Oneida County, New York, which he received from the legislature of that state on June 27, 1786.

By 1787, Steuben's finances were at low ebb. Bankrupt, he placed his affairs under the administration of Ben Walker. In 1788, he moved into rooms in the house of his friends, Benjamin and Polly Walker, on King Street. In May 1788, he set out for his vast estate in the Mohawk country, 100 miles northwest of Albany. To pay off his debts and gain some much-needed capital, Baron Steuben wrote to Captain Walker on May 23, 1788, giving him full authority to sell his Jersey estate at New Bridge. At about this time, his close friend and advisor William North confided: "The Jersey Estate must be sold and the proceeds sacredly appropriated to paying his debts and with the remainder he must live a recluse till the new Government (then forming under the Constitution) decides his affairs. Accordingly, on September 5, 1788, the New Jersey legislature repealed its previous acts and invested Baron von Steuben with full title to the former Zabriskie estate. Recognizing his predicament and hoping to save himself from further financial embarrassment, Steuben wrote to North in October 1788, saying: "The jersey Estate must and is to be sold. Walker is my administrator, all debts are to be paid out of it." On November 6, 1788, Steuben again wrote to William North at his new home in Duanesburg:

New-Jerfey confifcated Lands.

To be Sold at Public Sale,

THAT well known and valuable place or farm, commonly called Zebrifkie's Mills, formerly the property of John Zebrikie, fituate, lying, and being, at a place called the New-Bridge, in the county of Bergen, and ftate of New-Jerfey, containing about 60 acres, chiefly of the beft meadow land.

There are on this place a well built, fpacious and commodious dwelling houfe, and a grift mill with two pair of ftones, and other good accommodations for a ftore keeper, having water carriage to and from the city of New-York; and in a fine grain country, thickly inhabited.

The fale of the above confifcated property is to be on Friday, the firft day of April next enfuing, beginning at ten o'clock in the morning, on the premifes.

CORNELIUS HARING,

Jan. 25, 1785.   Agent for Bergen county.

N. B. Nothing but fpecie will be accepted in payment for the above faid property.

Before improving his estate at New Bridge, General Steuben first intended to acquire title to the property in fee simple. On December 24, 1784, the New Jersey legislature responded to his overtures by passing a supplement to its previous act (which had awarded use of the Zabriskie estate to General Steuben) by authorizing the agent for forfeited estates to sell the property to the highest bidder and deposit the money in the State treasury. Interest upon the sum was to be paid to the Baron during his lifetime. Cornelius Haring, Agent for Confiscated Lands in Bergen County, placed an advertisement in the New Brunswick *Political Intelligencer* on February 15, 1785, advertising for sale "the valuable farm called Zabriskie's Mills, at New Bridge, containing 60 acres, formerly property of John Zabriskie. It has a gristmill with two pair of stones, and has water carriage to and from New York." Accordingly, the Zabriskie estate at New-Bridge was sold on April 1, 1785, but its purchaser was none other than the Baron himself acting through his agent, Captain Benjamin Walker. The purchase price was £1,500.

My jersey Estate is Advertised but not yet Sold, from this Walker Shall immediately pay to you the money, you so generously lend me and all my debts in New-York will be paid. I support my present poverty with more heroism than I Expected. All Clubs and parties are renounced, I seldom leave the House.

Steuben's extensive repairs to the premises are openly stated in his advertisement of sale, published in the *New Jersey Journal* on December 3, 1788:

Long-noted as the best stand for trade in the state of New Jersey. Large well-built stone house, thoroughly rebuilt lately, a gristmill with two run of stone; excellent new kiln for drying grain for export built lately; other outbuildings, and 40 acres of land, one-half of which is excellent meadow. Situated on the bank of the river by which produce can be conveyed to New York in a few hours, and sloops of 40 tons burden may load and discharge alongside of the mill.

On December 4, 1788, the Major-General Frederick Wm. Baron de Steuben of New York City, conveyed his Jersey Estate, comprising forty-nine acres at New Bridge, formerly belonging to John Zabriskie, to John Zabriskie, Jr. (1767–1793), of New Barbados Township, for £1,200. He was the son and namesake of the loyalist who

Major General Baron von Steuben. (*Maquette by sculptor Albert Jaegers, the full-size version is in Lafayette Park across from the White House. Artifact in the Bergen County Historical Society Collections, photo by Deborah Powell*)

lost the property. Steuben happily reported in a letter dated December 12: "My Jersey Estate is sold for twelve hundred Pounds N.Y. Money (about $3,000). Walker and Hamilton are my Administrators."

Steuben hoped that the proceeds from the sale would more than satisfy his creditors and thus stave off the threatened forced sale of his Oneida tract. His hopes for a fresh start in the Mohawk Valley were frustrated by the inaccessibility of the vast undeveloped estate and his perennial lack of capital and credit. Contrary to his original expectations, several perilous waterfalls on a tributary of the Mohawk River isolated the New York grant, making the water transport of agricultural products virtually impossible. On June 4, 1790, Congress finally granted him an annual pension of $2,500 but declined to award him an additional $10,000 bonus. Thus, we can say that the proceeds from the sale of his property at New Bridge were the most valuable compensation for his war service to the nation. In 1794, the Baron von Steuben died in poverty while resident in a crude log-house erected in the midst of an untamed wilderness. Per his direction his loyal *aide-de-camp*, Ben Walker, buried him without ceremony in a plain pine coffin, wrapped in his military cloak. There are circumstantial references that Steuben was a gay man.[2]

The tax assessments for 1786 list Walker and Zabriskie as merchants. On December 4, 1788, the Honorable Major-General Frederick Wm. Baron de Steuben of New York City conveyed his Jersey estate, comprising 49 acres at New Bridge formerly belonging to John Zabriskie, to John Zabriskie, Jr., of New Barbadoes Township for £1,200.[3] A subscription list for 1790, kept by John Terheun, treasurer of the Hackensack Reformed Church on the Green included John Zabriskey, £10; John Zabriskey, Jr., £5; John Seamen, £5; Albert J. Van Voorhis, £10; David Brower, £1; Abraham D. Brower, £1; Caetey £1. 4; John Van Norden, £1.4; John Brower, £5; and Uzal Meeker, £4. In 1791, John J. Zabriskie was taxed for 30 acres, two gristmills, and one slave; John Zabriskie, Jr., was listed as a merchant and householder. John Seaman, a singleman, owned one vessel. On September 28, 1791, John Brower and his wife Mary sold two tracts upon Round Hook near New Bridge to John Zabriskie, Jr., for £53.[4] The boundary survey for the first of these tracts began on the south side of Tantaquas Creek (Cole's Brook) on the line of John Zabriskie's lands and ran thence over the round hill, thence by various courses until it reached Flat Creek, thence following along Flat Creek and Tantaquas Creek to the beginning point of the survey. The boundary for the second parcel began on the east side of land belonging to Jan Zabriskie Jr. at the edge of Flat Creek and ran to the south side of the "New dam," thence to the Hackensack River and finally northwest and south along Flat Creek to the beginning point. It seems that Jan Zabriskie, Jr., restored his father's gristmill to operation by reconstruction of a new dam on Flat Creek, apparently a tidal arm of Cole's Brook and the Hackensack River.

Jan Zabriskie, Jr., married Catharine Hoagland, daughter of New Bridge innkeeper Cornelius Hoagland, on October 13, 1792, at Schraalenburgh. Jan died less than a year later on July 6, 1793, aged twenty-five years, nine months, and twenty-five days. Tradition says John Zabriskie fell into the waterwheel while trying to free it from a jam and was crushed and drowned.

An inventory was made on July 17, 1793, of Jan's estate in the presence of Albert Zabriskie, administrator, by John Earle and Christian Zabriskie, appraisers. A list

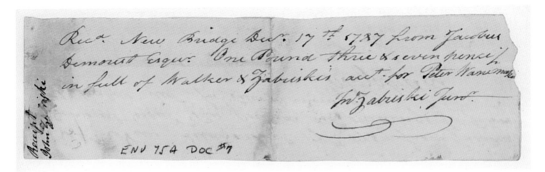

December 17, 1787, receipt "from Jacobus Demarest, Esqu, One pound three & seven pence in full of Walker & Zabriskie's acct. for Peter Wanemaker." Signed by Jn Zabriski Jr. (*Artifact in the Bergen County Historical Society Collections*)

follows of some of the items that appear in the store inventory and show a wide range of goods available at the trading post:

> 18 half gallon stone (ware) pots and jugs, 9 chamber pots, 6 earthen pots, 20 large earthen dishes, 4 carpenters adzes, 2 mouse traps, 242 lbs. of nails, 10 pairs of Smoothing Irons, 6 frying pans, 6 slates, 13 wool hats, 21 pairs of H hinges, 10 shoemakers' knives, a bundle of knitting needles, 29 bowls of pint (size) of cream color, 50 lbs. Bohea Tea, 13.5 yards of shalloon, 16 yards of Green Shalloon, 24 yards of jean, 14 yards of velvet, 15.75 yards of tow linen, 23.5 yards of brown Holland linen and 14 Latin books.

Interestingly, the inventory includes 8,150 of black wampum and 27,350 wampum in the hands of Abraham Van Buskirk.[5]

On October 1, 1793, John E. Seaman, of New York City, mortgaged "those tracts devised unto John E. Seaman by the Last Will and Testament of John Zabriskie, deceased, lying and being near the New Bridge and now occupied by P. Christopher as Tenant, Also all those tracts at Steenrapie, at Sluckup, at Pascack and Werimus ¼ by Estimate 170 Acres" to David P. Demarest, blacksmith, for £300. He discharged this mortgage on June 6, 1794. The tax ratables for August 1793 included John Zabriskie, Jr., deceased, as owner of 47 acres and two gristmills; John Zabriskie was also listed as owner of a slave. In 1794, Abraham Collins, who married John Zabriskie's widow, Catherine Hoogland, was taxed for 40 acres, two gristmills, and one vessel (this property being identified as the estate formerly belonging to John Zabriskie, Jr., deceased, and inherited by his widow). On March 28, 1795, John E. Seaman of New York City mortgaged his interest in the dwelling house, grist mills and lands at the New Bridge, formerly the property of John Zabriskie, Jr., as well as the woodland at Sluckup, to Abraham Collins for £700. He discharged this mortgage on June 2, 1798. In September 1795, the list of tax ratables indicates that Thomas Howard had taken possession of the 40 acres, two gristmills and one slave, formerly owned by the Zabriskies.

On February 23, 1796, Edmund Seaman, Jr., of New Barbadoes Township conveyed two lots of land (113 acres) to John Anderson for £1,500.[6] The first tract,

Jan Zabriskie, Jr., lies buried at the French burying ground in New Milford. He died July 6, 1793, aged twenty-five years, nine months, and twenty-five days. Family tradition says he fell into the waterwheel at his tide mill. (*Photo by Deborah Powell*)

comprising 74.5 acres, included that "certain message, tenement and tract whereon the said Edmund Seaman, Jr., now lives near New Bridge." Today, the site of this dwelling house would be where Main Street intersects Route 4 (where the south curb of Main Street intersects the east curb of Route 4). The tract including Seaman's residence encompassed all the ground between Cole's Brook and the south side of Main Street, extending east to what is now Hackensack Avenue. The second tract sold by Seaman to Anderson in 1796, comprising 38.5 acres at Steenrapie, extended west from Kinderkamack Road on the south side of what is now Reservoir Avenue.

The tax lists for September 1796 mention Derrick Banta as owner of 60 acres and one gristmill while John S. Banta was included as a merchant owning one gristmill, one-half a vessel. In 1797, John S. Banta owned 40 acres, one gristmill, and one-half vessel; Derrick Banta owned 20 acres and one gristmill. On February 7, 1798, John S. Banta, yeoman, and his wife, Rachel, of the Precinct of New Barbadoes conveyed five tracts to Derreck Banta of the same place, yeoman, for $7,875.[7] The five tracts comprised: first, 11 acres of woodland and meadow on the east side of the Hackensack River in present-day New Milford; second, a parcel of land near Round Hook, on the south side of Tantaquas Creek (Cole's Brook), across from the Zabriskie-Steuben House; third, another small parcel of land, also on Round Hook, bounded upon Flat Creek, Tantaquas Creek, and the Hackensack River; fourth, 7 acres of woodland at Sluckup; and fifth, all that part of the real estate at New Bridge, formerly belonging to Jan Zabriskie, that had been presented to the Baron von Steuben, comprising 49 acres. On April 20, 1798, these same five tracts, including the Steuben House, were sold by Derreck Banta, yeoman, of New Barbadoes to Luke Van Boskirk of the same place for $7,250.[8] The list of tax

140

ratables for September 1802 includes Luke Van Buskirk, shopkeeper, as owner of 49 acres and two gristmills.

David Anderson sold 49.57 acres situated on the south side of the road leading from New Bridge to Hackensack (now Main Street), nearly opposite John Van Orden's Grist Mill, to John Anderson on January 7, 1805, for $2,875.[9]

Andrew A. Zobriskie

Andrew A. Zobriskie (1771–1837), a cousin to Jan, purchased the stone mansion, gristmill, and 49-acre farm at New Bridge in 1815 and opened the first commercial brickyard in the Hackensack valley. The brick gable infill on the south-end of the house is probably his handiwork. The north-end, out of view, was shingle and bricked in a modern "restoration."

Andrew was the son of Andres Albert Zobriskie (1746–1771) and Jannetje Lozier, the daughter of Hildebrant Lozier and Christina De Baun. Andres married Jannetje on August 4, 1769. Daughter Christina was born on May 9, 1770, and baptized at Schraalenburgh Church on June 8, 1770. Andres A. Zobriskie died on March 10, 1771, at only twenty-four years of age. According to his last will and testament, Andres realized, "My wife Jenny is expecting." In keeping with standard practice of the time, he allowed his wife the use of his real and personal estate for so long as she remained his widow. If the expected child was a boy, then he was to inherit all of his real estate; if a daughter, then she would inherit half of his real and personal estate while Christina was to receive the other half.

Andrew A. Zobriskie was born on June 15, 1771, and baptized at Schraalenburgh Church on July 2, 1771, three months after his father's death. Jane, Andrew's widow, soon married Peter Valleau (1733–1845), a loyalist who joined the British Army in 1776. She and her second husband had a son, Hildebrand Valleau, born at Bergen on June 5, 1775, and a son, Cornelius Valleau, born at Bergen on March 7, 1777. Lieutenant Peter Valleau, his wife, their two sons, and eleven-year-old stepson, Andrew, removed to Nova Scotia when the British army evacuated New York City in 1783. There a daughter named Mary was born on February 10, 1787. Jane Lozier died at Sophiasburgh, Prince Edward, Ontario, Canada, in 1814, aged sixty-three years. On January 30, 1784, Garret Hopper was appointed Andrew A. Zabriskie's guardian. Upon reaching eighteen years of age in 1790, Andrew A. Zobriskie chose Aert Cuyper (Cooper) as his legal guardian.

On July 21, 1793, Andrew Zobriskie, of Oppenheim, New York, married Elizabeth Anderson of St. Johnsville, Montgomery County, New York. The marriage was recorded in New Jersey. Elizabeth was born July 7, 1774, a daughter of David Anderson and his wife, Antie Demarest. In 1800, Andrew Zobriskie was residing in Palatine, Montgomery County, New York. In 1806, the militia records for Montgomery County, New York, list Andrew Zobriskie as an adjutant in Lieutenant-Colonel Andrew Gray's Regiment.[10] Andrew Zabriskie was lieutenant-colonel of the Nineteenth Regiment in 1814, but in 1815, Frederick Getman was listed in place of Andrew Zabriskie, who was noted as "moved." The Zobriskies also used the name Zabriskie.

Andrew Zobriskie's signature from a store journal. (*Artifact in the Bergen County Historical Society Collections, photo by Deborah Powell*)

On August 23, 1810, Andrew Zobriskie sold 49.57 acres on the south side of Main Street, bounded south by Cole's Brook, to John Anderson, of New Barbadoes Township, for $1,125.[11] Five years later on January 2, 1815, John and Caty Anderson conveyed these same premises back to Andrew Zobriskie, yeoman, of New Barbadoes Township, for $1,125.[12]

Gristmiller John Van Orden's son and surviving executor, Theodorus Van Orden, a merchant banker on Maiden Lane in New York City, sold the mill property on the outlet of Zabriskie's Pond at New Bridge to Andrew Zobriskie of New York in November 1813. On January 3, 1815, Lieutenant Daniel Denniston, who served during the Revolution in the Second New York Regiment, conveyed five tracts of land, formerly belonging to Lucas Van Buskirk (including the Steuben House), to Andrew Zobriskie for $5,000.[13, 14] In 1820, Andrew Zobriskie, shopkeeper, was taxed for 200 acres, three to eight tan vats, one fishery, one sawmill, and three gristmills.

Andrew seems to have made a deliberate move to settle at the Zabriskie home and expand the estate at a place associated with the Zabriskie family although not his direct line ancestor.

Andrew Zobriskie and his wife, Elizabeth, had eleven children, comprised of four sons and seven daughters, including John A. Zabriskie, born July 9, 1807, who married Maria Anderson. David Anderson Zobriskie was born in Montgomery County, New York, on October 8, 1809.

Andrew A. Zobriskie died May 7, 1837 and is buried in Hackensack Cemetery. He ordered that his real estate be sold for the best price that it would bring but suggested that his heirs purchase it. On January 1, 1838, his executors sold the

Image of the Steuben House date stone with 1813 carved in the center spokes. Unknown is when and why this date was removed or what it represented. Around that time, Andrew Zobriskie is acquiring tracts of land including the mill and the Steuben House.

property at New Bridge to Richard W. Stevenson for $14,000. On the same day, the grantee sold several tracts back to Andrew's children. David A. and John A. Zobriskie purchased the homestead farm at New Bridge for $4,000. On December 5, 1839, John A. Zobriskie sold his interest to brother David for $6,000.

In 1839, his son, David A. Zobriskie, took ownership of the family homestead. Captain Dave, as he was familiarly known, owned and commanded a schooner named *The Farmer*. He also built a frame store wing adjoining the south gable-end of the stone house, where farmers would exchange cord wood for groceries. He made other improvements, including replacement of the front porch, for the *Bergen Democrat* reported in March 1872 that "Anderson Zabriskie is effecting considerable improvements by adding a handsome verandah, &c, to the front of his dwelling house."[15]

Andrew's widow, Elizabeth Anderson Zobriskie, died at the Steuben House on December 25, 1852, aged seventy-eight years.

In 1909, a gentleman provided the following interesting facts to *The Hackensack Republican* regarding the house, the property, and the former owners:

About 1835 the house was owned and occupied by David A. Zabriskie and Jane Anderson, his wife. At that time it was quite an important business center. Capt. Dave, as he was familiarly known, owned and commanded a schooner named "The Farmer." He also had a large store adjoining the present building, which has since been removed. Here the farmers would bring in loads of cord wood and exchange it for groceries to supply their family needs, and the schooner would transport the wood to New York, and return with groceries to supply the store. In addition to this he operated a large gristmill, which was situated across the road and south of the present dock. As it was a

Oldest known photograph of the Steuben House, about 1890. Notice the store wing and the three dormers, *c. 1880–90. (Artifact in the Bergen County Historical Society Collections, photo by Deborah Powell)*

tide water mill it could only be operated when the tide had fallen a couple of feet, and often the solemn stillness of the night would suddenly be broken by the clatter of "Take it, Bob. Take it, Bob—it's better than tea." About 1852 the mill was totally destroyed by fire, and all that remains today (that is to say, in 1909) are a few burned piles and the iron driving shaft which projects above high water; the lower end of the shaft to which the wheel is attached, is deeply embedded in the sand.

Captain David A. Zobriskie and Jane Anderson married (1812–1880) on March 5, 1835. Their four sons and a daughter were born and reared in the family homestead.

The 1860 census for New Bridge included David A. Zobriskie, fifty years old, a farmer; his wife, Jane, forty-seven years old; son David A. Zobriskie (generally known by his middle name of Anderson), twenty-two years old and "Master of Schooner"; daughter Christina, fourteen years old; and son John, eleven years old. Hannah (Durie) Zobriskie, nineteen years old, and Mary Casey, a "Domestic", also resided there. Another part of the dwelling, perhaps the south end including the store wing, seems to have been occupied by the family of Ezra Smith, a merchant, forty-eight years old, a native of Ridgefield, Connecticut. His wife Emma was born in New York City. This household also included Emma, twenty-two years old; her husband, Jacob Demarest, thirty years old and master of a schooner; daughter

144

Mary Demarest, three years old; daughter Emma, nine months old; Eynia (spelling unsure) Bogert, a three-year-old boy born in New York City; and Gilbert Conklin, forty-seven years old, a boatman. Life at New Bridge still centered around the river.

D. Anderson Zobriskie was born April 4, 1837. He married Hannah Durie (born October 3, 1836) on July 7, 1859. They had three sons and two daughters. For many years, Capt. D. Anderson Zobriskie commanded schooners, and in later years, the tug boat *Wesley Stoney*, on the Hackensack River.

By 1880, widower David A. Zobriskie, then seventy-one years of age, resided with his son D. Anderson Zobriskie, forty-three years of age, in Anderson's residence at the intersection of Hackensack Avenue and Main Street with family in a newer house. D. Anderson Zobriskie acquired title to the old family homestead at a sheriff's sale on October 7, 1891. He removed the store wing, the so-called Trading Post, located at the south-end of the house, shortly afterwards.

By 1895, the household included only D. Anderson Zobriskie and his daughters, Madgdelena (born August 1868) and Jennie (born May 1874). That same year on July 13, 1895, three people were killed and houses on Main Street were demolished by the Cherry Hill Tornado, but the Steuben House was unscathed.

D. Anderson Zobriskie died May 27, 1907, at seventy years of age, bequeathing his estate to his daughter Magdelena. On October 1, 1909, Magdalena Zobriskie of New Barbadoes Township sold a tract in Riverside Borough, part of the Anderson Zabriskie estate at North Hackensack, comprising thirty acres of land including the old Baron Steuben house facing the bridge, to Charles W. Bell of New Barbadoes Township. Mr. Bell, a former president of the Common Council of Dayton, Ohio,

Looking west from along the river from Brett Park, Teaneck. Horses and wagon crossing on the 1889 bridge. Notice the two barns just north of the Steuben House. Three men and two children standing on the bridge bumpers, the Pell-Zabriskie House on the hill in the distance, obscured by bridge. (*Bergen County Historical Society Collections*)

Capt. D. Anderson Zabriskie is pictured in front of his well-maintained Steuben House after the store wing (1891) is removed. Notice the four dormers; later photographs show three. He died May 27, 1907. The boy is not named. (*Bergen County Historical Society Collections*)

was a businessman who moved to Hackensack and built a home on West Anderson Street in 1906. According to a report in *The Hackensack Republican* on October 7, 1909, "It is the purpose of Mr. Bell to build on the property a large mill for the manufacture of cardboard." A large sum of money was to be invested and the enterprise will be of great importance, especially to that vicinity. The property acquired by Mr. Bell has an important water front, and plans are already prepared for running in a spur from the New Jersey and New York railroad so as to give direct freight facilities. Mr. Bell was familiar with the business, having acted as receiver for a similar plant at Bogota and placed it upon a paying basis.

In May 1911, Mayor Charles W. Bell of Hackensack transferred his interest in the 50-acre tract at North Hackensack (on which it was proclaimed that a large paper mill would be erected) to the American Ink Company. The Ink Factory, a small brick structure, was still standing near the intersection of Hackensack Avenue and Main Street as recently as 1952.

In 1916, the old Zobriskie estate at New Bridge was sold to the Veronica Realty Corporation (formerly the Veronica Ink Company) of New York. In 1919, it was sold again to Mrs. Hanna L. Willson, of Manhattan, William Randolph Hearst's mother-in-law. Later that year, she died September 14, 1919. Millicent V. Hearst and her father, George L. Willson, renounced their rights and the property passed to her sister, Anita Irwin, wife of Walter W. Irwin, of Manhattan. On May 29, 1929, William Randolph and Millicent Hearst and her father, George L. Willson, conveyed all their real estate at New Bridge to Anita Irwin.

8

Saving a Historic Site

Our journey begins with the Sesquicentennial of American Independence (1776–1926) and the accompanying surge in interest in Revolutionary War sites. Few surviving relics of the American Revolution in New Jersey were more intriguing or deserving of preservation that the old Baron Steuben House in River Edge, a cynosure of Jersey Dutch architecture, steeped in associations with the great American struggle for self-government. Here, Washington had headquartered for ten days in September 1780. This was New Jersey's gift to the German baron who had trained the first American army. Here was an American battleground certainly worthy of preservation, but all was not well. In 1923, its owners had leased the old stone mansion for a tea room, serving the touring car trade out of New York City and its suburbs. To accommodate the restaurant, an interior stone wall and chimney, including a jamless Dutch fireplace, were removed to turn two parlors into one large room. This poorly conceived renovation threatened the very integrity of the structure, weakening the roof and threatening an invasion of the elements. What could and should be done?

In June 1920, the Women's Auxiliary of the Bergen County Historical Society toured the Steuben House, reporting that "in spite of its fall from its past estate, has many interesting features still to be seen." The group returned on June 11, 1921, hosting local chapters of the Daughters of the American Revolution. They had some momentum; the Society created a list of Historic Places that included the "Baron Steuben House at New Bridge" in 1905. They raised funds for the base for General Poor's statue in Hackensack (1904), had seventeen members on the executive board for the Fort Lee monument (1908), helped make plans for the Camp Merritt obelisk monument and dedication (1919), marked the Lutheran Church location at New Bridge (1920), and participated in the dedication of the Liberty Pole (1921).

On January 26, 1926, Bergen County's Senator William B. Mackay, Jr., introduced a bill to preserve the Baron von Steuben House in River Edge under auspices of the

The Bergen County Historical Society and Daughters of the American Revolution, William Paterson Chapter, visit the Steuben House in 1921. Also pictured are John Schwarzman and family, tenants of the house. (*Bergen County Historical Society Collections*)

State of New Jersey, saying, "this so-called Steuben House is a place of national significance dear to the heart of every Jerseyman who wishes it to be preserved." Without a single dissenting vote, the legislature passed a bill (Chapter 15, Public Laws of 1926) on Washington's birthday, 1926, to establish the three-member Steuben House Commission for the purpose of acquiring the old stone mansion and its grounds as a historic memorial. The commission was specifically charged with buying the property for a sum not to exceed $12,000 and invested with the full responsibility of caring for it and keeping it open for public inspection under the supervision of a caretaker. It was further empowered to permit such persons and societies as it saw fit to occupy the historic house, once it was acquired. The commissioners were to serve without compensation and were required to make an annual report to the Legislature.

Upon the recommendations of Senator Mackay and Judge George Van Buskirk, Governor A. Harry Moore appointed Joseph Kinzley, Jr., of Teaneck, former Republican sheriff of Bergen County, and Margaret Porch Hamilton of Leonia former Democratic Assembly candidate, to the Steuben House Commission. After conferring with Louis Auerbacher, Jr., of Newark, chairman of the legislative committee of the Steuben Society, he also named Dr. Robert F. Mautner, of Elizabeth as the commission's third member. The Steuben House Commission first met in Governor Moore's office on June 2, 1926.

From the outset, the Steuben House Commission experienced difficulty in locating Mrs. Walter W. Irwin, sister-in-law of William Randolph Hearst, the wealthy owner of the property who traveled extensively. It was originally hoped that the owners might deed the property to the state of New Jersey as a patriotic act. Instead, they demanded the full $12,000 appropriation for the house alone, even though the property on which it stood was then valued at $3,500 to $4,000 per acre. The owners repeatedly declined offers based upon valuations from qualified realtors and, after a year of fruitless negotiation, Joseph Kinzley, chairman of the Steuben House Commission, conferred with Governor Moore, and asked for an amendment to the law in February 1927 "so as to clothe the Commission with the necessary power to condemn if we are unable to acquire it by gift or purchase." The legislature accordingly granted use of the power of eminent domain to take the property. Condemnation proceedings were initiated to take title to the old house, as well as to the water frontage on the Hackensack River owned by Walter Benson. In May 1928, the Hearst interests decided to contest the condemnation proceedings. While the Steuben House Commission prevailed, it cost the astounding sum of $12,000 to acquire the house on only an acre of ground, frustrating efforts to preserve the surrounding battleground as a public historical park.

Acting through the Steuben House Commission, the State of New Jersey formally took title to the Steuben House and one acre on Sunday, October 21, 1928. Some 3,000 people attended the dedication of the Steuben House as a state historic site, including members of the Steuben Society, the Daughters of the American Revolution, the Boy Scouts, veterans' associations, and others. A large crowd applauded as Joseph Kinzley handed the deed to Assemblyman Ralph W. Candless, who represented the state. It was hoped that renovations of the interior and its surroundings might "establish an institution of some sort that may be maintained for generations to come."

In February 1929, former county sheriff Joseph Kinzley, Jr., chairman of the Steuben House Commission, asked for an appropriation of $100,000 to repair and restore the building, expecting that even a smaller amount could do much good. *The Bergen Evening Record* called attention to the fact:

> The Steuben house as it now stands and the property nearby are a disgrace to the state and an eyesore to the county. If the relic and its immediate surroundings are put into decent condition, enough will have been accomplished for the present.

The hope was that the historic landmark and acreage in the rear of the house could be developed into a public park. The *Record* concluded, "efforts to restore the old Steuben house and the adjoining grounds to some semblance of respectability will be approved by most Bergen County residents."

Bergen County assemblyman Robert W. Purdy supported the requested appropriation as the building was "in such dilapidated condition that it must be rebuilt in part to prevent it from collapsing." This dire state of affairs apparently came about by the removal of an interior stone wall in 1923, which included a jambless Dutch fireplace and chimney, set in the original end wall of the 1752 house, to open two parlors into one large tea room for restaurant purposes. Assemblywoman Agnes Jones, of Essex County, a leading member the joint appropriations committee, opposed the appropriation.

Ye Old Colonial 1752 House, Restaurant and Tea Room, New Bridge-North Hackensack N.J. (*Bergen County Historical Society Collections*)

On July 17, 1929, *The Bergen Evening Record* reported, "The State of New Jersey has never contributed a cent toward the upkeep of the Steuben House, a historical North Hackensack building of Revolutionary War times, despite the fact that two years ago it bought the old building for memorial purposes." The neglect continued despite chairman Joseph Kinzley's best efforts to secure a state appropriation. In an editorial published on August 7, 1929, and headlined "Steuben House a Disgrace," *The Bergen Evening Record* opined:

When the State of New Jersey purchased the old Steuben House for preservation as a historic relic, it assumed a moral obligation for its upkeep. This responsibility our lawmakers in Trenton shunned by refusing to appropriate the necessary money to make repairs to the building and keep the grounds in order. The structure, about which much romance lingers, stands today a disgrace to the state and a disgrace to the county. What are patriotic organizations of Bergen County going to do about it? Several methods are open. One of the best, it would seem, would be for the Bergen County Historical Society to demand action by Governor Larson. The Sons of the Revolution with hundreds of members in Bergen County, might join in a vigorous protest. It is a matter of concern to every patriotic resident. Are there not among the Boy Scout executives those who will lead the troops to the Steuben House, cut down the weeds and put the grounds in some semblance of decency? Who might better assume this task until the state is shaken from its lethargy? It should be a matter of county pride to see that the

Steuben House is given the care it deserves and we hope for prompt action to that end on the part of several organizations and individuals.

As the house that survived more of the American Revolution than any other in America was "nearing a state of ruin," the Frank J. Van Wetering Post, V. F. W., undertook the task of reclaiming the building, which had virtually disappeared behind an overgrowth of weeds. Hiram B. Blauvelt, president of the Bergen County Historical Society, joined the Veterans of Foreign Wars in denouncing state neglect. It was learned that Kinzley was only able to contribute funds on repairs and general maintenance. The Bergen County Historical Society therefore urged Governor Morgan F. Larson to appropriate $25,000 in a timely manner to preserve the ancient fabric of the building.

On August 7, 1929, the *Bergen Evening Record* asked, "Has the state senator from Bergen or any of the assemblymen moved to provide for the Steuben House through any of the customary legislative channels?" Its editor insisted, "Regrettable though it would be, the Steuben House might better be demolished than continue to stand, a disgrace to the state and to the county, and an eyesore to the community." Patriotic folks were urged to continue their care because "the old house is fast going and needs a thorough overhauling if it is to be held for posterity." The bake house was demolished in 1931.

Efforts to get appropriations to repair the house were pursued by officials including Assemblyman Joseph Marini, Assemblywoman Emma Peters and the Veterans' Legislative Committee.

With its partial collapse imminent, the Steuben House Commission pleaded for the ongoing care and proper management of the Steuben House with reliable annual appropriations. Proponents of the historic site, including *The Bergen Evening Record*, noted:

> Old Dutch Colonial architecture, even with no historic significance, is fast disappearing. This antique building, state property, rich in legends and history, a shrine in its possibilities, has been ignored year after year by those charged with the responsibility of making financial provisions for the care of the state's interests.

Assemblywoman Emma Peters, a member of the joint appropriations committee, succeeded in May 1931 in at least obtaining an appropriation for emergency repairs. She said, "I believe that the $10,000 will help pay for a much-needed new roof for the Steuben House and will also help to meet the claims of the caretaker of the property and cover some other bills." Consequently, the Steuben House Commission received bids on June 18, 1931, to make emergency repairs. Civil service certification was also filed for the purpose of appointing a resident caretaker once repairs were completed. Plans were made "to enlist all patriotic support for the further improvement of the building looking toward establishing the house as a landmark of Washington's retreat through New Jersey."

To historically refute contentions made that the Steuben House was not authentic and that it was not standing during the American Revolution, Miss Saretta Demarest, of Teaneck, compiled a groundbreaking study of the historic fabric of the old structure, proving its antiquity. She was the first to explain how the house "really contains a house within a house," noting the additions were built before the

American Revolution. She pointed out that rat-tail nails were used in hand-split laths, window frames and door frames, attesting to its mid-eighteenth-century construction. In contrast, mill sawn laths were used in a later addition. She also noted the Holland brick and old clay mortar, tempered with straw, used in the low circular vault in the rear of the house. "Holy Lord" or "H L" hinges, predating 1770, were also found throughout the house. She concluded, "the Steuben House is not only an historical site in connection with Baron Steuben, but also a Revolutionary War site, and an outstanding one in Bergen County."

In July 1931, Chairman Joseph Kinzley expressed gratitude to Assemblywoman Emma Peters for her success in securing the emergency appropriation. Architect Wesley Bessell thought the house could be made "fairly habitable for next winter, though our plans make no provision for heating or sanitation." Despite these limitations, he hoped to set aside a room or two as caretaker's quarters. Kinzley promised to make the most of the emergency funding:

Tearing down decaying structures, removing accumulated debris, rebuilding stone walls, fireplaces and chimneys is costly and restoration is far more expensive than new work. Even in making emergency repairs, the contractor was "directed to preserve all the old Holland brick, hand-hewn beams, stone block and old sills in the building. A beamed ceiling which has been re-plastered is reputed to be one of the finest examples of the Colonial period in this section. An antique step, which for many years was used in the demolished Hackensack Courthouse, has been secured for the entrance."

Saretta Demarest is pictured on the left with Katherine Moore (Kitty), Marnie Demarest, and Lillian (Shan) Moore. They may be standing on Teaneck Road in front of her sandstone house, the Brinkerhoff-Demarest Homestead. The kitchen and beehive oven were removed at a later date for a ten-foot road widening. (Photo from *Teaneck Public Library*)

We are hopeful that next year there will be an awakening of those responsible for state property to a realization of the fact that many people in New Jersey believe this fine old colonial structure is worth what it will cost to restore and preserve. History proves that in years past state officials gave it concern. The present day records show that all patriotic organizations are desirous of its proper restoration. Our hope is that the legislature of 1932 will definitively and properly consider its obligation to complete what it started when it purchased the old structure for preservation. It will be a fitting monument to the memory of the man who, out of despair at Valley Forge, created the soldiery which enabled Washington to be the victor at Yorktown.[1]

Requests for rooms from the Steuben Society, the Bergen County Historical Society and the Daughters of the American Revolution were filed for future consideration. Meanwhile, large numbers of visitors were "making special trips to see it almost every day from all parts of the state."

If the Steuben House at New Bridge expressed an important link to the past and a salient connection to the land and a vanishing way of life, then it was being politely ignored.

Facing difficult economic times and the need to more efficiently organize its governmental functions, the New Jersey legislature formed a Historic Sites Commission in the Department of Conservation and Development in 1931 to administer the State's expanding historic sites program and to consolidate the powers previously exercised by independent commissions supervising State-owned historic parks and landmarks. Accordingly, the Steuben House Commission was dissolved in February 1932, its responsibilities passed to the Historic Sites Commission. In consequence of the shift of decision-making to Trenton, "local interest faded and the interior (of the Steuben House) was never completed. The Historical Society, the various orders of Revolutionary origin did not get a permanent meeting place. The Steuben Societies failed in securing its 'place in the sun' of New Jersey's scheme of things." In 1934, the Historic American Buildings Survey arrived to prepare detailed measured drawings of the house. With these completed, Francis Koehler, president of the Bergen County Historical Society, again urged a restoration of the Revolutionary War landmark.

The Bergen County Historical Society held its first program at the Steuben House on Constitution Day in September 1935, when caretaker Mrs. Gordon Brown Kynoch escorted members through the rooms. In August 1937, former county sheriff and assemblyman Joseph Kinzley, Jr., began to annunciate a plan to feature the Steuben House as the centerpiece of a historic park on the shoreline of an inland lake to be created by damming the Hackensack River.

He lamented the passing of such visionaries as Dr. Maximillen R. Brinkmann, a Hackensack dentist, who, while a member of the city's governing body, sought to secure title to most of Hackensack's river shoreline for park purposes. Kinzley also noted congressman and later county prosecutor Archibald Chapman Hart, who originally proposed a dam and locks at Little Ferry and later a dam at Anderson Street in Hackensack, in hopes of redeeming a once beautiful and abundant river from suburban waste. He remarked:

Francis C. Koehler, BCHS President 1931–1944. (*Bergen County Historical Society Collections*)

Over the years clear minded men, with thoughts of future and forlorn hopes of the present, have labored with mediocracy in governmental place of municipality and county. They have passed out of life but the torch they flung still flares. It will be seized by oncoming youth.... When more of the human energy seen in New York comes into this delightful section of the Garden State the lethargy of present day officialdom will be replaced by surging alertness. Stupid lack of initiative and co-operation will be replaced by unselfish action. 'Hope springs eternal in the human breast' and still prevails despite the weakness of the human equation. There is still hope of salvaging the Hackensack River.

Overlooking the smelly wasteland that then comprised the riverfront and bordering wetlands, he speculated:

Our on-coming young folks of today with less incentive to pile up personal possessions, with true valuation of leisure hours, with appreciation of the fact that meadow lands are valueless in a metropolitan area will build the dam, sewer the terrain above and create home sites along the shores of a beautiful sanitary lake.

On October 30, 1937, the Historic Sites Commission dedicated a bronze roadside marker and a bronze wall plaque at the Steuben House. At this time, Louis Sherwood, of the Historic Sites Commission, forecast an impending restoration of the house by the Works Progress Administration (WPA). At this date, two hills or embankments of dirt remained on each side of the river, marking the proposed location of a bridge across the Hackensack River, which was "abandoned in the borning..." Yet the need to replace the antiquated old swing bridge (1889) would have to be solved sooner or later.

On June 20, 1938, a crew of WPA workmen began a $20,000 renovation of the Steuben House with the New Jersey Historic Sites Commission contributing $3,000 and the WPA supplying $15,800 worth of labor. A new oil heating system, a bath, and lavatory were installed. Original floorboards of the ground level were removed and the floor level raised about 6 inches; new random-oak flooring was installed in the front rooms over concrete pads poured between the original floor joists. In the front rooms on the first floor, original plaster walls and ceilings were either removed or concealed as a sand-finish plaster was applied over expanded metal lath. A system of subterranean concrete conduits (called French drains) were installed to drain the grounds and the New Jersey Highway Department built an 18-inch driveway around the house (removed in 2001). A mid-nineteenth-century frame kitchen wing was torn off the southwest corner of the building. Lastly, whitewash coating the east and south elevations of the house was sandblasted and a temporary concrete porch pad was laid in front.

On October 14, 1938, Thomas Marple, assistant director of the Historic Sites Commission, invited the Bergen County Historical Society to occupy the restored Steuben House as their museum headquarters. The Society accepted on October 20, 1938. The Hackensack Boys Workshop of the National Youth Administration set about splitting rails and posts from condemned chestnut telephone poles to fence the Steuben House property on August 19, 1939. The renovated house was formally dedicated on September 23, 1939. Thomas Marple represented the state. A red oak, the official state tree, was planted near the northeast corner of the front porch, where it remains to this day.

The house was not restored in 1938–39 as a period home or as an artifact of its time, but rather the state converted its front rooms into a museum for showcases to display artifacts with an office and library on a part of the second floor in the rear, and four small rooms (originally two upstairs and two downstairs) for a caretaker's residence. The Society began meeting in the historic homestead in 1940. The museum regularly opened between 10 a.m. and 4.30 p.m. from Tuesday through Saturday. Admission was free and 3,000 schoolchildren visited during the first year.

Route 4 was built to connect the newly opened George Washington Bridge and Paterson as part of the original state highway system, spurring development on its periphery. Yet although the population of River Edge doubled between 1930 and 1940, 25 percent of the borough remained farm acreage when the Steuben House opened as a public museum on September 23, 1939. The dedication of the Steuben House "as a historical shrine and home of the Bergen County Historical Society" began a two-week celebration of the tercentenary of the settlement of the Hackensack valley. Some 300 people attended the dedication ceremony, which featured Francis C. Koehler, president of the Bergen County Historical Society, and Thomas Marples, director of the State Historic Sites Commission. According to newspaper accounts, Francis Koehler "spoke of the conversion of the building into a historical museum as the realization of a boyhood dream." Thomas Marples "declared that the Steuben House was one of the most interesting and important historical sites the State had acquired." The program also "included singing by three

Indians, who are in the vicinity in connection with the filming of a motion picture dealing with the history of a vanished New Jersey tribe." They were Chief Red Wing, a Cherokee; Chief Blow Snake, a Winnipeg; and Princess Naomi, a Sioux. It was noted at the time that "many ranking officers on both sides of the (Revolutionary) war were quartered at the Steuben House, including George Washington when in 1776 he led his forces in a retreat from Fort Lee toward Trenton and again in 1780 when his army occupied the village." Others included Light Horse Harry Lee, Mad Anthony Wayne, Lord Cornwallis, Sir Charles Grey, and Sir John Baird in 1778. General Lee started his expedition against Paulus Hook from the mansion.

Several hundred guests attended a reception and tea held in celebration of Washington's birthday in 1940. A bus and twenty-five cars brought members of the LeRoy S. Mead Post of the American Legion from Closter. Hostesses included Mrs. Elmer Blauvelt, Lida Bellis and Mrs. Isaac D. Demarest of Oradell; and Mrs. Cornelius V. R. Bogert of Bogota; Saretta Demarest and Mrs. Harry Bennett of Teaneck; Mrs. John M. Meyers of Woodcliff Lake; Mrs. Koehler, Mrs. Terhune and Mrs. Theodore Romaine of Hackensack; and Mrs. J. Pell Zabriskie of River Edge. In November 1941, plans for the construction of a large colonial barn on the property adjoining the Steuben House to display agricultural implements were discussed at the Society's semi-annual meeting on November 6, 1941, prompted by the donation of $50 from the Rutherford and Bergenfield Rotary Clubs towards the cost. Koehler noted that three thousand visitors came to the Steuben house during the previous year.

Some 200 citizens attended a combined celebration of American Independence Day and a naturalization ceremony at the Steuben House on July 4, 1942. Sponsored by several Hackensack civic organizations, three trucks conveyed Dr. Paul G. Mack's twenty-piece band and twenty new citizens from the Broadway school in Hackensack to the Steuben House. A highlight of the event was a minuet and Virginia reel danced by Josephine Criscione, Clorinda Di Lonado, Frances Ferraro, Anna Malatino, Velma Post, Isabel Romanelli, Mary Ruffino, Anna Sanzari, and Jeanne Williams.

Although the Zabriskie-Steuben House was regarded as "one of the most significant shrines in the State," an automobile junkyard to the west was expanding with the potential to reach the very back door of the house. Fires started in wrecked cars menaced the historic building several times. In April 1941, Koehler appealed for support for a bill that would authorize the Commission on Historic Sites to acquire eight acres adjoining the Baron von Steuben House, including some shore frontage, at a cost not exceeding $3,000 for a park. He had an option on it at the quoted price, expiring July 31, 1941. The land in question belonged to Mrs. Phoebe Hearst, mother of William Randolph Hearst, and was appraised at $1,100. It had been acquired many years earlier for industrial purposes. The extra property was needed partly for parking at the Steuben House as visitors to the house were then required to park along narrow New Bridge Road, creating a bottleneck. Construction of a large development on River Road in New Milford made it increasingly dangerous to park along the busy road approaches to the old bridge. Consequently, Koehler, Kinzley and Assemblyman Herbert F. Meyers introduced a bill to authorize the Commission on Historic Sites to acquire nearly 8 acres adjoining the Steuben House but the effort failed.

Above: Crowds visit the Steuben House. (*Bergen County Historical Society Collections*)

Right: William Randolph Hearst Interests say the offer of $12,000 was not enough in 1928 for the Steuben House and 1 acre. (*Bergen County Historical Society Collections*)

STEUBEN HOUSE AT NORTH HACKENSACK TO BE COURT ISSUE

Hearst Interests Contend That $12,000 Offered By State Is Not Enough for the Land Involved.

may 1928

The William Randolph Hearst interests will contest the condemnation proceedings of the North Hackensack property, the Steuben House, by the State of New Jersey through the Steuben commission.

Lawyer Louis Auerbacher, for the commission, has tendered offers based on valuations of real estate men. These have been declined by Mrs. Irwin's legal representative who contends that New Jersey by its legislative enactment placed an historic value of $12,000 on the old house with no reference to land, further than "a plot."

Members of the commission decided that the old building itself had little intrinsic value and that an acre of the property was all that could be consistently considered.

COURT ACTION RESULTS.

So a long drawn out court action is anticipated, Judge Parker having been petitioned to apoint a condemnation commission and consented to do so.

It may be decided by the Steuben commission to take possession as soon as legal action is started, with the hope that the celebration of Baron Steuben's birthday this year may be celebrated by the Steuben societies on the site of the old house at New Bridge.

If this is done it will be a Mecca for many pilgrimages next September.

As to the significance of the ground, Koehler notes, "History seldom records the fact that the crossing of the Delaware in December 1776 was made possible by the safe crossing of the Hackensack a month previous." He contended Washington's retreat across the New Bridge on November 20, 1776, was a turning point since "the Revolutionary War was decided at the location on the Hackensack River rather than at the crossing of the Delaware a month later in 1776." Ironically, it would be another sixty-four years before the auto salvage yard would be acquired.

On July 4, 1942, a new steel flagpole was dedicated in the backyard of the Steuben House. The War of 1812 cannon named "Old Bergen" was permanently relocated to a concrete mount in front of the Steuben House (the cannon was stolen in 1978). In 1944, a sandstone well and well sweep were constructed in the backyard (removed in 1983).

Mrs. Olga Atkins, supervisor of the Historic Sites Section, decided after an initial inspection of the property in 1950 that the well and four-seat outhouse should be restored. The state subsequently dismantled the outhouse for its preservation and reconstruction.

The Bergen County Historical Society took the initiative and responded to the threat of encroachment of the expanding auto salvage yard and the lack of even parking facilities by purchasing the adjacent 7.3 acres to the west of the Steuben House. Acting in trust for the Bergen County Historical Society, David D. Bellis acquired the property on April 18, 1944, thereby saving a large portion of the Revolutionary War battleground. The Society vigorously contested the county's revived plans to build a new river crossing adjacent to the Steuben House in 1947. The right of way for the approaching roadway on the west side of the river is still evident on the tax map, showing the road corridor as it would have crossed immediately south of the Steuben House to the river's edge.

The State Historic Sites Commission's functions and properties were transferred to the Division of Forestry, Geology, Parks, and Historic Sites in 1945. Twenty historic sites, either partially or wholly supported by the State, were placed under the Division's administrative jurisdiction and a Bureau of Historic Sites was created for their management and care. In the re-organization of State government following the adoption of the new State Constitution in 1947, "Historic Sites" was ominously dropped from the Division's title. The Division was absorbed into a Division of Planning and Development, Department of Conservation, and Economic Development. In 1961, the name was changed to the Division of Resource Development.

The population of River Edge tripled between 1940 and 1950, increasing from three to nine thousand. Within this time frame, the Steuben House, sitting upon an acre of ground, quickly lost the open surroundings of centuries past. Kiddie Wonderlands, an amusement park, opened on the largely wooded grounds of the old ink factory between Main Street and Cole's Brook. The auto salvage yard, an eyesore for decades, occupied the northeast corner of the intersection of Hackensack Avenue and Main Street. The slatted chain-link fence and piled-up cars obscured the historic site for years.

The building boom of the post-war years and a swelling population gave urgency to replacing the antiquated iron 1889 swing bridge across the river connecting River

Above: Photograph taken when members of the BCHS and the Daughters of the American Revolution visit in 1921. The group poses by the Steuben House four-seater outhouse. (*Bergen County Historical Society Collections*)

Right: James Bellis, Sr. and James Bellis, Jr., by the Westervelt-Thomas barn. The Blauvelt-Demarest Foundation funded its restoration in 2014. The Bellis family has been supportive of the musem site beginning in the 1940s. (*photo by Deborah Powell*)

Kiddie Wonderlands, located where the apartments are on Main Street, River Edge. It operated in the 1950s. (*Bergen County Historical Society Collections*)

Edge, Teaneck and New Milford. In 1949, the Bergen County Freeholders attempted unsuccessfully to secure federal aid to build a new bridge across the Hackensack River above the historic crossing at New Bridge to safely accommodate the growing flow of traffic. To redirect the location of the proposed new span away from the dooryard of the Steuben House, the Bergen County Historical Society deeded a right of way, 60 feet wide, with 10-foot slope rights, across its property for $1 on January 13, 1953, to provide for an extension of Hackensack Avenue northeast from the intersection of Main Street in River Edge to the site of a proposed new bridge. In December 1953, the Bergen County Board of Freeholders announced plans to replace the narrow iron bridge with a modern span as part of a proposed military highway to connect Hackensack and Englewood. County engineer Roscoe P. McClave designed a new structure that would cross the river about 300 feet north of the old New Bridge, permitting an extension of Hackensack Avenue in River Edge to connect with Brookside Avenue in New Milford, just beyond Roosevelt Avenue, thus straightening out what was described as "perhaps the most crooked overland route in Bergen County" (*Bergen Evening Record*, December 13, 1954).

The new roadway and bridge, projected to cost $500,000, was declared a military route to gain federal dollars. On November 11, 1954, the Freeholders applied to the Federal Bureau of Public Roads for approximately $250,000 in federal aid for the project. The new bridge was designed 44 feet wide and 250 feet in length.

In comparison, the old iron swing bridge was 20 feet wide and 100 feet long. A strike delayed the arrival of steel needed for construction of the new fixed-span bridge, which finally opened in June 1956. The bridge alone cost $218,000. The Army Corps of Engineers considered the old bridge an impediment to navigation and tried to make its removal a permit requirement for erection of its replacement. The Woman's Club of Bergen County joined the Bergen County Historical Society in a call to preserve the 1889 swing bridge across the Hackensack River. Colonel John T. O'Neill, of the Army Corps of Engineers, yielded to Freeholder Walter M. Neill, who promised that the County of Bergen would henceforth maintain the old bridge, if it were spared. The bridge is still an important pedestrian and commuter crossing for area residents in River Edge, Hackensack, New Milford, Teaneck, and Bergenfield.

Once the location of the new bridge and its approaches was settled, plans developed for a historical park centering upon the Steuben House. In 1954–56, the Demarest Memorial Foundation (now the Blauvelt-Demarest Foundation) painstakingly disassembled the Demarest House on its original site, where the Elks Club now stands behind the present New Milford Borough Hall at 1 Patrolman Ray Woods Lane, and reconstructed it on Main Street, River Edge, directly behind the Steuben House, taking a ninety-nine-year lease for 2,800 square feet from the Bergen County Historical Society. The Red Barn (an 1889 English-style dairy barn or "cow house," also known as the Westervelt-Thomas Barn) was moved from Ridgewood Road, Washington Township and reconstructed in its present location behind the Steuben House in November 1954. The Old Red Barn featured an assemblage of ancient farming implements, old sleighs, a picnic wagon or runabout, harness and saddles. Farming implements included a wooden shovel found in the 1776 House in Tappan, NY; yokes for oxen, sheep, and pigs; a plowshare carved from the crutch of a tree; a broom-making machine; a corn-shucker; a wheat separator; an automatic seeding machine (1864); a cobbler bench; axes; saws; traps; a wagon jack; and even an old divining rod. Parking was available south of the Steuben House on the Society's property. The Westervelt-Thomas Barn was opened to the public on October 14, 1956.

Drainage remained a problem on the grounds, but construction of embankments to carry the roadways to the new bridge aggravated the problem. When the County decided to extend Hackensack Avenue beyond its intersection with Main Street to a new river crossing north of the Steuben House, a drainage system was laid in the abandoned right of way for the originally proposed route, straightening Main Street in River Edge, immediately south of the Steuben House. The Bergen County Historical Society granted a drainage easement, 10 feet wide, across its property, to the County of Bergen on July 28, 1955, together with all cross basins, catch basins and future storm-water drains. Using earth from the embankment built for this abandoned bridge approach, 18–22 inches of fill was spread around the Steuben House, helping considerably to raise the grade and to alleviate tidal flooding. The County installed a new drainage pipe with a "tidal flap" on its outlet, thus allowing run-off from storm drains to empty into the Hackensack River. As the septic tank in the backyard of the Steuben House was subject to recurrent back filling by high tides, repairs were continually made to address the problem. On November 17,

Demarest House shown during reconstruction behind the Steuben House. William Demarest and Hiram B. Blauvelt, BCHS president, are pictured, *c.* 1955–56. (*Bergen County Historical Society Collections*)

1954, a contract for the installation of a new 500-gallon septic tank, Orangeburg leach lines, and gravel beds was awarded. While digging percolation test holes, old brickwork was discovered along the north driveway on the edge of the marsh, about thirty feet from the northwest corner of the Steuben House, revealing the location of a former out building.

The Bureau of Architecture, Department of the Treasury, put out specifications for restoration of the roof framing, structural reinforcement, and roof repairs to the Steuben House in March 1955. Most original roof trusses were consequently removed and replaced with circular-sawn oak timbers; a new wooden shingle roof was installed; the first floor was painted; electrical repairs were made; fixtures added; a kitchen installed; and sewage disposal upgraded. Sadly, the old roof trusses were replaced to raise headroom in the garret level, enabling the space to be used for exhibits. The carpenters found it impossible to cut the new oak for mortise and tenon work, so most trusses are nailed together with fake pegs inserted in auger-holes. In October 1955, while the replacement of the roof rafters was progressing, architect Lawrence Moon decided at the urging of the Bergen County Historical Society not to replace the rafters and other timbers at the south end of the house in order to preserve some of the original work and to save the small bedroom. The garret was thus opened up (by the removal of old board partitions) in the summer of 1956 to make a 25 feet by 50 feet space for exhibits that had been previously displayed downstairs in the large museum room. The large room downstairs was then furnished in a more homelike setting. The entrance was moved to the front porch and the Dwelling-Room converted from an entry and office to a "Colonial kitchen." There were 4,536 visitors to the house in 1955.

Attendance at the Zabriskie-Steuben House reached 6,624 in 1956, including three thousand school children from much of Bergen County. Visitors came from almost every state and foreign visitors arrived from England, Germany, Canada, France, Holland, Denmark, Netherlands, and Italy. On December 4, 1956, the Distaff Committee of the Bergen County Historical Society was organized "to assist in preservation and display of such valuable treasures and to aid in securing additions to the Society's collection of Americana." The Society's collections were begun in 1902 when the organization was founded.

On January 13, 1959, the Bergen County Historical Society deeded part of its lands, just south of the house, to the State of New Jersey, acting through the Division of Planning and Development in the Department of Conservation and Economic Development, to provide the first parking lot for the Steuben House, adjacent to its south gable end. The Maintenance Division of the State Highway Department completed construction of the parking area in May 1960. The project also included installation of a brick walk with a "basket-weave pattern" on a 4-inch concrete base, leading from the new parking lot to the south end of the Steuben House. In July 2001, a portion of this walkway was re-laid to form a ramp to the level of the new wooden porch.

Bit by bit, the Zabriskie farm atop Cherry Hill in River Edge, with its resplendent views of the Hackensack valley and the historic crossing at New Bridge, was sold off, starting with the property fronting Main Street at the foot of the hill, where builder Ercole Tamburelli tore down eight rented homes along Kinderkamack Road and Main Street and constructed the Huffman and Boyle store and an A & P store. J. Pell Zabriskie next sold the farm surrounding the old homestead, where Tamburelli built River Edge Gardens, Hillcrest Manor and Yolanda Court, which, upon completion, housed 500 families or an estimated 1,500 residents. In 1949, J. Pell Zabriskie sold his antique homestead atop Cherry Hill, which was soon torn down to make way for three-story garden apartments. The departing owner and occupant, who looked forward to residing in one of the new garden apartments, told how his grandfather John C. Zabriskie had purchased the property in 1849 from Abraham Van Buskirk.

The lowland along the river succumbed to suburban development. After the old iron swing bridge was replaced by a fixed concrete-and-steel span on an extension of Hackensack Avenue to New Bridge Road, the way was laid for intensive development of what had long been a quiet backwater hamlet. Bloomingdales was built on the north side of Route 4 in Hackensack in 1959, forming the core of what would later become the Riverside Square Mall. The New Bridge Inn, across the river from the Steuben House, built in 1823, burned on May 30, 1964.

Bergen County freeholder D. Bennett Mazur (D), of Fort Lee, an avid historian, initiated a million-dollar project, to be financed through a 20-year bond issue, in October 1967, to build a Hall of History, using a portion of the Bergen County Historical Society's land and purchasing the adjacent auto junkyard, whereon the County would put up a building to display the collections of the Bergen County Historical Society and the Bergen Community Museum (which also was looking for a home to house its growing collections). The central block of the proposed Hall of History was to feature a 200-seat auditorium, office space, a reception area, conference room and a library and archives. Exhibits would be displayed in two

A&P supermarket at the corner of Main Street and Kinderkamack Road. Brower Hill in background. (*Photo by Elizabeth Benedict Timpson née Zobriskie, Bergen County Historical Society Collections*)

River Edge Gardens, apartments being built before the demolition of the J. Pell Zabriskie House. (*Photo by Elizabeth Benedict Timpson née Zobriskie, Bergen County Historical Society Collections*)

New Bridge Inn, before it burned down in 1964, sketch by BCHS member Lewis Blackwell. (*Bergen County Historical Society Collections*)

symmetrical lateral wings, one intended for the Bergen County Historical Society and the other for the Bergen Community Museum. Plans also included a 200-car parking lot, accessible from New Bridge Road. Albert L. Gazzola, president of the Bergen Community Museum, endorsed the project and announced the Community Museum was prepared to spend $30,000 to purchase and prepare artifacts and exhibits to add to what it already possessed. On the opposite side of the river, the Township of Teaneck acquired 10.54 acres of land through the Federal Open Space and New Jersey Green Acres programs in 1968–69. Once the site of Rekow's truck farm and several summer bungalows composing Benson's Campground, the new parkland was named to honor Clarence W. Brett, a former member of the Teaneck Planning Board.

Along partisan lines, a Democratic resolution to create an advisory committee to study the proposed Hall of History passed the Board of Chosen Freeholders, six to three. The following individuals were then named: T. Robert Krammer of Saddle River, president of the Bergen County Historical Society; Dr. Byron C. Lambert, dean of Fairleigh Dickinson University's Rutherford campus and a member of the board of the Bergen Community Museum; Ridgewood attorney Albert B. Dearden, a trustee of the Historical Society; Richard Adinare of Waldwick, an assistant professor of political science and history at Seton Hall University; and Albert L. Gazzola, of Rivervale, president of the Bergen Community Museum. *The Bergen Evening Record* believed the project deserved "thoughtful discussion:"

D. Bennett Mazur, taken at the time of the Campbell-Christie House move to BCHS property in River Edge. (*Bergen County Historical Society Collections*)

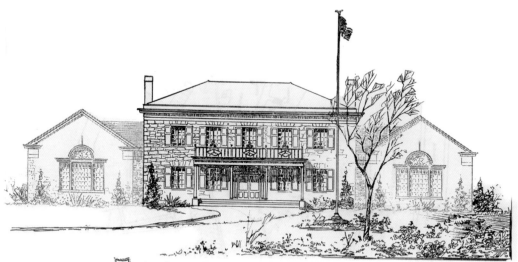

Artists' concept of initial building of Historical Museum with shaded areas indicating future additions. Architecture and design reflect early colonial and Bergen County culture.

The Bergen County Historical Society had plans for a Hall History at New Bridge. The plans included facilities to house collections. (*Bergen County Historical Society Collections*)

There are good reasons for the County to preserve reminders of its historical past in a central location. Rapidly increasing population creates the illusion that everything in this area is new or almost new, but scattered through the older towns are buildings that have plainly stood for centuries, and it would be good if the way of life they represent could be recalled by exhibits and artifacts and perhaps meetings of such groups as the Community Museum.

Republican freeholders, however, balked at bonding for the expected cost, saying the project should be located on land the county already owned rather than on property it would have to purchase; they recommended using Overpeck Creek Park in Leonia. Noting its presentation came only three weeks before a general election, they denounced what they considered a "hasty and foolish plan, in light of already huge county spending increases." Republican freeholder Henry L. Hoebel, of Fort Lee, suggested the whole idea was just an expensive way of getting rid of a junkyard. Freeholder D. Bennett Mazur countered, saying the county was already twenty-five years late in building such a facility and noting the historic battleground surrounding the Steuben House at New Bridge made the site the most appropriate location.

At their meeting on February 27, 1968, freeholder director William J. Dorgan (R) said the proposal would have to be scaled down considerably from former freeholder D. Bennett Mazur's original million-dollar plan, suggesting, "We're talking in the vicinity of one-half to two-thirds that price." The Bergen County Historical Society, which originally offered to sell 3.5 acres of its land, where the Campbell-Christie House now stands, to the county for $45,000, then dropped its offering price to

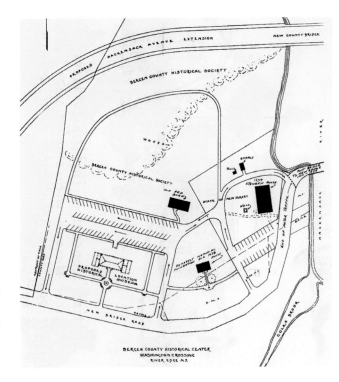

The Bergen County Historical Society had plans for a Hall History at New Bridge calling it "Washington Crossing." (*Bergen County Historical Society Collections*)

$25,000, considerably lower than the value of surrounding property. The adjoining 2.2-acre auto junkyard was offered for sale to the county for $90,000. In the end, the county offered the old County Poor House on Ridgewood Avenue in Paramus, which was converted to a museum in 1969, but the Society withdrew its participation when the county wanted the Society's artifact collection turned over to the county.

In December 1967, archeologist Roland Robbins excavated a section of the tidal mill wharf in front of the Steuben House, hoping to discover evidence of what the eighteenth-century dock looked like. Fighting the tides and high-water table, he suggested there had been at least three different boat landings on three different levels, one succeeding the next as business expanded. The dig retrieved hundreds of artifacts, including a shoe sole and a fragment of pig iron stamped LON "Long Pond." Using plans developed by Harry Dobson, the Bergen County Historical Society awarded a contract in July 1968 to spread topsoil, grade, and seed with grass, a strip of their land, 50 feet wide, extending from the auto-salvage yard to the Demarest House. The first floor of the Steuben House was changed into a "colonial" house museum and the Victorian items placed in storage.

As envisioned, Lake Hackensack would have been a 200-acre freshwater lake, extending 7.1 miles from the Oradell dam to a concrete dam, rising 10 feet above sea level, to be built across the Hackensack River between Hackensack and Bogota at a point lying between the Midtown and Susquehanna Railroad bridges. The river bed between these two dams would have been dredged from its current depth of 3–6 feet to a depth of 20 feet and the water maintained at three feet above sea level, the existing mean high-tide mark. What planners intended to create was a continuous recreation system on about 527 acres of the proposed lake shoreline, thereby linking a variety of recreational, cultural, and commercial attractions on what would have been the largest piece of open space in the heart of Bergen County. While boating and fishing would be allowed, other recreational uses, such as swimming, would have to wait until all sources of pollution—most notably the combined storm and sanitary sewers in the City of Hackensack—were eliminated.

Estimates of the engineering costs for Lake Hackensack reached as high as $10 million. The project also required acquisition of 51 acres in three separate parcels, including 33 acres in Hackensack, 11 acres in River Edge, and 9 acres in New Milford. The owners of the land required for the project in Hackensack included the Vornado Corporation, which operated the Two Guys discount chain; a family owning the land on which the Bloomingdales store on Route 4 stood; and George Levitin, who owned 12.5 acres sloping down to the river behind the Oritani Motel, where he had his office. Here the project ran into opposition; George Levitin opposed the project, calling instead for more housing, more shops and wider roads. He had already applied for County permission to build high-rise apartments on land already zoned for residential, commercial and office development. He also noted he had been offered $3.5 million for his property bordering the river. Donald L. Clark, executive director of the Bergen County Planning Board, however, insisted three independent appraisers had arrived at a figure of one million dollars for Levitin's property. At the same time, Donald L. Clark announced the County had expended about $221,000 on preliminary engineering studies and indicated that a portion of the land in River Edge, surrounding the Steuben House, would be preserved for its historic value and developed in time for the American Bicentennial (1976). Oscar Epstein of Teaneck chaired the Hackensack River Coordinating Committee, which had been established five years earlier by representatives of Oradell, New Milford, River Edge, Teaneck, Hackensack, and Bogota (the six towns that would border the proposed lake). As one can readily see today, it was the vision of residential, commercial, and office development that would succeed; Cole's Brook was straightened and Commerce Way developed as an industrial park. The Steuben Arms apartments were built on the south side of Main Street, River Edge, in 1967. Continental Plaza, comprising three office towers with an attached parking garage, was built in 1972 on the old driving range, west of Hackensack Avenue. In 1978, the Riverside Square Mall was built around Bloomingdales, less than a quarter mile south of the Steuben House. Shortly thereafter, the County of Bergen designed and built a riverside park, with public access from the rear of the parking garage of the new mall.

In April 1974, the firm of Miceli, Week & Kulik presented a Lake Hackensack shoreline plan to the Bergen County Board of Chosen Freeholders. Planner Luciano Miceli proposed construction of a historical "village" and extensive recreational facilities in Brett Park. His proposal envisioned a river front beach, bath house and snack bar, multi-use athletic fields, tennis courts, boat rentals and docks, foot paths, family picnic area, a "historical village," shops and village green, a restaurant, and parking for seventy-six cars. Old buildings were to be moved to the site, or antique reproductions built, on the flood plain in Brett Park, opposite the Steuben House. The plan called for "a unifying village motif ¼ to provide a compact yet appropriate setting for the buildings." Office rental space was to be offered as a partial adaptive reuse of these historic buildings. In May 1975, Teaneck's own park consultant, Robert B. Kinsey, concluded the proposed County projects "would constitute an over-development of the Brett Park site—an attempt to include many crowd-producing areas and facilities into a site not large enough to accommodate them." He further noted, "a substantial part of the total acreage does not lend itself to development for active (or even passive) recreational development." Left unsaid was the protection of a Revolutionary battleground, especially on the east side of the river in what is New Milford and Teaneck, which could have been damaged or lost in an ill-considered rush to develop a "historical" theme park.

Would Lake Hackensack have worsened flooding in the upper valley by maintaining the level of mean high-tide? Environmental concerns doomed the projected tidal barrier and freshwater lake and the plan lost its unifying purpose. Elements of the plan would haunt us into the present.

Across the river, the state of New Jersey was to more fully develop the museum potential of the Steuben House through a plan of extensive renovations and its grounds were to be screened from incompatible adjacent land uses. The state was also to acquire the junkyard at the west edge of the property, making possible a more attractive approach and to allow the removal of the existing road and parking lot, located immediately south of the house. Integral to the proposed park design, the Bergen County Historical Society made plans for a museum and Society headquarters building on the site where the Campbell-Christie House now stands. The County of Bergen also acquired marshland on the river's edge, north of Hackensack Avenue, where it planned to build an environmental center.

The County of Bergen and the Bergen County Historical Society cooperated to relocate the Campbell-Christie House from its original site at the intersection of River Road and Henley Avenue in New Milford to the Society's lands at New Bridge on September 27, 1977. The County leased the plot of ground that the house occupies from the Society, leasing the interior to the Society for its use. After extensive reconstruction, the Campbell-Christie House opened to the public in 1980. The original kitchen wing, damaged by fire, was not salvaged and reconstructed on the new site in River Edge.

Due to flood damage to the caretaker's living room and kitchen, located in the rear basement rooms of the Steuben House, the Division of Parks and Forestry asked the Bergen County Historical Society to remove their library collections from the northwest room. A new kitchen and living room were then installed in the rear rooms on the second floor in 1979, placing the caretaker's residence on one floor and above the reach of tidal flooding for the first time. Kevin Wright was employed as "caretaker" on October 31, 1981, and became the site's first professional Historic Preservation Specialist on July 18, 1984, a position he wrote the description for and was used as other state sites were professionalized. Our family resided in the Steuben House until February 1996. Our oldest child, Ivan, was two and a half years old when we moved there in 1981, Ben and Anna followed.

John Spring, president of the Bergen County Historical Society, working closely with Kevin Wright, assembled a Site Management Committee in September 1983

The Campbell-Christie House was moved to the present site in 1977 on a flat-bed truck. Junked cars piled in the background in the adjacent Bergenfield Autoparts property. (*Bergen County Historical Society Collections*)

to examine the site and structures at New Bridge, to make plans for their care and development, and to report to the Society on findings and priorities. The Committee also made a study of "Society lands and State lands on the west bank of the river as well as an investigation of areas on the east bank of the river." In *The New Bridge Landing Historic Park Site Management Plan* (August 1984), Wright suggested the name of Historic New Bridge Landing Park as a way to integrate the various historic buildings and their respective owners into a single coordinated entity, saying that the "name represents a recognition that the resources, and organizations which participate in their preservation, are partners in the management of the area." To this end, the committee deliberately included representatives of the Bergen County Historical Society, the Division of Parks and Forestry, the Blauvelt Demarest Foundation, and, to the extent possible, from the three neighboring communities at New Bridge.

Columnist Mark Stuart wrote:

> The society's idea is to recreate this whole collection (of historic buildings) as a historic-cultural park, the heritage of every resident of Bergen County. The park would include not only the society's property but Brett Park in Teaneck, just across the river; the corner of Hackensack Avenue and Main Street, now occupied by an auto junkyard; and a small stretch of New Milford that includes the street on which the New Bridge Inn now stands. [2]

The site management plan also identified "a need for a Visitor Center" to "display large items from the collection and provide space for group audio-visual presentations on Bergen County history, architecture, crafts and natural environs." It was to include space for a research library, sales area and rest rooms. Thus, the Historic New Bridge Landing General Management Plan of the Historic New Bridge Landing Park Commission is a direct and complete fulfillment of the Bergen County Historical Society's own wishes and plans.

After the BCHS Board of Trustees adopted the site management plan in June 1984, a copy was officially presented to the Division of Parks and Forestry for its approval. BCHS President John Spring personally handed a copy to Governor Thomas Kean on his visit to the site during the Hackensack River Festival in June 1985. The Society discussed the plan with the New Jersey Department of Environmental Protection, seeking Green Acres purchase of the junkyard, and also discussed the rehabilitation of the iron swing bridge with the County Engineer. Kevin Tremble made presentations before the municipal officials of River Edge, Teaneck and New Milford (See "$1.7M plan for historic park," *The Record*, March 25, 1985).

The Society encouraged the various stakeholders to act upon this plan. In response, the Division of Parks and Forestry added the board reading "Historic New Bridge Landing" to the entrance sign at the Steuben House. BCHS Trustee Harold Syverson conducted a membership fund drive to erect the rail fencing around the grounds and river landing. To mark the bridge's centennial in 1989, the BCHS Site Committee successfully applied for the Iron Swing Bridge to be included on the New Jersey and National Registers of Historic Places and asked the County of Bergen to paint it and clear away vegetation that obscured it from view. At this time, the County of Bergen also erected the two brown historical markers on the river landing explaining the history of the bridge and tide mill. The County also placed directional signs to Historic New Bridge on the surrounding streets and highways.

The Division of Parks and Forestry undertook a major maintenance project to repair the exterior of the Steuben House in 1984, doing extensive repointing of masonry joints, reconstructing the chimneys above the roof line, replacing the wood shingle roof, and making other much needed repairs and painting.

In evaluation of its open space and recreational needs, the Township of Teaneck adopted a master plan and summary of background studies, prepared by the firm of Queale & Lynch, Inc., in June 1985. Two important guidelines, recommended in the Draft Revision of 1993, were adopted:

> (1) that appropriate zoning standards should allow for a natural buffer of about 100 feet along the Hackensack River and that the township should require future development on land fronting the river to provide for a river pathway in conformance with the Hackensack River Pathway concept plan
>
> (2) that any development of Brett Park should be made with regard to plans for the entire New Bridge Landing area being developed by the Bergen County Historical Society, the County and the State.

PSE&G installed an extended service line to the Demarest and Steuben Houses in 1991, providing gas heat. At this time, a 275-gallon tank was removed from the root cellar of the Steuben House. The basement location of the furnace continued to be a problem, however, due to repeated flood damage. We (Kevin Wright and family) moved out of the residence in the Steuben House in March 1996.

The Site Committee's efforts to co-ordinate planning at Historic New Bridge foundered because of the Society's lack of resources and an inability to compel participation from the disparate governmental entities that needed to be involved. The creation of the Historic New Bridge Landing Park Commission solved these defects and legally established the very centralized coordinating committee that the Site Committee struggled to be.

The Historic New Bridge Landing Park Commission was established by legislation (PL. 1995, Chapter 260) in 1995 to coordinate and implement federal, State, county, municipal and private development policies, and other activities incidental to the preservation, maintenance, restoration, and interpretation of historic buildings, structures, sites, and features of Historic New Bridge Landing, so as to develop and promote their optimal educational and recreational benefit to the public. The Commission provides the regular interface needed to inform and coordinate decisions made by diverse public and private entities having ownership of land, buildings, structures, or roadways within the Commission's jurisdiction.

The Historic New Bridge Landing Park Commission consists of a representative from the County of Bergen, a representative from the Blauvelt-Demarest Foundation, a representative from the Borough of River Edge, a representative from the Borough of New Milford, two representatives from the Bergen County Historical Society, and two representatives from the Township of Teaneck. Each of these eight members is appointed by resolution of the respective governing bodies they are to represent and serve for a term of three years. The Director of the Division of Parks and Forestry

Kevin Wright and Deborah Powell with children Ivan, Benjamin, and Anna Wright taken about 1991 by the Westervelt-Thomas Barn. (*photo by Kevin Wright with a photo timer*)

is the ninth member. The Commission's business is organized and conducted by annually elected officers, namely a chairperson, vice-chairperson, a secretary, and a treasurer.

After years of meetings, seeking public input, and building consensus, final approval of the Historic New Bridge Landing General Management Plan on February 4, 1999, set the stage for remarkable progress. Through the intercommunicative forum provided by the Historic New Bridge Landing Park Commission, several effective and changing partnerships have formed to achieve the master plan goals, turning a diversity of stakeholders into a positive asset.

The Borough of River Edge enacted Ordinance No. 1334 on May 12, 2001, vacating the dead end of Main Street (approximately 213 feet in length) between the entrance to the PSE&G Substation and the 1889 Swing Bridge. A portion of the former westbound lane was incorporated into the design of the new parking lot at the Steuben House. The deeds vacating a portion of Main Street and transferring title to the lands from the Borough of River Edge to the State of New Jersey and to the Bergen County Historical Society, the contiguous property owners, is dated September 17, 2001.

On October 27, 2000, the NJ Department of Environmental Protection purchased the former Saw shop property at 1 Old New Bridge Road in New Milford (Block No. 113, Lot No. 10 on the New Milford Tax Map) from Joseph Van Hook.

Through the intercession of Senator Robert Torricelli, the Secretary of the Interior was authorized (by Public Law 106-554) to provide $1,097,580 to purchase and clean property including the autoparts salvage yard at Historic New Bridge Landing. Authority to implement the appropriation was delegated to the National Park Service. Administrative oversight and stewardship responsibilities were accordingly assigned to the National Park Service Regional Director at the Northeast Region Office in Philadelphia. An agreement to transfer administration of this fund was signed with the New Jersey Department of Environmental Protection on August 17, 2000.

The Green Acres Program has been willing and able to secure properties for historic park purposes in a densely settled corner of the State. In July 2001, the County of Bergen joined Green Acres in securing the right of way to make the necessary road improvements on or near the site of the proposed entrance and visitor facilities. The County of Bergen also initiated and funded important improvements to its properties at Historic New Bridge Landing, namely, the 1889 Swing Bridge and the Campbell-Christie House. The participating municipalities have also lent their talent, enthusiasm, and support to the project. The Blauvelt-Demarest Foundation provided timely support at the inception of the Historic New Bridge Landing Park Commission and greatly advanced the cause by funding a professional concept development prospectus.

The Division of Parks and Forestry has committed its resources and talent to the project. When the Borough of River Edge vacated the dead end of Main Street, the Division designed and installed a new parking area (increasing its capacity from sixteen to twenty-one parking spaces), by incorporating a lane of the vacated roadway. The antiquated heating system in the Steuben House irreparably broke in January 2000. Due to the loss of heat, the house closed in November 2000, while

Ribbon cutting for the end of the Autoparts property and fence. Pictured here is HNBLSPC Chairman (at the time) Bob Griffin, Senator Loretta Weinberg, Assemblywomen Charlotte Vandervalk and Valerie Huttle, and former Freeholder and HNBLSPC Commissioner Mary Donohue. Reenactor Todd Braisted pictured in background. (*photo by Deborah Powell*)

awaiting repairs. The Bergen County Historical Society removed and safely stored its valuable historic collections from the Steuben House in April 2001 to allow for the extensive renovations.

Green Acres acquired the Sutton and Lys property (0.1 acre) on the tip of the traffic island, south of the intersection of Main Street and Hackensack Avenue, on May 14, 2001. The adjacent Pizza Town property was acquired, with 0.45 acres to the State of New Jersey and .15 acre to the county of Bergen for a right of way. The Sutton and Lys house was demolished in September 2002.

The Division of Parks and Forestry completed a major exterior restoration of the house in August 2001, according to plans and specifications prepared by historic restoration architects Holt, Morgan & Russell. With a small gas furnace removed to the attic level, well above the flood level, a new heating system became operational in October 2001. The renovated Steuben House reopened in October 2001, just in time for the 225th anniversary of Washington's retreat. The "Retreat to Victory" was held on November 17–18, 2001.

On March 25, 2002, the State House Commission approved trading a strip of land on the Lys & Sutton property, located on the traffic triangle, to the County of Bergen in exchange for small neighboring plots of land. The exchange was made to facilitate the widening of Hackensack Avenue as part of the anticipated road improvements to enhance the gateway to Historic New Bridge Landing.

The 2010 park master plan was written by Kevin Wright for the Historic New Bridge Landing Park Commission. The plan provides further guidance on planning alternatives, existing conditions, visioning, and heritage tourism.[3] The Historic New Bridge Landing Park Commission is a unique example of public and private partners working together to save a historic park with complex, layered stories and different property ownership.

Epilogue

Kevin Wright went on to retire from his position as Regional Historic Preservation Specialist in the Department of Environmental Protection in 2008. As a volunteer, he served as Bergen County Historical Society president for three years beginning in June 2004 and was president for a second set when he passed away in October 2016.

Kevin said many times, 'you save a historic site not once but every day.' He left us with much vision, history, and planning; his handprint is everywhere one looks at the museum site and beyond in the state historic sites system.

We continue to make progress at the historic park we now know as Historic New Bridge Landing.

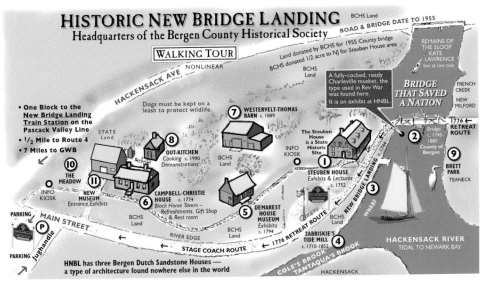

Bird's eye view map of Historic New Bridge Landing today. Brett Park is not pictured. (*Original sketch by Claire K. Tholl, updated by Deborah Powell*)

Endnotes

Chapter 1

1. According to Arthur James Weise, author of *The Discoveries of America to the Year 1525* (p. 348), "the noun *berge*, besides meaning an elevated border of a river, a scarp of a fortification, a steep side of a moat or of a road, is a designation for certain rocks elevated perpendicularly above the water. In an old French lexicon it is said: 'They likewise call in marine phraseology *berges* or *barges* those great rocks, rugged and perpendicularly elevated, that is to say, uprightly and plumb, as the *berges* or *barges* of Clone: such rocks as are Scylla and Charybdis, toward Messina.'" *Bergen* is the Dutch plural.
2. The Helix of the Lincoln Tunnel spirals down a natural offset or fault in the Palisades, long used to provide passage down the steep esarpment through a stream-worn ravine. To this day (2016) you can still see the outlet of the old Ferry Creek, lying northeast of Harbor Boulevard and east of Port Imperial Boulevard, where travelers took water passage to or from Manhattan. While somewhat set back to the south, the Palisades steeply crowd the riverfront immediately to the north. I strongly suspect that "Awiehacken," now Weehawken, may be a Dutch approximation of the Algonquian "*wequae-achtenne*," describing "the limit, edge, or point of the hill."
3. Kummel, H. B., 'The Newark System,' *Annual Report of the State Geologist for the Year 1896*, p. 30 (Trenton: MacCrellish & Quigley, 1897).
4. Lewis, J. V. and Kummel, H. B., *Bulletin 50, Geological Series, The Geology of New Jersey*, p. 50 (Bayonne: The Jersey Printing Company, 1940); Sullivan, Walter, *Landprints*, p. 41 (New York: Time Books, 1984).
5. *Ibid.*, p. 50.
6. Darton, N. H., 'The Relations of the Traps of the Newark System in the New Jersey Region,' *Bulletin of the United States Geological Survey, No. 67*, p. 37 (Washington, D.C.: Government Printing Office, 1890).
7. Westervelt, F. A. 'Study of the Soil,' *History of Bergen County, New Jersey 1630–1923*, Vol. I, p. 5 (New York: Lewis Historical Publishing Company, Inc., 1923).
8. Salisbury, R. D., *Physical Geography of New Jersey, Geological Survey of New Jersey, Volume IV of the Final Report of the State Geologist*, pp. 39, 83, 104, 237 (Trenton: The John L. Murphy Publishing Co., 1898).
9. Salisbury, R. D., Volume V, *op. cit.*, p. 519 (1902).

10. Reeds, C. A., *Geology of New York City and its Vicinity*, American Museum of Natural History, Guide Leaflet, No. 56; Reed, Chester A., "The varved clays at Little Ferry, New Jersey," *American Museum Novitates*, No. 209.

11. Salisbury, R. D., Volume IV, *op. cit.*, p. 105 (1898).

12. Nelson, W. (ed.), *The New Jersey Archives, Vol. V, Laws of the Royal Colony* (Paterson, NJ: The Press Printing and Publishing Co., 1900), pp. 161–163; see also, Winfield, Charles, H., *History of the County of Hudson, New Jersey*, p. 363 (New York: Kennard & Hay Stationery M'Fg and Printing Co., 1874).

13. The old route actually departed Route 23 in Wantage, taking Libertyville Road and the Deckertown Turnpike across Kittatinny mountain to Montague, where it crossed the Delaware River into Milford, Pennsylvania.

14. Jameson, J. F. (ed.), 'Journal of New Netherland, 1647,' *Narratives of New Netherland 1609–1664, Original Narratives of Early American History*, pp. 272–273 (New York: Charles Scribner's Sons, 1909).

15. One end of the *bouwhuys* is living apartments, and the other end is a barn with cattle stalls.

16. Mistakenly reported as 17 and 18 September.

17. Brodhead, J. R., 'Documents Relating to the Colonial History of the State of New-York,' Volume 13, p. 17 (Albany: Weed, Parsons, 1881).

18. Van Der Donck, A., 'Description of the New Netherlands.' *Collections of the New-York Historical Society*, p. 81 (New-York: Printed for the Society, 1841). Second Series. Volume 1.

19. In 1759, John Zabriskie, of New Bridge, advertised "a Boat carrying seven Cord, all in good Order to attend a Mill; when deeply loaded won't draw above four Feet, eight Inches Water; Sails and Rigging all in complete Order. The Boat to be seen every Week at New-York; for Price enquire of Richard Waldron, at the Great Dock; or of John Zabriski, at Hackinsack." *The New York Mercury*, October 1, 1759.

Chapter 2

1. Benson, A. B. (translator and editor), *Peter Kalm's Travels in North America*, p. 463.

2. Van Der Donck, Adriæn, *A Description of the New Netherlands*, p. 97 (Syracuse, New York: Syracuse University Press, 1968).

3. Kenton, E. (ed.), 'Relation of what occurred among the Hurons in the year 1635, Sent to Quebec to Father le Jeune by Father Brebeuf,' *The Jesuit Relations and Allied Documents*, p. 113 (New York: Albert & Charles Boni, 1925).

4. *Ibid.*, p. 111; Agnierrhonons is probably based upon *Ongwe-houwe*, meaning "men surpassing all others, superior to the rest of mankind," from which Mengwe or Minquaas is probably derived; these people were also known as the Aniez, Maquaas, or Mohawks.

5. Fernow, B., *Documents Relating to the History and Settlements of the Towns along the Hudson and Mohawk Rivers from 1630 to 1684*, p. 112 (Albany: Weed, Parsons, 1881); Kenton, *op. cit.*, p. 304.

6. Jameson, *op. cit.*, p. 279.

7. According to Edward Manning Ruttenber's *History of the Indian Tribe of Hudson's River*, the Tankitekes occupied lands now embraced in the towns of Darien, Stamford; New Canaan, Connecticut; Poundridge, Bedford; and Greenbush in Westchester County, New York.

8. Jameson, J. F. (ed.), 'A Short Account of the Mohawk Indians, by Reverend Johannes Megapolensis, Jr., 1644' *Original Narratives of Early American History, Narratives of New England 1609–1664*, p. 172 (New York: Charles Scribner's Sons, 1909).

9. A version of the *Dutch Figurative Map* (1616) shows them occupying the tidal shores of Bergen Neck, while an earlier version shows them on what may be the Raritan, Passaic or Hackensack River. The Sankikans were included as a nation of Indians inhabiting the South (Delaware) River, according to De Laet's *Nieuwe Wereldt* (1625, 1630).

10. Brodhead, J. R, 'History of the State of New York, First Period 1609–1664', p. 633 (New York: Harper & Brothers, 1853).
11. Now occupied by Ridgefield Park, Bogota, and Teaneck.
12. Since the Tappans were the inland neighbors of the Hackensacks, this reply offers clear evidence that these two bands or *affines* were not closely affiliated; the Tappans were part of the Minisink superaffine, whereas I suspect the Hackensacks were Sanhicans.
13. Jameson, J. F. (ed.), *Narratives of New Netherland 1609–1664*, 'Letter of Isaac De Rasieres to Samuel Blommært, 1628,' p. 104 (New York: Barnes & Noble, Inc., 1909).

Chapter 3

1. Bartlett, B. J. and Jameson, J. F., (eds.), 'Journal of Jasper Danckaerts 1679-1680,' *Original Narratives of Early American History*, p. 77-78 (New York: Charles Scribner's Sons, 1913).
2. Wright, K. W., *1609: A country that was never lost, 400th Anniversay of Henry Hudson's Visit with North Americans of the Middle Atlantic Coast*, p. 1 (Franklin, TN: American History Imprints, 2009).
3. Bartlett, B. J. and Jameson, J. F., (eds.), *op. cit.*, pp. 77–78.
4. Benson, A. B. (trans. and ed.), *Peter Kalm's Travels into North America*, pp. 686–687 (London; T. Lownes, 1750).
5. *Ibid.*, pp. 686-687.
6. Jameson, J. F. (editor), 'Journal of New Netherland, 1647,' *Narratives of New Netherland 1609–1664, Original Narratives of Early American History*, p. 281 (New York: Charles Scribner's Sons, 1909).
7. Bird, E. K., 'First Lutheran Church in Bergen County,' *Papers and Proceedings of the Bergen County Historical Society, Number Three*, 1906–1907, pp. 41–44.
8. Demarest, D. D., 'The Lutherans of the Hackensack', *Papers and Proceedings of the Bergen County Historical Society, Number Eleven*, 1916–1917, p. 98.
9. *Ibid.*, p. 105.
10. 'Lourence Van Boskeark's Deed,' *Papers and Proceedings of the Bergen County Historical Society, Number Twelve*, 1916–1917, p. 19.
11. Demarest, D. D., 'Lutherans On The Hackensack,' *Papers and Proceedings of the Bergen County Historical Society*, 1915–1916, p. 99–100.
12. *Collections of the New York Genealogical and Biographical Society, Vol. IX, Marriages in the Dutch Reformed Church in New York City 1639–1801*, p. 141 (New York, 1940).
13. *New Jersey Archives, Vol. XII, Newspaper Extracts Vol. II 1740–1750*, p. 283.
14. *Ibid.*, p. 437.
15. Demarest, D. D., *The Huguenots On the Hackensack*, p. 5 (New Brunswick: The Daily Fredonian Steam Printing House, 1886).
16. Riker, J., *Harlem (City of New York), Its Origin and Early Annals*, pp. 114–115 (New York: 1881).
17. *Ibid.*, pp. 117–118.
18. *Ibid.*, p. 245.
19. In church services, the Voorleser read the Decalogue and Creed, a chapter from the Bible and prayers, then a sermon from a noted Dutch Domine, and lead Psalm singing.
20. Riker, *op. cit.*, pp. 114–115.
21. *Ibid.*, p. 377.
22. Demarest 1886, *op. cit.*, p. 12.
23. From *pemapeek*, referring to a body of water with no current.
24. From *assiskuju*, referring to marshy ground.
25. This stone dwelling was erected in 1670 by Captain William Sandford, but included in that portion of New Barbados ceded to Major Nathaniel Kingsland a year after its construction.

It reportedly stood "within a few feet of where the D. L. & W. shops are now [in 1927] located" on Union Avenue in Lyndhurst, but it was demolished in 1906.

26. From *Menach'hen*, meaning, "island"; now Moonachie.

27. Also Aquepoch, derived either from *wipochk*, "a brush meadow" or from *ukque-pek*, "at the head of a bay or body of water." Now the Overpeck Creek and Meadows.

28. Myndert Myndertsen van Keren and Godard van Reeds, Lord of Nederhorst, received a patroonal grant for land extending sixteen miles northward from the head of Newark Bay. A thatch-roofed trading post, erected in 1641 by Johannes Winkelman, patroonal agent and manager, had been burnt in a dispute with the natives in 1643.

29. Also Ackingh-sack, from *achtshingi hacki*, meaning "stony ground"; later corrupted into Hackensack.

30. Tradition places these villages along Fyke Lane in Teaneck, where Glenwood and Cedar Parks are now located.

31. From *woapak*, water beech or sycamore. Along the Hackensack River near present-day Anderson Street, in the City of Hackensack.

32. Later known as Rond Hook, in the northeastern most section of the City of Hackensack.

33. From *tachtschaunge*, also *woaktschachne*, meaning, "Where the river bends around a hill," or "the narrows of a river." Now the New Bridge section of River Edge and Teaneck.

34. From *schejawonge*, meaning "hill-side," the earliest name for French Creek on the present boundary between New Milford and Teaneck.

35. The Demarests probably erected wooden houses upon their settlement of the upper Hackensack Valley. Such frame dwellings were commonly built in New Harlem during their residence there. For example, to provide a new house for the *Voorleser*, the Constable and Magistrates of New Harlem decided in July 1678 to purchase the heavy timbers of a house frame, originally contracted for by Maria Vermilye, widow of Johannes Montagne, and hewn by carpenter Daniel Tourneur, to wit: "five beams twenty feet long, broad in proportion; twelve posts ten-feet long; four sills twenty-two and twenty feet long; two rafters, two girders, one other spar, all twenty-two feet; also split shingles for the roof; all finished to deliver at the stumps..." These timbers would have framed a one-story frame house 22 feet by 20 feet.

36. Demarest 1886, *op. cit.*, p. 10.

37. *Ibid.*, p. 127.

38. Budke, G. H. (Compiler), *Indian Deeds 1630–1748, BC—88 of the Budke Collection*, pp. 60–61 (New City, New York: Library Association of Rockland County, 1975).

39. Road return dated March 9, 1743/4—Jacob Ferdon, Aryea Blinkerhof, HA Hendrick van Alen, his mark, HH Hendrick Hopper, his mark, AR Allebart Romyen, his mark, IK Isaac Kip, his mark.

40. Budke, G. H., *op. cit.*, pp. 137–138.

41. *New Jersey Archives, Vol. XXI, Calendar of NJ Records, East Jersey Deeds*, p. 70.

42. Salisbury 1902, *Volume IV, op. cit.*, p. 105.

43. See *A. H. Walker's 1776–1876 Atlas of Bergen County, New Jersey* p. 33. (Reading, Pa.: Reading Publishing House, 1876), "History of the Townships and Villages," The name has changed over time: Slokeup (1774), Slokup (1792), Sluckup (1793), Slockup (1806).

44. *Marriages from 1639 to 1801 in the Dutch Reformed Church, New Amsterdam, New York City*, Vol. IX, p. 27 (New York: New York Genealogical and Biographical Society, 1940).

45. Pierce, C. H., *New Harlem Past and Present*, pp. 25, 33–34 (New York: New Harlem Publishing Co., 1903).

46. David Ackerman and wife Hillegond Ver Plancken had the following children baptized in the Dutch Reformed Church at New York, namely, David, on April 1, 1681; Johannes, on February 7, 1683; Johannes, on April 16, 1684; Gelyn, on January 7, 1686; and Gelyn, on April 11, 1688.

47. The Bollen Release of 1720 to the heirs of David Demarest mentions the outlet of French Creek (this brook being the division line between lands of Peter Van Boskerk and Peter Demarest) as lying "opposite the house of Johannis Ackerman."

48. *New Jersey Archives, Vol. XV, Journal of the Governor and Council, Vol. III 1738–1748*, p. 284.

49. Maresca, V., Hunter, R. W. and Liebeknecht, W. B., "Archaeological Investigations in Connection with Exterior Repairs at the Zabriskie/Steuben House Historic New Bridge Landing, River Edge Borough, Bergen County, New Jersey." (tDAR id: 333020: 2001).

50. *New Jersey Archives, Vol. XII, Newspaper Extracts Vol. II 1740–1750*, p. 283.

51. Now Chernyakbovsk, near Kalingrad.

52. *Passengers to New Netherland 1654 to 1664 From the Copyrighted Year Book of the Holland Society of New York for 1902* (arranged by Theodore M. Banta, Secretary), p. 21.

53. Memsche (also *Mamche*) was the "sackamaker of Tappan" who signed the deed for a "certaine tractt of Land lyinge and beeinge in ye province of East Jersey knowne by ye name of Tappan" on March 17, 1681. Memsha (also Memmess, Sackemacker, Mettatoch and Seytheypoey) signed a deed conveyed lands in the northern valley of the Hackensack and along the Peskeckie Creek to the Governor and Proprietors of East Jersey on October 16, 1684.

54. Nelson, W., 'Bergen Church Marriage Records,' *New Jersey Archives, First Series, Vol. XXII Marriage Records, 1665–1800*, p. 581 (Paterson: The Press Printing and Publishing Co., 1900)

55. A tract on the Hackensack River, near Warepeake (Anderson Street, City of Hackensack) extending north to Tantaquas Creek (Cole's Brook) encompassing the Fairmount section of City of Hackensack. Aschatking is an approximation of Woaktschachne, "a bend in the river," describing the sinuous curve of the stream below New Bridge, later called Rond Hook by the Dutch.

56. Also Warepeeke. A parcel of land on the east side of the Hackensack River, extending from Anderson Street in the City of Hackensack northward to Tantaquas Creek (Cole's Brook). Warepeake is probably an approximation of Woapak, "water beech" (Plane Tree, *Plantanus occidentalis*, more commonly known as Buttonwood or Sycamore). Peter Kalm (*circa* 1750) noted that it grew on lowland marshes, especially along the edges of rivers and brooks. He also reported that the Swedes of the lower Delaware Valley had boxes, pails and other wooden ware made of this wood by native Americans who also "made little dishes of the bark for gathering whortleberries." He is probably referring to woven splint baskets rather than dishes, since he also mentioned that "the bark was a line in thickness."

57. *East Jersey Deeds, Liber A*, p. 328.

58. When Albert Sobrisco sold 224 acres to Jacob Vansan on October 29, 1695, the deed was given under a corrected survey and did not agree with the boundaries of the patent of April 24, 1682.

59. Also spelled Memmess, and undoubtedly the same Mamshier of his earlier dealings.

60. Probably the same individual called Chechepowas in 1675.

61. *East Jersey Deeds, Liber 1*, p. 200.

62. *East Jersey Deeds, Liber A*, p. 173.

63. The New Barbadoes Patent of Captain Sandford extended seven miles north of Newark Bay, to what became known as Boiling Spring, now Rutherford.

64. Hanayahame, Capitamme, Tantaqua and Thamago; the claim may be fraudulent on Berry's part since Warepeake was apparently a place upon the Hackensack River and was not a name used in association with the Saddle River. Rerakanes is probably derived from Lechauhanne, meaning "fork of a river."

65. *New Jersey Archives, Vol. XXI, Calendar of NJ Records, East Jersey Deeds*, p. 70.

66. *East Jersey Deeds*, Liber E, p. 313.

67. Son of Cornelius Matheus, the original purchaser.
68. Also Whirimins (in 1696), Weerommensa, Wierimus. Samuel Bayard's deed, dated September 16, 1703, for part of the Kakiak Patent, mentions "Vacant Land within Our County of Orange Called by the Indians Whorinims [Wieremis], Perseck [Peskeck], Gemackie [Gomagkie], Narrashunk [Narasonk]." Weromensa is probably an approximation of Woapiminschi, *chestnut tree.* The upland in this neighborhood was later known as Chestnut Ridge.
69. McMahon, R., 'Wierimus' *Bergen County History 1974 Annual,* pp. 38–51.
70. *Bergen County Deed Book A, p. 26.*
71. Joost's son, Albert J. Zabriskie, erected the high-style mansion, now known as the Zabriskie-Kipp Homestead (River Road, Teaneck), the largest Bergen Dutch sandstone dwelling house built as a single unit, in 1787, but he died in 1791. His son George Zabriskie, an infant in the guardianship of his mother, inherited the premises from his grandfather in 1794. As a river merchant, he prospered during an embargo and coastal blockade preceding and during the War of 1812. George Zabriskie sold the homestead to Henry Kipp, a fisherman, in 1816. Upon his death in 1847 it passed to his son Jacob H. Kipp and later to grandson, Henry J. Kipp. After his death in 1899, the farm was inherited by Henry's children, namely, Sophia, Helena and Henry. In 1923, Helena and her husband, Henry Cadmus, purchased from the other heirs. May Cadmus sold the old house in 1959.
72. The children of John (b. May 17, 1704) and Theodosia Van Orden were Abigail Van Orden, born June 15, 1730; John Van Orden, born March 2, 1732; Elce or Elsje Van Norden, born January 30, 1735, died 1736; Gabriel Van Norden, born October 25, 1737; Elce or Elsje Van Norden, born September 17, 1742; Adam Van Norden, born July 30, 1744; and Annatje Van Norden, born February 3, 1747.
73. The children of John and Rebecca Van Norden were John, born July 14, 1755; David, born March 20, 1757; Lucas, born March 20, 1759; Theodosia, born June 29, 1761; Gabriel, born April 5, 1763; Mary, born December 26, 1764; Theodorus William, born January 4, 1767; Hanna, born February 6, 1769; Abigail, born November 16, 1770; Elizabeth, born October 29, 1772; Richard and Elsje, born February 1774 but died in infancy; Richard, born June 28, 1775 and died in infancy; Jain, born January 1, 1777; and Richard, born August 12, 1778.

Chapter 4

1. *New Jersey Herald and Sussex Democrat,* January 10, 1863, microfilm.
2. Mulenberg, H. M., *The Journals of Henry Melchior Muhlenberg* (Philadelphia: Lutheran Historical Society, 1982).
3. Niemcewicz, J. U., *Under their Vine and Fig Tree: Travels through America in 1797–1799, 1805, with some further accounts of life in New Jersey,* (Newark, N. J.: Grassmann Publishing Co., 1965).
4. McMahon, R., 'The Achter Col Colony on the Hackensack', *New Jersey History, Winter 1971,* pp. 221–240.
5. Glassie, H., *Pattern in the Material Folk Culture of the Eastern United States,* p. 146 (University of Pennsylvania Press: Philadelphia.) The roof was thatched with river reeds indigenous to the area. Owing to the incompleteness of the contract, further details of construction are left to speculation.
6. Brodhead, J. R. (Compiler), Documents relative to the Colonial History of the State of New-York p. 67 (New York, Albany: Weed, Parsons), Brodhead, *op. cit.,* 1853.
7. Pierce, C. H., *New Harlem Past and Present,* pp. 112–113 (New York: New Harlem Publishing Co., 1903).
8. *Ibid.,* p. 112–114.
9. Brodhead, *op. cit.,* p. 367.

10. *Geological Survey of New Jersey, Annual Report of the State Geologist, for the Year 1880*, p. 41 (Trenton: John J. Murphy: 1880).

11. Nelson, W., *History of the City of Paterson and the County of Passaic, New Jersey*, p. 4 (Paterson: The Press Printing and Publishing Co., 1901).

12. Thacher, James, M.D., *Military Journal During the American Revolutionary War, From 1775 to 1783*, p. 244 (Boston: Richardson and Lord, 1823).

13. Raleigh, W., 'From the Raleigh Register. Agriculture of North-Carolina, Letter VI.—Free Stone, Coloring Drugs, Slates and Ores, To Charles Fisher, esq., Secretary of the Rowan Agricultural Society.' *The Hillsborough Recorder*, No. 174, p. 1 (Hillsborough, North Carolina: June 11, 1823).

14. Gordon, T. F., *History and Gazetter of New Jersey*, p. 100 (Trenton: Daniel Fenton, 1834).

15. *New Jersey Archives, Vol. XXVI, Newspaper Extracts Vol. VII 1768–1769*, pp. 274, 339.

16. *New Jersey Archives, Vol. XXVII, Newspaper Extracts Vol. VII, 1770–1771*, pp. 371–372.

17. *New Jersey Archives, Vol. XXVII, Newspaper Extracts Vol. VII, 1770–1771*, p. 434.

18. *New Jersey Archives, Vol. XXVIII, Newspaper Extracts Vol. IX 1772–1773*, p. 150.

19. *New Jersey Archives, Vol. XXVIII, Newspaper Extracts Vol. IX 1772–1773*, p. 461.

20. *New Jersey Archives, Vol. XXV, Newspaper Extracts Vol. VI 1766–1767*, pp. 69–70; 355–356.

21. *New Jersey Archives, Vol. XXVI, Newspaper Extracts Vol. VII 1768–1769*, p. 177.

22. *New Jersey Archives, Vol. XXVI, Newspaper Extracts Vol. VII 1768-1769*, pp. 9, 528.

23. *New Jersey Archives, Vol. XXVII, Newspaper Extracts Vol. VII, 1770–1771*, p. 575, 602.

24. *New Jersey Archives, Vol. XXVIII, Newspaper Extracts Vol. IX 1772–1773*, p. 405–406.

25. *New Jersey Archives, Vol. XXXI, Newspaper Extracts Vol. XI 1775*, p. 63.

26. *Bergen County Deed Book K*, p. 128.

27. *Ibid.*, p. 131. In 1786, the tax ratables for Hackensack Township list Yelles Mead as owner of a house on 6 acres. According to the tax assessment rolls of August 1788 and July 1789, Mead owned a tanyard. On October 26, 1790, Giles Mead, Tanner and Currier, sold the premises to Caleb Wade, Jr., of Essex County, for £150. In the tax assessment of July–August 1791, Caleb Wade owned a tanyard.

28. *Bergen County Deed Book X10*, p. 31.

29. *The Bergen Democrat*, January 30, 1891.

Chapter 5

1. Gordon, T. F., *History and Gazetteer of New Jersey*, p. 36 (Trenton: Daniel Fenton, 1834).

2. Northrup, A. Judd, 'Act of the Director and Council of New Netherland', quoted in *State Library Bulletin*, History No. 4, May 1900, 'Slavery in New York', p. 247 (University of the State of New York, 1900).

3. Jameson, 'Letters of the Dutch Ministers', *op. cit.*, p. 407.

4. Northrup, *op. cit.*, pp. 246–247.

5. *Ibid.*, p. 250. An account of the *Tamandare*, the first African slave ship of record to reach New Netherland. I am indepted to Arnold E. Brown of Englewood for bringing this important piece of research to my attention.

6. Hart, A. B. (ed.), *The Representation of New Netherland* (1650), New York Historical Society Collections (New York, 1849), Second Series II, as cited in American History as told by *Contemporaries*, Vol. I, *Era of Colonization 1492–1689*, p. 535 (New York: MacMillan Company, 1900).

7. Dankers, J. and Sluyter, P., *Journal of a Voyage to New York in 1679–1680*, p. 172 (Brooklyn, 1867) cited in American History told by Contemporaries.

8. *New Jersey Archives, First Series, Vol. XXI, Calendar New Jersey Records 1664–1703*, pp. 261, 282 (Paterson: The Press and Publishing Company, 1899).

9. *New Jersey Archives, First Series, Vol. XXII, Bergen Church Marriage Records*, p. 571 (Paterson: The Press and Publishing Company, 1899).

10. *The Minutes of the Board of Proprietors of the Eastern Division of New Jersey from 1725 to 1744, Vol. II*, p. 114 (Perth Amboy: 1960).

11. *Ibid.*, p. 173.

12. *Ibid.*, p. 198.

13. *Ibid.*, p. 223.

14. *Ibid.*, p. 241–42.

15. *Ibid.*, p. 242.

16. Gordon, T. F., *History and Gazetter of New Jersey*, pp. 29–33 (Trenton: Daniel Fenton, 1834).

17. Pomfret, J. E., *The Province of East Jersey 1609–1702*, p. 292 (Princeton: Princeton University Press, 1962).

18. Bangs, E. (ed.), *Journal of Lieutenant Isaac Bangs, April 1 to July 29, 1776*, p. 51 (Cambridge: John Wilson and Son, 1890).

19. *Proceedings of the Bergen County Historical Society for the Year 1915–16*, p. 25.

20. Gordon, *op. cit.*, p. 36.

Chapter 6

1. 'From George Washington to John Hancock, 19–21 November 1776,' *Founders Online*, National Archives, accessed April 11, 2019, https://founders.archives.gov/documents/Washington/03-07-02-0128. (Original source: *The Papers of George Washington, Revolutionary War Series, vol. 7, 21 October 1776–5 January 1777*, Chase, P. D. (ed.), pp. 180–186 (Charlottesville: University Press of Virginia, 1997).

2. Ewald, Captain J., Field Jager Corps, *Diary of the American War, A Hessian Journal*, translated and edited by Joseph P. Tustin, p. 16 (New Haven and London Yale University Press, 1979).

3. 'From George Washington to John Hancock, 19–21 November 1776,' *op. cit.*, p. 180–186.

4. Ewald, Captain J., *op. cit.*, p. 17.

5. Paine, T., *The Writings of Thomas Paine, Vol. I, Collected and Edited by Moncure Daniel Conway, 1774–1779*, Project Gutenberg, Produced by Norman M. Wolcott and David Widger. gutenberg.org/files/3741/3741-h/3741-h.htm

6. *Ibid.*, fourth paragraph.

7. Report of James Hogg, made at Ramapo on July 26, 1777.

8. Leiby, A. C., *The Revolutionary War in the Hackensack Valley, The Jersey Dutch and the Neutral Ground*, p. 94 (New Brunswick: Rutgers University Press, 1980).

9. *Ibid.*, p. 125.

10. *Ibid.*, p. 127.

11. *Ibid.*, pp. 122–124.

12. *Ibid.*, p. 142.

13. *New Jersey Archives, Second Series, Vol. II, 1778*, p. 43.

14. Near the crest of the hill at Bogert Avenue and Reservoir Avenue, River Edge.

15. Extracts of letters, Sudduth, James, *The Remembrancer; or, Impartial Repository of Public Events, For the Year 1778, and Beginning of 1779*, p. 295 (Printed for J. Almon, 1779).

16. *National Archives and Records Administration, Papers of the Continental Congress, Washington, DC.* founders.archives.gov/documents/Washington/03-17-02-0166

17. Extracts of letters, Southward, James, *The Remembrancer, op. cit.*, p. 295.

18. *New Jersey Archives, Second Series, Vol. II, 1778*, p. 485.

19. *Ibid.*, pp. 210–212.

20. *New Jersey Archives, Second Series, Vol. III, 1779*, pp. 621–629.

21. *New Jersey Archives, Second Series, Vol. II, 1778*, p. 13.
22. *New Jersey Archives, Second Series, Vol. III, 1779*, p. 592.
23. Leiby, *op. cit.*, p. 224.
24. *New Jersey Archives, Second Series, Vol. IV, 1779-1789*, pp. 253–254.
25. Leiby, *op. cit.*, p. 243.
26. Leiby, *op. cit.*, p. 245.
27. Barber, J. and Howe, H., *Historical Collections of the State of New Jersey*, p. 82 (Newark: Benjamin Oldis, 1844).
28. Romeyn, Rev. T. B., *Historical Discourse Delivered on Occasion of the Re-Opening and Dedication of the First Reformed (Dutch) Church at Hackensack, N. J.*, pp. 35–36 (New York: Board of Publication, R. C. A., 1870).
29. *New Jersey Archives, Second Series, Vol. IV, 1779-1789*, pp. 306–308.
30. *Ibid.*, pp. 378–381.
31. *Revolutionary History of State of New Jersey, Vol. IV., Extracts from American Newspapers relating to New Jersey, Nov. 1, 1779–Sept. 30, 1780*, N.J., p. 434 (Trenton, N.J., State Gazette Publishing Co., 1914).
32. In August 1893, William Ely tore down the old James Ely Homestead, preparatory to erecting a fine modern residence (now No. 1141 River Road, New Milford) on the site. The old stone house had been a landmark in this section for many years.
33. 'Revolutionary War Days, Some Occurrences at New Bridge', *Relics*, Vol. 18, No. 103, November 1974, pp. 2–3 (Park Ridge: Pascack Historical Society).
34. Leiby, *op. cit.*, pp. 257–260.
35. *Revolutionary History of State of New Jersey, op. cit*, p. 586.
36. See Alexander Hamilton's 'A Letter to Colonel John Laurens,' from New Bridge, Sep. 12, 1780, transcribed by Kevin W. Wright (New York Public Library Digital Collections) digitalcollections.nypl.org/items/b917eb3b-decb-ad32-e040-e00a18060e3e

Chapter 7

1. *Selections from the Correspondence of the Executive of New Jersey from 1776 to 1786*. p. 358 (Newark, N. J.: The Newark Daily Advertiser, 1848).
2. Lockhart, P. D., *Drillmaster of Valley Forge: The Baron de Steuben and the Making of the American Army*, p. 203 (New York: HarperCollins).
3. *Bergen County Deed Book F*, p. 2.
4. *Bergen County Deed Book G*, p. 62.
5. Jan Zabriskie Estate Inventory, 1793, (Bergen County Historical Society, BergenCountyHistory.org).
6. *Bergen County Deed Book H*, p. 219.
7. *Bergen County Deed Book J*, p. 369.
8. *Bergen County Deed Book J*, p. 351.
9. *Bergen County Deed Book V*, p. 126.
10. The 1810 Federal census for Oppenheim, Montgomery, New York, includes Andrew Zobriskie as a householder. He is listed as serving in the same regiment in 1811. In 1812, he is listed as first major in Lieutenant-Colonel Jacob Snell's Regiment.
11. *Bergen County Deed Book E2*, p. 129.
12. *Bergen County Deed Book K2*, p. 480.
13. Lieutenant Daniel Denniston, of the New York Artillery, was one of the original members of the New York State Society of the Cincinnati, founded in the Temple at New Windsor in 1783.
14. *Bergen County Deed Book K2*, p. 482.
15. *Bergen Democrat*, March 15, 1872.

Chapter 8

1. *The Record*, July 16, 1931.
2. Stuart, M., 'History needs a face lift', *The Record*, April 17, 1985.
3. *Historic New Bridge Landing Park Master Plan,* Historic New Bridge Landing Park Commission, (2010).

Bibliography

'From George Washington to John Hancock, 19–21 November 1776,' *Founders Online*, National Archives, accessed April 11, 2019, https://founders.archives.gov/documents/Washington/03-07-02-0128. (Original source: *The Papers of George Washington*, Revolutionary War Series, vol. 7, *21 October 1776–5 January 1777*, Chase, P. D. (ed.), pp. 180–186 (Charlottesville: University Press of Virginia, 1997)

'Lourence Van Boskeark's Deed,' *Papers and Proceedings of the Bergen County Historical Society*, Number Twelve, 1916–1917, p. 19

'Revolutionary War Days, Some Occurrences at New Bridge', *Relics*, Vol. 18 No. 103, November 1974, pp. 2–3 (Park Ridge: Pascack Historical Society)

Bangs, E. (ed.), *Journal of Lieutenant Isaac Bangs, April 1 to July 29, 1776*, (Cambridge: John Wilson and Son, 1890)

Barber, J. and Howe, H., *Historical Collections of the State of New Jersey*, (Newark: Benjamin Oldis, 1844)

Bartlett, B. J. and Jameson, J. F., (eds.), 'Journal of Jasper Danckaerts 1679-1680,' *Original Narratives of Early American History*, (New York: Charles Scribner's Sons, 1913)

Benson, A. B. (trans. and ed.), *Peter Kalm's Travels into North America*, (London; T. Lownes, 1750)

Bergen County Deed Book A, p. 26

Bergen County Deed Book E2, p. 129

Bergen County Deed Book F, p. 2

Bergen County Deed Book G, p. 62

Bergen County Deed Book H, p. 219

Bergen County Deed Book J, p. 351

Bergen County Deed Book J, p. 369

Bergen County Deed Book K, p. 128

Bergen County Deed Book K2, p. 480

Bergen County Deed Book K2, p. 482

Bergen County Deed Book V, p. 126

Bergen County Deed Book X10, p. 31

Bergen Democrat, March 15, 1872

Bird, E. K., 'First Lutheran Church in Bergen County,' *Papers and Proceedings of the Bergen County Historical Society, Number Three, 1906–1907*, pp. 41–44

Bibliography

Brodhead, J. R., 'History of the State of New York, First Period 1609–1664', (New York: Harper & Brothers, 1853)

Brodhead, J. R., 'Documents Relative to the Colonial History of the State of New-York,' Volume 13, (Albany: Weed, Parsons, 1853–1887)

Budke, G. H. (Compiler), *Indian Deeds 1630–1748, BC—88 of the Budke Collection*, pp. 60–61 (New City, New York: Library Association of Rockland County, 1975)

Dankers, J. and Sluyter, P., *Journal of a Voyage to New York in 1679–1680*, (Brooklyn, 1867) cited in American History told by Contemporaries

Darton, N. H., 'The Relations of the Traps of the Newark System in the New Jersey Region,' *Bulletin of the United States Geological Survey*, No. 67, p. 37 (Washington, D.C.: Government Printing Office, 1890)

Demarest, D. D., 'Lutherans On The Hackensack,' *Papers and Proceedings of the Bergen County Historical Society, 1915–1916*, p. 99–100

Demarest, D. D., 'The Lutherans of the Hackensack', *Papers and Proceedings of the Bergen County Historical Society, Number Eleven, 1916–1917*, p. 98

Demarest, D. D., *The Huguenots On the Hackensack*, (New Brunswick: The Daily Fredonian Steam Printing House, 1886)

East Jersey Deeds, Liber 1, p. 200

East Jersey Deeds, Liber A, p. 173

Ewald, Captain J., Field Jager Corps, D*iary of the American War, A Hessian Journal*, translated and edited by Joseph P. Tustin, (New Haven and London Yale University Press, 1979)

Extracts of letters, Sudduth, James, *The Remembrancer; or, Impartial Repository of Public Events, For the Year 1778, and Beginning of 1779*, p. 295 (Printed for J. Almon, 1779)

Fernow, B., *Documents Relating to the History and Settlements of the Towns along the Hudson and Mohawk Rivers from 1630 to 1684*, p. 112 (Albany: Weed, Parsons, 1881);

Geological Survey of New Jersey, Annual Report of the State Geologist, for the Year 1880, p. 41 (Trenton: John J. Murphy: 1880)

Glassie, H., *Pattern in the Material Folk Culture of the Eastern United States*, (University of Pennsylvania Press: Philadelphia)

Gordon, T. F., *History and Gazetteer of New Jersey*, (Trenton: Daniel Fenton, 1834)

Hamilton, A., 'Letter to Colonel John Laurens', written from New Bridge, transcribed by Kevin W. Wright (New York Public Library Digital Collections, Sep. 12, 1780)

Hart, A. B. (ed.), *The Representation of New Netherland* (1650), New York Historical Society Collections (New York, 1849), Second Series II, as cited in American History as told by *Contemporaries, Vol. I, Era of Colonization 1492–1689*, (New York: MacMillan Company, 1900)

Historic New Bridge Landing Park Master Plan, Historic New Bridge Landing Park Commission, (2010).

Jameson, J. F. (ed.), 'A Short Account of the Mohawk Indians, by Reverend Johannes Megapolensis, Jr., 1644' *Original Narratives of Early American History, Narratives of New England 1609–1664*, (New York: Charles Scribner's Sons, 1909)

Jameson, J. F. (ed.), 'Journal of New Netherland, 1647,' *Narratives of New Netherland 1609–1664, Original Narratives of Early American History*, (New York: Charles Scribner's Sons, 1909)

Jan Zabriskie Estate Inventory, 1793, (Bergen County Historical Society, BergenCountyHistory.org)

Kenton, E. (ed.), 'Relation of what occurred among the Hurons in the year 1635, Sent to Quebec to Father le Jeune by Father Brebeuf,' *The Jesuit Relations and Allied Documents*, (New York: Albert & Charles Boni, 1925)

Kummel, H. B., 'The Newark System,' *Annual Report of the State Geologist for the Year 1896*, (Trenton: MacCrellish & Quigley, 1897)

Leiby, A. C., *The Revolutionary War in the Hackensack Valley, The Jersey Dutch and the Neutral Ground*, (New Brunswick: Rutgers University Press, 1980)

Lewis, J. V. and Kummel, H. B., Bulletin 50, *Geological Series, The Geology of New Jersey,* (Bayonne: The Jersey Printing Company, 1940), Sullivan, Walter, Landprints, (New York: Time Books, 1984)

Lockhart, P. D., *Drillmaster of Valley Forge: The Baron de Steuben and the Making of the American Army,* (New York: HarperCollins)

Maresca, V., Hunter, R. W. and Liebeknecht, W. B., "Archaeological Investigations in Connection with Exterior Repairs at the Zabriskie/Steuben House Historic New Bridge Landing, River Edge Borough, Bergen County, New Jersey." (tDAR id: 333020: 2001)

Marriages from 1639 to 1801 in the Dutch Reformed Church, New Amsterdam, New York City, Vol. IX, p. 27 (New York: New York Genealogical and Biographical Society, 1940)

McMahon, R., 'Wierimus' *Bergen County History 1974 Annual,* pp. 38–51

McMahon, Reginald, 'The Achter Col Colony on the Hackensack', *New Jersey History, Winter 1971*

Mulenberg, H. M., *The Journals of Henry Melchior Muhlenberg* (Philadelphia: Lutheran Historical Society, 1982)

National Archives and Records Administration, Papers of the Continental Congress, Washington, DC. founders.archives.gov/documents/Washington/03-17-02-0166

Nelson, W. (ed.), *The New Jersey Archives, Vol. V, Laws of the Royal Colony* (Paterson, NJ: The Press Printing and Publishing Co., 1900), pp. 161–163; see also, Winfield, Charles, H., *History of the County of Hudson, New Jersey*, p. 363 (New York: Kennard & Hay Stationery M'Fg and Printing Co., 1874)

Nelson, W., 'Bergen Church Marriage Records,' *New Jersey Archives, First Series, Vol. XXII Marriage Records, 1665–1800,* p. 581 (Paterson: The Press Printing and Publishing Co., 1900)

Nelson, W., *History of the City of Paterson and the County of Passaic, New Jersey,* p. 4 (Paterson: The Press Printing and Publishing Co., 1901)

New Jersey Archives, First Series, Vol. XXI, Calendar New Jersey Records 1664–1703, pp. 261, 282 (Paterson: The Press and Publishing Company, 1899)

New Jersey Archives, First Series, Vol. XXII, Bergen Church Marriage Records, p. 571 (Paterson: The Press and Publishing Company, 1899)

New Jersey Archives, Second Series, Vol. II, 1778, p. 13

New Jersey Archives, Second Series, Vol. II, 1778, p. 43

New Jersey Archives, Second Series, Vol. II, 1778, p. 485

New Jersey Archives, Second Series, Vol. III, 1779, p. 592

New Jersey Archives, Second Series, Vol. III, 1779, pp. 621–629

New Jersey Archives, Second Series, Vol. IV, 1779-1789, pp. 253–254

New Jersey Archives, Second Series, Vol. IV, 1779-1789, pp. 306–308

New Jersey Archives, Vol. XII, Newspaper Extracts Vol. II 1740–1750, p. 283

New Jersey Archives, Vol. XII, Newspaper Extracts Vol. II 1740–1750, p. 283

New Jersey Archives, Vol. XV, Journal of the Governor and Council, Vol. III 1738–1748, p. 284

New Jersey Archives, Vol. XXI, Calendar of NJ Records, East Jersey Deeds

New Jersey Archives, Vol. XXI, Calendar of NJ Records, East Jersey Deeds, p. 70

New Jersey Archives, Vol. XXV, Newspaper Extracts Vol. VI 1766–1767, pp. 69–70; 355–356.

New Jersey Archives, Vol. XXVI, Newspaper Extracts Vol. VII 1768-1769, pp. 9, 528

New Jersey Archives, Vol. XXVI, Newspaper Extracts Vol. VII 1768–1769, pp. 274, 339

New Jersey Archives, Vol. XXVI, Newspaper Extracts Vol. VII 1768–1769, p. 177

New Jersey Archives, Vol. XXVII, Newspaper Extracts Vol. VII, 1770–1771, pp. 371–372

New Jersey Archives, Vol. XXVII, Newspaper Extracts Vol. VII, 1770–1771, p. 434

New Jersey Archives, Vol. XXVII, Newspaper Extracts Vol. VII, 1770–1771, p. 575, 602

New Jersey Archives, Vol. XXVIII, Newspaper Extracts Vol. IX 1772–1773, p. 150

New Jersey Archives, Vol. XXVIII, Newspaper Extracts Vol. IX 1772–1773, p. 461

New Jersey Archives, Vol. XXVIII, Newspaper Extracts Vol. IX 1772–1773, p. 405–406

New Jersey Archives, Vol. XXXI, Newspaper Extracts Vol. XI 1775, p. 63

New Jersey Herald and Sussex Democrat, January 10, 1863, microfilm

Niemcewicz, J. U., *Under their Vine and Fig Tree: Travels through America in 1797–1799, 1805, with some further accounts of life in New Jersey*, (Newark, N. J.: Grassmann Publishing Co., 1965)

Northrup, A. Judd, 'Act of the Director and Council of New Netherland', quoted in *State Library Bulletin*, History No. 4, May 1900, 'Slavery in New York', p. 247 (University of the State of New York, 1900)

Paine, T., *The Writings of Thomas Paine, Vol. I, Collected and Edited by Moncure Daniel Conway, 1774–1779*, Project Gutenberg, Produced by Norman M. Wolcott and David Widger

Pierce, C. H., *New Harlem Past and Present*, (New York: New Harlem Publishing Co., 1903)

Pomfret, J. E., *The Province of East Jersey 1609–1702*, p. 292 (Princeton: Princeton University Press, 1962)

Proceedings of the Bergen County Historical Society for the Year 1915–16, p. 25

Raleigh, W., 'From the Raleigh Register. Agriculture of North-Carolina, Letter VI.—Free Stone, Coloring Drugs, Slates and Ores, To Charles Fisher, esq., Secretary of the Rowan Agricultural Society.' *The Hillsborough Recorder*, No. 174, (Hillsborough, North Carolina: June 11, 1823)

Reeds, C. A., *Geology of New York City and its Vicinity*, American Museum of Natural History, Guide Leaflet, No. 56; Reed, Chester A., "The varved clays at Little Ferry, New Jersey," *American Museum Novitates*, No. 209

Revolutionary History of State of New Jersey, Vol. IV., Extracts from American Newspapers relating to New Jersey, Nov. 1, 1779–Sept. 30, 1780, N.J., (Trenton, N.J., State Gazette Publishing Co., 1914)

Riker, J., *Harlem (City of New York), Its Origin and Early Annals*, (New York: 1881)

Romeyn, Rev. T. B., *Historical Discourse Delivered on Occasion of the Re-Opening and Dedication of the First Reformed (Dutch) Church at Hackensack, N. J.*, (New York: Board of Publication, R. C. A., 1870)

Salisbury, R. D., *Physical Geography of New Jersey, Geological Survey of New Jersey, Volume IV of the Final Report of the State Geologist*, pp. 39, 83, 104, 237 (Trenton: The John L. Murphy Publishing Co., 1898)

Selections from the Correspondence of the Executive of New Jersey from 1776 to 1786, (Newark, N. J.: The Newark Daily Advertiser, 1848)

Stuart, M., 'History needs a face lift', *The Record*, April 17, 1985

Thacher, James, M.D., *Military Journal During the American Revolutionary War, From 1775 to 1783*, (Boston: Richardson and Lord, 1823)

The Bergen Democrat, January 30, 1891

The Minutes of the Board of Proprietors of the Eastern Division of New Jersey from 1725 to 1744, Vol. II, p. 114 (Perth Amboy: 1960)

The Record, July 16, 1931

Van Der Donck, A., 'Description of the New Netherlands.' *Collections of the New-York Historical Society*, p. 81 (New-York: Printed for the Society, 1841). Second Series. Volume 1

Walker, A. H., *Atlas of Bergen County New Jersey 1776–1876*, (Reading, Pa.: Reading Publishing House, 1876)

Weise, J., *The Discoveries of America to the Year 1525* (HardPress Publishing (December 11, 2013)

Westervelt, F. A. 'Study of the Soil,' *History of Bergen County, New Jersey 1630–1923*, Vol. I, p. 5 (New York: Lewis Historical Publishing Company, Inc., 1923)

Wright, K. W., *1609: A country that was never lost, 400th Anniversay of Henry Hudson's Visit with North Americans of the Middle Atlantic Coast*, (Franklin, TN: American History Imprints, 2009)